MOON

MAR - - 2021

HOUSTON & THE TEXAS GULF COAST

ANDY RHODES

CONTENTS

Although every effort was made to make sure the information in this book was accurate when going to press, research was impacted by the COVID-19 pandemic. Some things may have changed during this crisis. Be sure to confirm specific details when making your travel plans.

1. Contemporary Arts Museum of Houston

2. Saturn V rocket at the NASA Space Center in Houston

3. San Jacinto Battleground State Historic Site monument

4. Caddo Lake

5. The *Elissa*

6. Pleasure Pier amusement park

DISCOVER
HOUSTON & THE TEXAS GULF COAST

Everything about Houston and the Texas Gulf Coast is larger than life. From towering skyscrapers to endless stretches of sandy coastline, this region of the Lone Star State exemplifies grandiosity, all with a hearty sense of Texas pride.

Houston offers travelers a cosmopolitan playground with a Texas flair that sets it apart from other urban landscapes. Its thousands of restaurants specialize in far beyond most cities' standard fare. The multifaceted nightlife ranges from down-home honky-tonks to stylish, sophisticated dance clubs.

Just down the road, the Gulf Coast boasts more than 350 miles of shoreline, appealing to all types of recreational travelers. Salty fishermen escape to Galveston or Mustang Island near Corpus Christi for no-frills fishing while South Padre Island draws visitors from the opposite extreme: road-tripping families and spring breakers who frolic on the pristine white beaches.

This cosmopolitan Southern city has an independent spirit befitting Texas's colossal charm, making it a worthy destination for anyone seeking a memorable escape.

5 TOP
EXPERIENCES

1 See the Sea: Get away to the longest remaining undeveloped stretch of barrier island in the world at **Padre Island National Seashore** (page 140).

2 Learn Something New: Houston is home to some of the preeminent museums in the country, where you can explore **natural history and the arts** (page 29 and 30). Or head to the Gulf Coast to experience **seafaring life** (page 104) or **WWII aircraft** (page 127).

3 Take in Historic Views: Enjoy the stunning panorama from atop the 570-foot-tall monument that commemorates the **San Jacinto Battleground**, a triumphant battle site where Texas earned its independence (page 40).

>>>

4 Taste Texas Cuisine: Texas's holy trinity of cuisine—**barbecue, Tex-Mex, and Southern**—provide a culinary journey. Also, be sure to try the excellent **seafood** found along the Gulf Coast (page 13).

5 Explore Space: Feel your goosebumps rise as you gaze upon the awe-inspiring original Mission Control Center at the **NASA Space Center** (page 38).

PLANNING YOUR TRIP

WHERE TO GO

HOUSTON AND EAST TEXAS

With historic oil boomtowns, five national forests, and the megalopolis of Houston, this enormous region is an ideal place to experience the legacy of the Lone Star State. East Texas has a distinct Southern bayou influence, reflected in the food, heritage, and even the accents. Standing apart is Houston, the fourth-largest city in the country and home to NASA, oil-related industries, and some of the most preeminent restaurants, museums, and humidity in the nation.

South Padre Island National Seashore

Corpus Christi Beach

THE GULF COAST

Stretching 350 miles (560 km) along the Gulf of Mexico, this region's moderate beaches and waves draw casual beachcombers, salty anglers, and frolicking families. The biggest city on the gulf, Corpus Christi, offers plenty of recreational activities to accommodate a quick weekend getaway and the ubiquitous Winter Texans. Once a year, students from across the country invade South Padre Island for a rollicking spring break, but otherwise, the region remains as low-key as the gulf's lightly lapping waves.

KNOW BEFORE YOU GO

WHEN TO GO

The region is downright pleasant in spring and fall, quite tolerable during the mild winter months, and absolutely hellish during the summertime.

Spring is the ideal time to visit, so plan for **March or April.** Vegetation is blooming in parks and gardens, festivals capitalize on sunny 73-degree days, and people enjoy the final few months they'll be able to spend outside. **Fall** is the next-best season. By **late October,** things begin to "cool" down to the 80s, drawing cabin-fever sufferers out of their homes to restaurant patios and neighborhood parks.

Winter is a distinct season, but snowflakes and icy roads are rare. Temperatures can be erratic, jumping from the 30s to the 70s in just a few hours. This is a good time to plan a trip to South Padre Island.

surfing on the Gulf Coast

Houston has gone to great lengths to accommodate its sweltering humid weather during **summer (May through mid-October),** mainly via overpowered air-conditioning systems and subterranean downtown tunnels. The constant flow of air-conditioning and water recreation allows residents and visitors to (barely) tolerate the heat. The coastal communities don't have these fancy amenities, but he constant 15-mph wind coming off the water is a welcome change from oppressive urban humidity.

TRANSPORTATION

Air travel is the best option for getting to Texas, and Houston is a hub for United Airlines. It's wise to reserve a rental car before arriving, and to specify a fuel-efficient vehicle, since you'll likely be driving a lot. If you wait to rent a vehicle on arrival, there's a good chance you'll have to choose from the remaining fleet—typically an SUV or a minivan.

In a state this big, **a vehicle is virtually a necessity,** despite some recent advances in metropolitan public transportation systems. Fortunately, the interstate highway system is impressive—you can drive between major cities in a few hours.

EXPLORE
HOUSTON & THE TEXAS GULF COAST

HOUSTON'S BEST 2-DAY GETAWAY

With dozens of worthy attractions and hundreds of notable restaurants in greater Houston, planning a weekend getaway may be challenging. But who can complain about having too many good options?

DAY 1

Kick the day off in the **Museum District** to get a feel for the city's cultural story. Prioritize the **Houston Museum of Natural Science,** the **Contemporary Arts Museum of Houston,** and the **Museum of Fine Arts, Houston.** For a nearby lunch, go with new-school Vietnamese cuisine at **Lua Viet Kitchen** or old-school comfort food at **Benjy's.**

Lua Viet Kitchen

Continue discovering Houston's cultural legacy at the **Menil Collection** (the Rothko Chapel will provide welcoming serenity), then venture a few miles southeast of town to experience unique folk art at **The Orange Show.** Afterward, enjoy an incredible Southern dinner at **Lucille's,** then head down to Main Street for cocktails at **Dean's Credit Clothing.**

DAY 2

Skip the hotel breakfast and beat the lines at **Breakfast Klub,** where the delectable chicken and waffles are still drawing crowds. Then hit the road for an out-of-this-world experience at **NASA,** where you can see the recently restored **Mission Control Center** and learn about the Apollo and Space Shuttle programs.

Then head north for an afternoon of history at the **San Jacinto Battleground.** Drive back to Houston for some strolling along **Buffalo Bayou** then have a hearty dinner—for Mexican food, head to **Hugo's;** for a traditional Houston steakhouse, go to **Pappas Brothers Steakhouse.** Top off the evening with craft beers at **Hay Merchant** or live music at the **Continental Club.**

A TASTE OF TEXAS CUISINE

Houston has more than 8,000 restaurants – the array of options is overwhelming, from lowly fast food to lofty haute cuisine. This being Texas, the options also include a fair number of home-grown varieties, including some of the state's finest barbecue, Tex-Mex, and good ol' fashioned down-down Southern cookin'. Seafood is the favored item for most Corpus Christi and Galveston diners. Both cities are brimming with quality restaurants where you can eat your fill of shrimp, oysters, and snapper.

Here's the best of the bunch.

BARBECUE

- **Gatlin's Barbecue** (3510 Ella Blvd., Houston) is one of the best barbecue joints in the city, just don't be deterred by its location in an uninspiring strip mall. Try the Gatlin sandwich.

- **Stanley's Famous Pit Bar-B-Q** (525 S. Beckham Ave., Tyler) is must for barbecue fans looking to try ribs that frequently make "best of" lists across Texas. Try the smoked ribs.

TEX-MEX AND MEXICAN

- **Irma's Original** (22 N. Chenevert St., Houston) has authentic recipes that are the ultimate Texas comfort food. Try the *caldo* (corn-based chicken soup).

- **La Playa** (5017 Saratoga Blvd.; 7118 S. Padre Island Dr., Corpus Christi) is the place to go for top-notch traditional Tex-Mex. Try the stuffed fried avocados.

- The legendary **Hugo's** (1600 Westheimer Rd., Houston) serves trendy Mexican dishes sizzling with flavor. Try the squash-blossom quesadillas and flan with freshly roasted cocoa beans.

SOUTHERN COOKING

- **Dolli's Diner** (116 S. Pecan St., Nacogdoches) is a classic small town diner and the best lunch spot around. Try the chicken-fried steak (it's the best in the region).

- **Courthouse Whistlestop Café** (318 N. Washington Ave., Livingston) is the perfect place for a hearty breakfast before heading out for a day of hiking or paddling. Try the fried okra.

- **Vautrot's Cajun Cuisine** (13350 Hwy. 105, Beaumont) is where the locals line up for delectable Cajun food. Try the fried catfish.

SEAFOOD

- **Gaido's Seafood Restaurant** (3800 Seawall Blvd., Galveston) is a venerable institution serving memorable meals since 1911. Try the shrimp bisque or the full snapper, bones and all, if they have it

- **BLVD Seafood** (2804 Ave. R½, Galveston) offers fresh and contemporary seafood dishes. Try the fish tacos with a red bell-pepper sauce and avocado.

- **Saltwater Grill** (2017 Post Office St., Galveston) utilizes a bizarre steam-kettle device to rapidly cook fresh seafood. Try the fried asparagus topped with crabmeat.

- **Water Street Seafood Co.** (309 N. Water St., Corpus Christi) combines fresh seafood, Mexican influences, Cajun flavors, and Southern cooking. Try the fresh catch of the day.

- **Snoopy's Pier** (13313 S. Padre Island Dr., Corpus Christi) offers tasty food and a place on the water to soak up the laid-back beach life. Try a plate of fried or boiled shrimp (with a cold beer).

GULF COAST ESCAPE

Combining a Houston trip with excursions along the Gulf Coast is not only possible, it's encouraged. For those with limited time who need a quick saltwater fix, there's nearby **Galveston Island,** just 50 miles south-east of Houston on the Gulf Freeway (I-45). Though the beaches aren't exactly pristine, they're close and easily accessible. Less crowded and more inviting is **Mustang Island** near Corpus Christi, offering steady waves and wide-open stretches of sand. Texas's preeminent beach – think soft white sand and surfable waves – is on **South Padre Island,** a nearly five-hour drive from Houston but well worth the effort to truly kick back, relax, and soak up the warm Texas sun.

The following itinerary offers a solid introduction, but most visitors may prefer to enjoy these coastal towns at their leisure. To truly experience more than one of these destinations, plan for at least five or six days. Factor in driving time: from Houston, it will take about three-and-a-half hours to reach Corpus Christi via U.S. Hwy. 59 through Victoria (State Hwy. 35 along the coast is more picturesque but takes about 45 minutes longer). The five-and-a-half-hour drive to South Padre Island on U.S. Hwy. 77 is pretty lengthy, but absolutely rewarding once your feet hit the soft sand.

Pleasure Pier

the tall ship *Elissa*

DAYS 1-2
GALVESTON ISLAND

Just an hour southeast of Houston, welcoming waves beckon at Galveston Island. Visit **The Strand** district, a 36-block National Historic Landmark District that features New Orleans-style hotels, restaurants, art galleries, boutiques, and a seaport museum with the 1877 tall ship *Elissa*. Enjoy a local lunch at **Mosquito Café.** In the afternoon, you can choose your adventure based on the weather—if it's nice outside, visit **Pleasure Pier** for the amusement park rides; if it's too hot, windy, or rainy, head to the indoor pyramids at **Moody Gardens** for aquariums and exhibits. Dinner and drinks await at the tremendous **Tortuga's Saltwater Grill.**

If you want to extend your stay, consider spending the night at **Tremont House,** a stunning 1879 Victorian hotel in The Strand district. Spend the morning at Broadway Street's stately historical mansions—**Bishop's Palace** and **Moody Mansion**—then enjoy lunch at **Fisherman's Wharf,** with a deck overlooking the bay, before heading to your next coastal stop.

DAYS 3-4
CORPUS CHRISTI

A few hours down the coastline, Corpus Christi offers wide-open beaches on **Mustang Island.** Named for the wild horses that once roamed free on the island, the park offers five miles of outstretched beach, perfect for swimming, fishing, sunbathing, and beachcombing. Those seeking recreational fun can rent a kayak or windsurfing equipment and tackle the gulf waters. Be sure to schedule time for a meal at **Water Street Seafood Co.** Stay at the **Radisson,** located right on the sand of Corpus Christi Beach.

On your next day, hit one of the top-notch cultural attractions like

STEP BACK IN TIME

Despite all the new-fangled sprawl and a notorious penchant for teardowns, Houston and its Gulf Coast neighbors retain impressive historical charm.

HOUSTON

- **Buffalo Soldiers National Museum** is dedicated to the African American Army troops who protected the Texas frontier in the late 1800s (page 32).

- **San Jacinto Battleground Historic Site** boasts a remarkable 570-foot-tall monument on a 1,200-acre site commemorating the legendary battle that secured Texas's independence (page 40).

- **George Ranch Historical Park** is a working cattle ranch on an 1890s pioneer farmstead (page 41).

PINEY WOODS

- The **Aldridge Sawmill's** enormous concrete walls are all that remain of the century-old lumber operation (page 76).

- The **Texas Forestry Museum** and the **History Center** in the Lufkin area offer a fascinating look at the growth of the region's lumber industry (page 79).

- The **Texas State Railroad** allows you to ride the rails on an enchanting steam locomotive, which chugs and charms its way through the Piney Woods (page 83).

GALVESTON

- The **Strand** district was once Texas's second-busiest port, the "Wall Street of the South" (page 103).

- The *Elissa*, a ship from 1887, is the second-oldest operational sailing vessel in the world (page 104).

- The **Bishop's Palace**, an 1866 Victorian castle, exudes elegance, from its ornate fireplaces to its spectacular stained-glass windows (page 105).

- The **Moody Mansion** is worth a visit, given its manicured grounds and exquisite furnishings, as well as the dining room's gold-leaf ceiling (page 106).

CORPUS CHRISTI

- The **USS *Lexington* Museum** is a decommissioned World War II naval aircraft carrier now serving as a 33,000-ton floating museum (page 127).

- **Corpus Christi Museum of Science and History** celebrates maritime heritage with authentic recreations of Christopher Columbus's three ships, nautical exhibits, and a Children's Wharf (page 128).

- **King Ranch** tells the story of the Lone Star State's first cattle drives and legendary brands that forever changed Texas (page 146).

the USS *Lexington* or **Texas State Aquarium.**

DAYS 5-6
SOUTH PADRE ISLAND

Serious beachcombers should alter their schedules to spend a few days on South Padre Island.

Soft white sand and **bright blue water** are major attractions, and so is the marine life at **Sea Turtle, Inc.** It's also well worth the 74-step climb up the tight spiral staircase to experience the breathtaking views from the **Port Isabel Lighthouse.** The seafood

the Texas State Railroad

here is the best in Texas, so be sure to catch a lunch or dinner at **Pier 19** or **Sea Ranch Restaurant.**

EAST TEXAS

If you happen to be heading back from the coast along U.S. Hwy. 77, be sure to visit the legendary **King Ranch** to experience Texas's cattle culture where it was born. Then hightail it to one of East Texas's national forests for some camping or cabin time.

Another option—via U.S. Hwy. 59 and State Hwy. 103—is to explore the **Piney Woods** by bike or canoe, or hike to the abandoned Old Aldridge Sawmill in **Angelina National Forest.** Learn about the region's logging heritage at Lufkin's **Texas Forestry Museum,** or take a leisurely ride on the **Texas State Railroad.** At mealtime, be sure to sample a regional specialty like chopped beef barbecue or fried catfish. An East Texas day trip or overnight regional jaunt directly from Houston is also feasible.

HOUSTON FOR FAMILIES

Houston is the ideal stomping ground for frolicking families. The city is brimming with museums and recreational pursuits. From toddlers to great-grandparents, there are activities for all ages and interests.

DAY 1

Houston's Museum District is a natural place to get things rolling on a family road trip. Start things off at the **Museum of Natural Science,** where kids and parents can learn about dinosaurs, mummies, gems, and oil production through interactive exhibits. The museum's butterfly exhibit is worthwhile to see the colorful creatures in the towering domed rainforest habitat.

Another option is to actively participate in the fun exhibits at the **Children's Museum of Houston.**

The Museum District is surprisingly lacking in walking-distance restaurants, so head to the nearby Montrose-Kirby area for lunch at **Goode Co. Barbeque.** Then head back to the Museum District to visit the **Health Museum** next, where children are educated about the importance of health. The Amazing Body Pavilion lets you walk through a human body and learn about the various systems and organs.

Kemah Boardwalk

DAY 2

Head southeast of town for a day of family fun at **NASA**. Young children may not grasp the historical significance of viewing Mission Control, but they'll certainly appreciate Kids Space, a massive collection of exhibits, games, and hands-on activities. Grab some lunch on the bay and then head to **Kemah Boardwalk,** featuring restaurants, shops, fountains, and an impressive collection of amusement park-style rides at the water's edge.

DAY 3

Stick around Houston for an animal-themed day, staring with the **Houston Zoo.** Five thousand animals keep adult and children entertained on those 55 acres, including a world of primates, Asian elephant habitat, lion and tiger exhibit, and children's zoo. Afterward, head to the **Downtown Aquarium** for lunch – the seafood restaurant on the second floor is extremely kid friendly and surprisingly tasty. Plan to spend a few hours at the aquarium mingling with marine life. Families will marvel at the enormous tanks, Shark Voyage train ride, and outdoor midway rides.

tiger exhibit at Houston's Downtown Aquarium

If time permits, visit the **Buffalo Soldiers National Museum** dedicated to the African American troops who protected the Texas frontier (Native Americans gave them this noble name because of their immense bravery and valor).

HOUSTON AND EAST TEXAS

Like the mountains to the west, the pine forests of East Texas are a natural wonder not typically associated with the Lone Star State. Not surprisingly, the cultural gap between the two regions is as wide as their distance apart.

East Texas has a distinct Southern influence, reflected in the region's food, heritage, and even the dialect. Locals are much more likely to re-gale visitors with long stories in their laid-back, drawn-out speaking style than their twangy, tight-lipped West Texan counterparts. Standing apart from this rural Southern character is the

HIGHLIGHTS

✪ **WALK WITH BUTTERFLIES** at the most popular exhibit at the **HOUSTON MUSEUM OF NATURAL SCIENCE.** Covering everything from dinosaurs to ancient Egypt and Latin American cultures, it offers adventures for the family (page 29).

✪ **APPRECIATE THE EUROPEAN MASTERS** at Texas's largest art museum. Spanning several city blocks, **MUSEUM OF FINE ARTS, HOUSTON** boasts 64,000 works, ranging from antiquity to the present (page 29).

✪ **EXPLORE THE EVER-CHANGING EXHIBITS** at one of the country's most respected and compelling modern art facilities, the **CONTEMPORARY ARTS MUSEUM OF HOUSTON,** which is housed in a stunning stainless-steel building (page 30).

✪ **RE-LIVE THE APOLLO MISSIONS** in the meticulously restored Mission Control room at the otherworldly **NASA SPACE CENTER** (page 38).

✪ **CELEBRATE TEXAS INDEPENDENCE.** The legendary battle where General Sam Houston's troops defeated the Mexican Army in 1836 is commemorated at the 1,200-acre **SAN JACINTO BATTLEGROUND HISTORIC SITE** (page 40).

✪ **RECONNECT WITH NATURE.** A gaggle of species from the Gulf Coast, Central Plains, and Southeastern forests coexist alongside creatures from the deserts, bayous, woods, and swamps in the **BIG THICKET NATIONAL PRESERVE** (page 69).

✪ **RIDE THE RAILS.** A rickety locomotive from the historic **TEXAS STATE RAILROAD** chugs, clanks, and charms its way through the East Texas Piney Woods (page 83).

✪ **SWIM IN CADDO LAKE.** Texas's only natural lake offers hiking, fishing, and boating with a backdrop of wispy Spanish moss and outstretched cypress trees (page 94).

megalopolis of Houston, the fourth-largest city in the country and home to NASA, oil-related industries, a world-class medical district, and some of the preeminent museums in the country.

East Texas has long been the gateway to the Lone Star State: Native Americans, European explorers, Anglo settlers, and African Americans arrived primarily from the East. One of the first things they encountered was the dense acreage now known as the Piney Woods, which includes several national forests and the Big Thicket Preserve.

The first to inhabit the area were the Caddo People, an advanced society with sophisticated trade networks throughout the region. The Caddo are credited with inspiring the name Texas, as they welcomed the Spanish explorers by referring to them as *tejas,*

Houston and East Texas

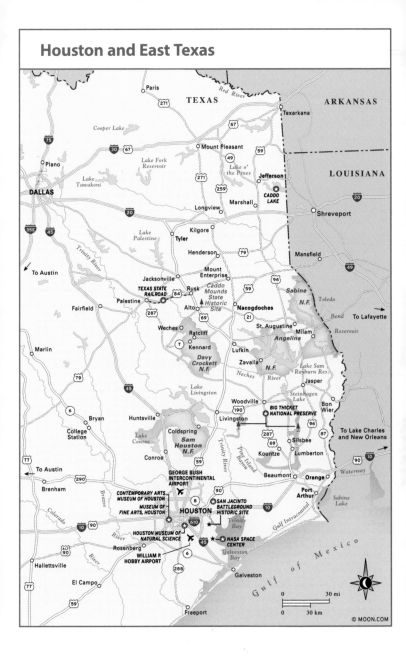

meaning "friends" or "allies." By the 1700s, Spain attempted to fortify its presence in the area by establishing a series of missions to protect their political interests, especially against France, and to convert the indigenous population to Catholicism. Neither of these ventures was very successful, and the land remained relatively unoccupied until Anglo homesteaders began arriving in large numbers in the early 1800s. In the southern portion of this region, just west of modern-day Houston, a group of settlers known as the Old Three Hundred established Stephen F. Austin's initial colony. After the fall of the Alamo in March 1836, droves of frightened frontier families fled to East Texas in an event known as the Runaway Scrape.

By the late 1800s, the region became associated with industry. Railroad expansion and European immigration brought an increased population and entrepreneurs, and the new railroad lines provided access to the Piney Woods's interiors, allowing the lumber industry to flourish. A few decades later, Texas's identity was forever changed when the 100-foot-high (30-m) oil spout known as the Lucas Gusher blew in (the industry term for "erupt") near Beaumont. As soon as word spread about the gusher's subterranean Spindletop oil field, tens of thousands of people flocked to the area. The colorfully named roughnecks and wildcatters worked the fields, while the entrepreneurial-minded investors made the money.

In 1901, the first year of the boom, three major oil companies—Gulf, Humble (later Exxon), and Texas (later Texaco)—formed in Beaumont, and by the following year there were 500 corporations in town. The impact of Spindletop and other oil fields

discovered near Tyler is immeasurable, as it brought billions of dollars to Texas through oil companies and related industry endeavors. Houston benefited the most, since the oil business ultimately shifted headquarters and shipping operations to the city, which grew at phenomenal rates throughout the mid-1900s.

As a result, East Texas has a remarkable number of heritage destinations to explore, including Caddo burial mounds, historic logging towns, Southern plantation homes, oil boomtowns, and five national forests.

PLANNING YOUR TIME

Houston has become a major destination for culinary-minded travelers and remains a popular convention location. Those who visit Houston will discover several days' worth of intriguing activities.

To maximize your time, first head to the Museum District, where nearly a dozen attractions, from the enormous Museum of Natural Science to the Buffalo Soldiers Museum, appeal to a wide spectrum. Visitors typically make it to about three destinations in a day before losing steam, so pick specific museums to make the most of them.

Nowhere else can claim Houston's distinctive connection to the space program. NASA is about a half hour from downtown, so you'll need at least half a day. Other uniquely Houston sites such as the impressive San Jacinto Monument and Battleship *Texas* also involve a 30-minute drive.

The remaining vast expanse of East Texas is worth three or four days of exploring. Beaumont is a fun day trip from Houston, less than two hours away, especially to learn about Texas's oil legacy. Naturalists should set aside a day or two to explore the Big Thicket National Preserve and other nearby national forests, and visitors interested in old-fashioned Southern culture can spend a few days in the northern portion of the Piney Woods, where the cities of Tyler, Lufkin, and Jefferson exude Texas heritage.

INFORMATION AND SERVICES

Knowledgeable staff members at the Greater Houston Convention and Visitors Bureau (701 Av. de las Americas, 713/437-5200, www.visithoustontexas.com, daily 7am-10pm) can handle almost any request. Similar services are southwest of town at Visit Bay Area Houston (604 Bradford Ave., Kemah, 281/474-9700, www.visitbayareahouston.com).

Tours of Houston and the surrounding area are available with Houston City Tours (832/388-8434, www.texascitytours.us) by activity types or location. Another company, Houston Tours Inc. (8915 Bellaire Blvd., 832/630-9188, www.houstontours.com) features traditional bus tours of downtown, outlying neighborhoods, and treks to Galveston.

To venture beyond Bayou City, the Texas Forest Trail Region (headquarters 202 E. Pilar St., Suite 214, Nacogdoches, 936/560-3699, www.texasforesttrail.com) is an ideal place to prepare for a Piney Woods adventure. Check out the website or drop by the main office to get help with an East Texas itinerary.

Entering East Texas by vehicle from Louisiana, look for the Texas Department of Transportation's Travel Information Center at two spots on the state border. The largest is in Orange (1708 E. I-10, 409/883-9416) on I-10 en route from New Orleans. The other is in Waskom (1255 N. I-20 E., 903/687-2547), on I-20 from Shreveport. Visit www.txdot.gov for road-related travel information.

GETTING THERE AND AROUND

Several East Texas cities have small regional airports, and Houston is so big it has two. Houston's major airport is George Bush Intercontinental Airport (IAH, 2800 N. Terminal Rd., 281/230-3100, www.airport-houston.com), just north of Houston and one of the major hubs for United Airlines. The city's old airport, William P. Hobby Airport (HOU, 7800 Airport Blvd., 713/640-3000, www.fly2houston.com), is now the center of activity for Southwest Airlines.

Super Shuttle (281/230-7275, www.supershuttle.com) offers shuttle service to and from area hotels and both Houston airports. If you're not using a ride-share, local cab companies include Houston VIP Taxi (281/616-5838), Liberty Cab Company (713/444-4444), and Yellow Cab (713/236-1111).

All the major rental car companies are accessible from the shared Rental Car Center (281/230-3000, www.fly2houston.com) at Bush Intercontinental Airport, about five minutes by bus from the terminals; the rental companies share a shuttle system that runs about every five minutes.

Buses and trains are a viable option in Houston. Buses arrive and depart at Houston Greyhound (2121 Main St., 713/759-6565 or 800/231-2222, www.greyhound.com). Amtrak's *Sunset Limited* trains arrive and depart three times a week at the Houston Amtrak station (902 Washington Ave., 713/224-1577 or 800/872-7245, www.amtrak.com).

Houston's public transportation system, the Metro, a.k.a. the Metropolitan Transit Authority of Harris County (713/635-4000, www.ridemetro.org), offers local and commuter light rail and bus service. Tickets are available from vending machines at each station. The Metro's red line serves 16 stations near downtown's busiest commercial and recreational sites.

Houston

Houston's humongous growth (population 2,325,502) has it closing in on Chicago as the third-largest city in the country, and it was recently named the nation's most diverse metropolis. The city is named after larger-than-life Sam Houston, president of the Republic of Texas, who led the fight for independence from Mexico as a general of the Texas Army.

The Bayou City is notorious for its lack of zoning ordinances and its high humidity, resulting in unmitigated sprawl and unbearably hot summers. But it's not without its charm—Houston has world-class cultural and medical facilities, and its international population contributes to a truly cosmopolitan setting with world-renowned services and restaurants.

The city started with grand ambitions: In the late 1830s, New York City brothers and entrepreneurs Augustus and John Allen claimed the town would become the "great interior commercial emporium of Texas," with ships from New York and New Orleans sailing up Buffalo Bayou. For most of the late 1800s, Houston was a typical Texas town, fueled by cotton farming and railroad expansion. The oil industry boom that started in 1901 changed Houston forever, with major corporations relocating to the city and using its deep ship channel for oil distribution.

Houston had another identity shift and financial surge in the mid-1900s, when it became headquarters for the aerospace industry. NASA established its Manned Spacecraft Center in 1961, which eventually became the epicenter of the U.S. space program's Gemini and Apollo missions.

With the proliferation of air-conditioning around that time, Houston's brutal humidity was no longer a year-round deterrent, resulting in corporations relocating from colder climes. The population boomed in the 1970s, when the OPEC oil embargo caused Houston's petroleum industry to become a vital asset. The world oil economy in the 1980s caused a recession in Houston, and it received another black eye in the late 1990s in the Enron fraud scandal.

A drive through Houston's central neighborhoods reveals what happens when a city doesn't prioritize zoning regulations. Depending on who you ask, it's good (Texans don't like to be told what they can or cannot do) or bad (significant historic neighborhoods and homes are routinely leveled to make room for McMansions). Regardless, it's part of Houston's character, even if that means a 150-year-old home sits in the shadow of a monstrous contemporary house across the street from a gargantuan pseudo-historic retail and residential complex.

Texans typically don't consider Houston a viable travel destination, but they should. Houston's sense of style is a step ahead of the rest of the Lone Star State, its restaurants specialize in the lesser-known international cuisine, and the city's public transportation system is surprisingly comprehensive. Houston may never equal San Antonio in visitor numbers, but its distinctive characteristics—a Southern cosmopolitan city with an independent spirit—make it a worthy destination.

ORIENTATION

Known for its endless suburban sprawl, Houston is defined by its highways and loops. The three loops are "the" Loop—Loop 610, the original and inner loop; the Belt, a.k.a. Beltway 8, Sam Houston Parkway, and Sam Houston Tollway; and the Grand Parkway, a.k.a. Highway 99, an unfinished outer loop that will be the longest in the United States when completed. The primary focus of this guide is the inner or near-Loop, in or around Loop 610.

With downtown as Houston's historical epicenter, the city's noteworthy attractions begin to expand mainly west, including the museums, Rice University, and mid-century modern architecture. To the north of these neighborhoods is Houston Heights (The Heights), a formerly low-key residential area that has transformed into a trendy place to live and do business. Well-heeled Houstonians have traditionally lived in ritzy suburbs to the west, most notably the Uptown area,

anchored by the high-end Galleria shopping district. Because the Houston Ship Channel was dredged eastward to provide access to the Gulf of Mexico, this side of the city is almost entirely industrial, with the exception of two large college campuses—the University of Houston and Texas Southern University—southeast of downtown.

DOWNTOWN

Once practically deserted after dark, downtown Houston is now a destination for reasons other than work. Major draws include sporting and entertainment facilities that host professional baseball, basketball, and soccer; the Downtown Aquarium; the George R. Brown Convention Center; and the Theater District. The addition of light rail—plus its continued expansion around downtown—has made it easier to get here. Downtown is vast, with pockets of nightlife, dining, and entertainment—and even a subterranean network of air-conditioned tunnels that functions as a shopping mall.

MIDTOWN

Bordering downtown to the northeast and Montrose-Kirby to the west, Midtown embodies the ethos of Houston: change. The revitalization of downtown has transformed Midtown from a commercial and low-income residential district into a commercial and high-income residential district. Expensive modern condos and townhomes abound, as do pockets of dining and nightlife. One unique district is Little Saigon, which has some of the city's best Vietnamese restaurants, as well as street signs in English and Vietnamese.

Houston

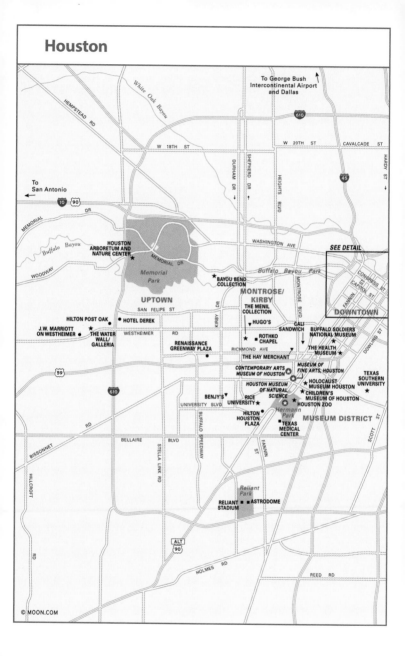

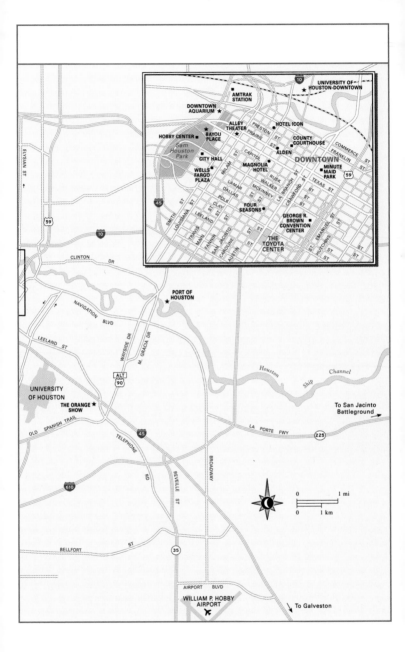

MUSEUM DISTRICT

The name gives it away: Museums are the main attraction in this area southwest of Midtown, and many major medical facilities are also here. With more than a dozen museums to explore within a manageable area, this is Houston's most-visited neighborhood, with welcoming greenery in manicured parks and lush tree canopies.

MONTROSE-KIRBY

Long the antithesis of Houston's sterile suburbs, the Montrose-Kirby area has been the bastion of the LGBT community, artists, hippies, punks, and bohemian types for decades. The scene has lost some of its edge of late: The forces of gentrification have been at work for decades, and Montrose-Kirby today is less seedy and has higher rents and upscale dining. That said, it remains an avant-garde and artsy hub, with world-class museums and galleries, eclectic nightlife, and renowned restaurants.

WEST UNIVERSITY

Officially known as West University Place or West U for its proximity to Rice University, this enclave is predominately residential, with a mix of cottages and bungalows attracting professorial types and wealthy families. The adjacent Rice Village is a 16-block zone packed with shops, restaurants, and bars.

THE HEIGHTS

If the Heights' Victorians and tree-lined roads could speak, they might report on the massive social changes in the district. The journey from streetcar suburb to city center has taken a predictable path: from desirable residential neighborhoods to postwar decline to revitalization and gentrification. The constant throughout has been the residential vibe. While it has a laid-back and somewhat bohemian feel like Montrose-Kirby, it is known more for its antiques shops and thrift stores than its of-the-moment clubs and boutiques.

UPTOWN

Anchoring Uptown is the Galleria, one of the largest shopping centers in the United States and a major Houston attraction. Just west of Loop 610, the Galleria's lavish sensibility infuses the district surrounding it, which features more upscale shops, hotels, and offices. Uptown is the second major business district in Houston after downtown. Beyond the business district, the vast and hard-to-define Uptown has many exclusive residential neighborhoods.

GREATER HOUSTON

Not surprisingly, this category represents the outlying parts of town, typically beyond Loop 610. Attractions include cultural sites like NASA, the Kemah Boardwalk, and the San Jacinto Battleground to the southeast and east. To the west are shopping and dining destinations Chinatown and the Kirby Outlet Malls. Otherwise, Greater Houston is mainly sprawling suburbs.

SIGHTS

A city of Houston's size offers countless cultural attractions. The Museum District is a loose collection (not logically planned, like most of Houston) just southwest of downtown. The urban core features occasional historic buildings and theaters among the modern skyscrapers, and offbeat spots outside town include the folk-art wonder of The Orange Show and the historically significant state park featuring the San Jacinto Battleground Historic Site.

MUSEUM DISTRICT

More inspiring than its name implies, the city's Museum District just south of Midtown spans several miles, with parks and medical facilities and 19 museum attractions. Realistically, visitors can make it to about three destinations each day before losing steam.

✪ Houston Museum of Natural Science

One of the best places in Houston for a family adventure is the Houston Museum of Natural Science (1 Hermann Circle Dr., 713/639-4629, www.hmns.org, daily 9am-5pm, $25 adults, $16 seniors and students, extra fees for some exhibits, free Thurs. 2pm-5pm). An overwhelming array of exhibits and artifacts covers everything from dinosaurs to gems and minerals to ancient Egypt. Its permanent collection is especially impressive in the Hall of the Americas, with exhibits on how people arrived, including Mayan, Aztec, and other Native American cultures, and their lifeways.

The museum's wing devoted to paleontology features dramatically lit dinosaur fossils and exhibits on evolution and early humans, with action-packed scenes of predators and prey.

Children won't want to leave the museum's Discovery Place on the lower level, featuring interactive exhibits dedicated to light and sound waves; machines with levers, pulleys, and gears; and a simulated weather studio. The Energy Hall is an extensive area showcasing the oil and gas industry. Interactive hands-on and touch-screen displays cover oil density, drilling, and delivery. Kids will be interested in the museum's large gemstone exhibit, featuring colorful and sharply cut gems in fascinating backlit displays.

The museum's butterfly exhibit ($10-12) is worthwhile to see the thousands of colorful winged creatures in the towering domed Mayan rainforest habitat. A lengthy waterfall flows gently in the background, and butterflies occasionally drop by for a personal visit.

✪ Museum of Fine Arts, Houston

Billing itself "the largest art museum in America south of Chicago, west of Washington, D.C., and east of Los Angeles," the Museum of Fine Arts, Houston (1001 Bissonnet St., 713/639-7300, www.mfah.org, Tues.-Wed. 10am-5pm, Thurs. 10am-9pm, Fri.-Sat. 10am-7pm, Sun. 12:15pm-7pm, $19 adults, $16 seniors and ages 6-18, free Thurs.) contains several buildings with 300,000 square feet of display space and 18 acres of public gardens drawing two million people annually. Look for the main entrance on Bissonnet Street, since the museum complex stretches over several blocks.

Museum of Fine Arts, Houston

The museum's collection of 64,000 pieces of world art dates from antiquity to the present. It's challenging to soak up the significance of each collection in a half-day visit, so consider visiting the museum's website ahead of time. European masters include Italian Renaissance paintings and the French impressionist works. The Arts of North America wing offers nascent American landscape paintings, black-and-white photographs, vintage jewelry, and renowned works of sculpture. The ancient Asian holdings are especially notable, including sculpture from Japan's pre-Buddhist days and a Chinese boat dating to circa 2400 BC. Other significant collections include masterworks by famed Western artist Frederic Remington, and the Glasswell Collection of African Gold, considered the best of its kind in the world.

✪ Contemporary Arts Museum of Houston

As big-city museums go, this is one of the best, with intriguing objets d'art down every hall. In the heart of the Houston Museum District, the Contemporary Arts Museum of Houston (5216 Montrose Blvd., 713/284-8250, www.camh.org, Tues.-Wed. and Fri. 10am-7pm, Thurs. 10am-9pm, Sat. 10am-6pm, Sun. noon-6pm, free) is unmistakable, in a distinctive stainless-steel building designed by architect Gunnar Birkerts.

As a non-collecting museum, the focus is on current and new directions in art, with changing exhibits. The museum grew steadily in the 1970s-1980s and features contemporary still-life painting, thematic installations, performance pieces, and other media. The museum's store is a step above similar shops, featuring whimsical toys, large posters, and decorative items.

The Health Museum

Since Houston is a leading medical center, it makes sense there's a corresponding Health Museum (1515 Hermann Dr., 713/521-1515, www. mhms.org, Mon.-Sat. 9am-5pm, Sun. noon-5pm, $10 adults, $8 seniors and ages 3-12, fees for some exhibits). In the Museum District, this modest-size facility educates mostly children about the importance of health. In the Amazing Body Pavilion, experience a human body by walking through it, entering through the mouth and exploring the various systems and organs via innovative interactive displays. Vocal cords, lung capacity, stomach acids, and blood content are portrayed through games, hands-on activities, and informative models. The museum also features traveling exhibits related to children's health and a gift shop with fun toys, games, and knickknacks.

Houston Zoo

Consistently rated a top attraction, the lush and welcoming Houston Zoo (6100 Hermann Park Dr., 713/533-6500, www.houstonzoo.org, daily 9am-5pm, $23 ages 12-64, $18 seniors and ages 2-11) has 5,000 animals on 55 acres of worldwide ecosystems. Drop by the World of Primates, the Asian elephant habitat, the lion and tiger exhibit, and the grizzly bear habitat.

Kids will love the Children's Zoo, featuring a petting area with farm animals, and the "Meet the Keeper" program, offering behind-the-cage insight. Families with children will want to set aside time for an excursion on the train, which takes a short journey through the park along the zoo's

Alley Theater's modern architecture

Now that modern architecture is becoming historic, the term "mid-century" is emerging as a distinctive style from the 1950s-1960s. Since Houston experienced one of its population booms during this era, the city known in architectural circles for its mid-century buildings that have so far survived the wrecking ball.

Houston Mod (www.houstonmod.org), an organization dedicated to 1960s architecture, is making impressive efforts to document and preserve dozens of the city's significant mid-century structures. Perhaps most iconic is the Astrodome, which opened in 1965 and served as home field for the Astros baseball and Oilers football during the teams' glory years. Finding a new use for the building, once hailed as the Eighth Wonder of the World, has been a challenge.

Another historically significant structure is the 1963 Humble Oil Building. The 600-foot-tall (180-m) 44-story edifice is one of downtown Houston's most recognizable mid-century buildings. For a short time, it even boasted the title of "tallest building west of the Mississippi."

Also instilling pride in Houston's mid-century fans is the Alley Theatre building, which opened in 1968. Known for its flowing and curvilinear use of raw concrete, the Alley is also associated with an architectural style known as Brutalism, coined in 1953 and referencing the French term *béton brut* (raw concrete).

border. If you have children in tow, consider bringing extra clothes, since most kids love the water play area and will undoubtedly get soaked.

Children's Museum of Houston

A must-see in the Museum District is the Children's Museum of Houston (1500 Binz St., 713/522-1138, www.cmhouston.org, Tues.-Wed. and Fri.-Sat. 10am-6pm, Thurs. 10am-8pm, Sun. noon-6pm, $12, $11 seniors). The building itself is a sight to behold—a playful take on classical architecture with giant colorful details. Inside, nine galleries engage children's minds in science, geography, performing arts, and history. One of the most popular and informative attractions is the multilevel exhibit *How Does It Work?* Parents may pick up a few pointers on how mobile phones function and how turning a key gets an engine running. Younger kids relish the opportunity to sit in a model car with the freedom to push and pull every button and lever in sight. Other fun activities include an interactive Mexican village, art stations, live shows, and a café with healthy snacks. An added bonus: The Teacher and Family Resource Center has loads of books and items related to child development and parenting.

Children's Museum of Houston

Buffalo Soldiers National Museum

The specialized Buffalo Soldiers National Museum (3816 Caroline St., 713/942-8920, www. buffalosoldiermuseum.com, Mon.-Fri. 10am-5pm, Sat. 10am-4pm, $10 adults, $5 students, free Thurs. 1pm-4pm) recently moved from a modest-size facility to a larger building. The name is derived from the term associated with the African American troops who served in the U.S. Army and protected the Texas frontier in the late 1800s. Native Americans reportedly called them as Buffalo Soldiers due to their bravery and valor. Fittingly, the museum honors the legacy of African Americans' contributions to military service for the past 150 years. This is a unique collection of materials dedicated to a compelling aspect of U.S. heritage. Two stories of exhibits feature artifacts, photos, and maps. It's

a true learning experience, and inspiring to see students making connections with the past as interpretive guides offer insight about the uniforms, flags, and equipment.

Holocaust Museum Houston

A somber subject is handled admirably at the Holocaust Museum Houston (5401 Caroline St., 713/942-8000, www.hmh.org, Mon.-Fri. 9am-5pm, Sat.-Sun. noon-5pm, $15 adults, $10 seniors, not recommended under age 10). The museum's mission is to educate people about the dangers of prejudice and hatred, and it makes an impact on everyone who walks through its doors. Visitors learn about the historical and personal stories associated with the Holocaust in the museum's permanent exhibit, called *Bearing Witness: A Community Remembers,* which focuses on the stories of Holocaust survivors living in the Houston area. Displays chronicle the Nazi rise to power and the concentration camps. Artifacts, photos, films, informative panels, and a research library serve as testament to the suffering, with the hope that this educational experience will help prevent similar future atrocities.

Houston Center for Photography

One of the best small museums in the region is the Houston Center for Photography (1441 W. Alabama St., 713/529-4755, www.hcponline.org, Wed.-Sun. 11am-7pm, free), in a funky building at the edge of the Museum District. The HCP's mission is to encourage and educate people about art and photography. Exhibits showcase local and national photographers, and programs stimulate dialogue about the art form through digital workstations and presentations about methods and critique.

Asia Society Texas Center

Even if you're not an architectural aficionado, you'll be impressed by the contemporary building that houses the Asia Society Texas Center (1370 Southmore Blvd., 713/496-9901, www.asiasociety.org/texas, Tues.-Sun. 11am-6pm, free, exhibits $5). In a residential neighborhood a block from the Museum District, the graceful structure blends in with its surroundings, offering panoramic views of downtown Houston from enormous second-story windows. Designed by Harvard-educated Yoshio Taniguchi, the 40,000-square-foot building is impeccable, with clean sight lines and exquisite materials. Research and community outreach are the center's primary focus, but there are public displays and an outdoor sculpture garden.

DOWNTOWN

There are plenty of shiny skyscrapers, hotel and convention facilities, and sports arenas downtown, but not many cultural sights for travelers. Regardless, the downtown area reveals Texas's version of cosmopolitan life—and a bizarre subterranean tunnel system.

Houston's Downtown Aquarium

Mingle with marine life at the modest-size Downtown Aquarium (410 Bagby St., 713/223-3474, www.aquariumrestaurants.com, Sun.-Thurs. 10am-9pm, Fri.-Sat. 10am-10:30pm, $15 adults, $13 seniors, $12 children, additional fees for rides and parking). Not as extensive or awe-inspiring as some big aquariums,

Houston's version is focused on fun. Families will marvel at the enormous tanks, touch pools, and midway rides outside.

It's awe-inspiring to stand face-to-face with a grouper, piranha, or shark. One of the aquarium's highlights is the Shark Voyage, where a train takes visitors into a clear tunnel surrounded by blacktips, whitetips, and zebra sharks. Other notable exhibits are the Gulf of Mexico tank, with barracuda and snappers, and the Discovery Rig, where kids can get a handle on horseshoe crabs and stingrays. The aquarium also includes an interesting exhibit with several majestic white tigers.

The on-site restaurant is better than expected, so plan your visit around a meal to enjoy a decent seafood plate while gazing at still-living sea creatures in the surrounding 150,000-gallon aquarium. Stick with the basics here: the flaky and flavorful whitefish or succulently seasoned shrimp.

Step outside and pony up for a few of the midway rides: A medium-size Ferris wheel offers spectacular views of downtown Houston, and the merry-go-round (with sea creatures in place of horses) will bring genuine smiles of delight to your family's faces.

Heritage Society at Sam Houston Park

Offering a welcome historical respite downtown is the Heritage Society at Sam Houston Park (1100 Bagby St., 713/655-1912, www.heritagesociety.org, Tues.-Sat. 10am 4pm, Sun. 1pm-4pm, museum gallery free, guided tours $15 adults, $12 seniors, $6 ages 6-18). Ten historic structures represent Houston 1823-1905. Although the buildings were relocated to the park from other parts of town, their collective stories illustrate life in the burgeoning boomtown. For a quick overview, the Kellum-Noble House gallery showcases the Heritage Society's early preservation efforts in a city that often didn't place value on protecting its past.

Saint Arnold Brewing Company

Just north of downtown in a semi-industrial neighborhood is the highly recommended Saint Arnold Brewing Company (2000 Lyons Ave., 713/686-9494, www.saintarnold.com, beer hall Sun.-Thurs. 11am-10pm, Fri.-Sat. 11am-11pm, free tours 1pm, 3pm, 5pm, and 7pm). Billing itself as Texas's oldest craft brewery, Saint Arnold's dates to 1994 and makes 10 different year-round beers, six seasonal varieties, and a handful of special series. The best place to sample them is in the beer hall—a welcoming room with long tables and German-inspired design. Bartenders are happy to offer suggestions based on personal tastes. Always reliable options include the Elissa IPA, Weedwacker hefeweizen, and 5 O'Clock Pils. Make a point to visit at lunch or dinner, since the beer hall's café serves German food; the bratwurst on a pretzel roll is superb.

Downtown Tunnels

Houston's bizarre Downtown Tunnels (713/650-3022, tour info 713/392-0867, www.houstonhistoricaltours.com) are more a local shopping destination than a tourist attraction. The 6-mile (9.7-km) subterranean system connects dozens of downtown buildings, offering an air-conditioned respite from triple-digit surface temperatures. The tunnels started by connecting three downtown theaters in the 1930s; now,

tunnel-goers can find scores of banks, restaurants, clinics, and boutiques, all 20 feet (6 m) below the surface.

The tunnel system is accessed by elevators, stairways, and escalators inside commercial buildings and parking garages. The only buildings offering direct access to the tunnels from the street are Wells Fargo Plaza (1000 Louisiana St.) and the McKinney Place Garage (930 Main St.). It's an appealing getaway on a sweltering summer day in Houston.

Once below ground, there are maps and wayfinding signs to help you get oriented. You'll need them to keep track of your location. Things move quickly in the tunnels, and you'll see that most people are mostly running errands and grabbing food. If you want to plan ahead, consult the maps on the website.

MONTROSE-KIRBY
The Menil Collection

What do you do when you have too much fine art? Renowned art collectors John and Dominique de Menil opened their own museum. The

The Menil Collection's Rothko Chapel

LITTLE SAIGON, THE SEQUEL

Traditional Vietnamese cuisine is available in many Houston neighborhoods.

In the 1960s, hundreds of Vietnamese residents fled their country and settled in and around Houston, where they found jobs in fishing, shrimping, manufacturing, and retail in a humid coastal environment reminiscent of their homeland. Today, Houston's Vietnamese community of more than 80,000 is the nation's largest outside California.

During the past few decades, tens of thousands of Vietnamese residents relocated from California and from Vietnam to purchase homes and open businesses, mostly along a 4-mile (6.4-km) stretch of Bellaire Boulevard in southwestern Houston. Comparatively cheap housing drew the Californians, many of whom lived in the Los Angeles area's famed Little Saigon district.

Word spread that Vietnamese families were selling their pricey California abodes and purchasing homes in Houston for a third the cost. The profits were often invested in new Vietnamese-centered businesses, including restaurants, real estate firms, medical facilities, and supermarkets.

The result is a vibrant community, and neighboring Chinese, Latino, and Pakistani enclaves add to Houston's cosmopolitan and diverse atmosphere. The Vietnamese restaurant scene is top-notch, with options ranging from inexpensive to upscale.

Menil Collection (1515 Sul Ross St., parking at 1515 W. Alabama St., 713/525-9400, www.menil.org, Wed.-Sun. 11am-7pm, free) is set among comfortable homes at the edge of the trendy Heights neighborhood, and it's an ideal place to spend a few hours soaking up some magnificent art spanning many ages. The grounds are expansive and inviting, with an abundance of trees, installation artwork, and even a wooden swing. The Menils left a legacy of 17,000 paintings, sculptures, prints, drawings, photographs, and rare books, most modern with an emphasis on surrealism, but there are also African pieces and works from the Byzantine period.

The compound includes several noteworthy structures near the main museum. Two blocks south of the main building is a fascinating Dan Flavin light installation, inside a former grocery store. The vertical-oriented fluorescent tubes on the side walls are a sensory delight, toying with color in your peripheral vision. Set aside at least 15 minutes to experience the **Rothko Chapel**, a block east of the main building. From the outside, the chapel is disarmingly stark, with bland rectangular brick walls. Inside, it's similarly subdued, but the silence screams reverence. Even if you're not religious, the experience of being completely quiet in a public space is absolutely sacred.

Bayou Bend Collection

The affluent home of the unfortunately named Ima Hogg, a respected Texas philanthropist, now houses the Bayou Bend Collection (6003 Memorial Dr., 713/639-7750, www. mfah.org, guided tours Tues.-Thurs. 10am-11:45am and 1pm-2:45pm, Fri.-Sat. 10am-11:15am, regular hours Tues.-Sat. 10am-5pm, Sun. 1-pm, guided tours $12.50 adults, $11 seniors, $6.25 ages 10-18). This spectacular 1928 home is one of Houston's cultural treasures, filled with nearly 5,000 antique objects showcasing American decorative arts 1620-1870. "Miss Hogg," as she was known, also had a hand in the design of the opulent home and grounds, featuring lush gardens and distinctive decorations spanning colonial to antebellum times. Call in advance to make tour reservations, and note that children under age 10 are not permitted in the home.

Rienzi

Another art museum in an impressive homestead is Rienzi (1406 Kirby Dr., 713/639-7800, www.mfah.org, tour only Wed.-Sat. 10am, 11am, 1:30pm, 2:30pm, 3:30pm, Sun. 1pm-4pm every 30 minutes, $12.50 adults, $10 seniors and students, free under age 13). Dedicated to European decorative arts, Rienzi features paintings, furnishings, and miniatures in the former home of local philanthropists Carroll Sterling Masterson and Harris Masterson III. The home was designed by Houston architect John Staub in 1952, and the museum is named after

Harris Masterson's grandfather Rienzi Johnston, a Houston newspaperman and politician.

The collection is best known for fine English ceramics and furniture, European jewelry, and sculpture, including the main attraction, an early-1800s white marble Venus. The surrounding four-acre grounds are impressive, with welcoming shade trees and lush gardens. Drop-in visits are welcome, but reservations are advised.

Rice University

One of the best universities in the South, Rice University is an oasis of intellectualism and vegetation in this sprawling metropolis. With an exclusive undergraduate enrollment of 6,700 students, the university has a reputation for high-quality instruction in medical, science, and engineering fields. Consider dropping by the Rice Student Center (6100 Main St., 713/348-4096) to pick up a T-shirt or ball cap, grab a coffee, visit the gardens, and even have a beer at Willy's Pub.

Garnering the most attention these days is the spectacular Skyspace building, adjacent to the university's Shepherd School of Music. The open-air structure was designed for music, but the visual effect of the two-story construction appears as a large grass-covered mound topped by a futuristic light show that projects LED-based colors onto the enormous 72-foot-wide (22-m) square roof, which opens to the sky.

UPTOWN
Houston Arboretum & Nature Center

Experience Houston's often forgotten natural side at the Houston Arboretum

& Nature Center (4501 Woodway Dr., 713/681-8433, www.houstonarboretum.org, grounds daily 7am-7pm, Discovery Room Tues.-Sun. 10am-4pm, free). On the west side of near-downtown Memorial Park, the 155-acre nature sanctuary is a green oasis in a city known for sprawling concrete. Native plants and animals are the focal point, with interactive exhibits and activities. The park area is beautifully landscaped, and kids will love the Discovery Room's pondering pond and learning tree. Stroll the 5 miles (8 km) of trails, hear the birds, and get a glimpse of Houston's version of the natural world.

The Water Wall

Houstonians take immense pride in their beloved Water Wall (2800 Post Oak Blvd., 713/621-2011, daily 8am-9pm). In a strangely unoccupied area among office buildings and Galleria parking garages, this six-story structure is a giant wall of cascading water that needs to be experienced to be appreciated. The structure is semicircular, and the hypnotic sound of falling water is mesmerizing. The gentle mist provides respite from a hot summer day, and the experience is even cooler at night thanks to the dramatic lighting and evening temperatures.

Considered the most romantic spot in town, the Water Wall is typically bustling with couples on dates, getting married, or taking selfies. The nearby 64-story Williams Tower offers an urban complement to the scene. Parking can be a hassle—instead of driving around in search of a street spot, head to the nearby West Drive parking garage, which is free on weekends.

Houston's Water Wall

HOUSTON, WE HAVE A LEGACY

Space exploration used to be major international news; now, we hardly know when a mission is taking place. Throughout the past four tumultuous decades, the **NASA Space Center** (1601 NASA Pkwy., 281/244-2100, www.spacecenter.org, Mon.-Fri. 10am-5pm, Sat.-Sun. 10am-6pm, summer longer hours, $30 adults, $28 seniors, $25 ages 4-11) in Houston has been the hub of American spaceflight. The facility was established in 1961 as the Manned Spacecraft Center and renamed the Lyndon B. Johnson Space Center in 1973. The center will forever be associated with its early Gemini and Apollo missions.

the iconic Mission Control building at NASA

The Mission Control Center is the nerve center of the U.S. piloted space program, and the facility's remarkable guided tours shed light on what took place here. In 2019, NASA reopened the meticulously **restored Mission Control room** for visitors. See restored details like the aquamarine-colored metal consoles, stark monitor screens, and even authentic ashtrays, bringing the Apollo missions to life as visitors absorb the significance of being in the same room where the words "The *Eagle* has landed" and "Houston, we have a problem" were first heard.

OUTER REACHES

Mission Control previously handled the activity related to the space shuttle and International Space Station programs. Training for these missions took place at an adjacent building, where astronauts and engineers prepared for their time in orbit using the Space Vehicle Mockup Facility. This enormous edifice still houses an International Space Station trainer, a precision air-bearing floor, and a partial-gravity simulator.

Although the future of the space program remains unclear (Mars missions are being discussed), NASA expects to play a role in space exploration. For over 50 years, the space center has helped humans transcend the physical boundaries of Earth to enhance our knowledge about the universe.

GREATER HOUSTON

✪ Nasa Space Center

Light-years from ordinary cultural attractions is the **NASA Space Center** (1601 NASA Pkwy., 281/244-2100, www.spacecenter.org, Mon.-Fri. 10am-5pm, Sat.-Sun. 10am-6pm, summer longer hours, $30 adults, $28 seniors, $25 ages 4-11). NASA is about as big as it gets for Houston attractions, and it's one of the few cities in the United States to host such a distinct icon.

Start at the far end of the main building with the open-air tram tour, which transports visitors to the space center's significant buildings, including the remarkably restored Mission Control Center. Here, visitors learn about the fascinating saga of the Apollo piloted spacecraft missions.

A knowledgeable and entertaining guide takes you on a descriptive tour spacecraft experience as you peer through a glass partition at the iconic aquamarine-paneled equipment and flat monitor screens. The entire room was meticulously restored and reopened in 2019 for the

50th anniversary of the first human moon landing.

Goosebumps may rise on your neck as you realize you're in the room where the words "The *Eagle* has landed" and "Houston, we have a problem" were first heard. Nearby, you'll get to see real astronauts in action at the Space Vehicle Mockup Facility, containing space shuttle orbital trainers, an International Space Station trainer, a precision air-bearing floor, and a partial-gravity simulator. One of the highlights of the tour is a visit to the enormous structure housing the immense Saturn V rocket, an awe-inspiring sight that must be seen to be believed.

Most of the NASA facility features educational and entertainment-related elements, including Starship Gallery, containing impressive space-related artifacts such as the Apollo 17 command module, the Gemini 5 capsule, lunar rovers, and even a moon rock. Additional attractions include interactive flight simulators and Independence Plaza, with a model of the space shuttle *Independence,* which visitors can walk through to see what astronauts experienced, including the robotic arms they operated and even the toilets they used.

The Orange Show

You know that occasional burst of inspiration that enters your brain? Jeff McKissack, a Houston postal worker turned artist, acted on it and built an enormous folk art monument dedicated to oranges. McKissack glorified his favorite fruit with 3,000 square feet of space filled with orange-related folk art now known as **The Orange Show** (2402 Munger St., 713/926-6368, www.orangeshow.org, usually Sat.-Sun. noon-5pm, $5). Standing among modest suburban homes just east of

The Orange Show

downtown, this bizarrely compelling artwork is primarily brick and concrete, accompanied by metal sculptures, mosaic tilework, and various objects that include birdhouses, windmills, and statues.

McKissack once delivered oranges throughout the South and became obsessed enough to fashion this whimsical collection of objects found along his mail route. The absurdity factor is fascinating, and the devotion to his subject is admirable. McKissack apparently believed his life work (it took him 25 years to assemble his collection into a publicly accessible venue) would become a major tourism destination. It never quite caught on, but it remains an intriguing folk art environment unlike any other you'll encounter. You'll know you're in the right spot when you see the colossal 70-foot-tall (21-m) blue saxophone, an enormous sculpture comprising oil-field pipes, an entire VW Beetle, and even a surfboard.

Kemah Boardwalk

About 25 miles (40 km) southeast of downtown on Galveston Bay, the popular Kemah Boardwalk (215 Kipp Ave., 281/535-8100, www. kemahboardwalk.com, open daily, amusement rides Mon.-Thurs. noon-7pm, Fri. noon-9pm, Sat. 10:30am-10pm, Sun. 10:30am-9pm, all-day ride pass $25 adults, $19 children) features restaurants, shops, fountains, and an impressive collection of amusement park rides at the water's edge. Touristy by nature, it draws suburbanites by the thousands for a summertime diversion of nostalgic family fun. The restaurants are more notable for their bayside views than the food, but there's plenty of excitement in rides, including a roller coaster, a Ferris wheel, and a double-decker carousel. Other attractions include a 50,000-gallon aquarium with 100 species of tropical fish, a marvelous meandering train, and an interactive stingray reef.

TOP EXPERIENCE

✪ San Jacinto Battleground State Historic Site

A significant historical attraction lies near the Houston Ship Channel, just 20 miles (32 km) east of the city. After driving through miles of stark petroleum plants, visitors to San Jacinto Battleground State Historic Site (3523 Hwy. 134, 281/479-2431, www. thc.texas.gov, daily 9am-6pm, free) encounter the welcoming beacon of Texas independence, where the stories of valiant warriors defending Texas's independence come alive.

The battleground site, with its remarkable 570-foot-tall (174-m) monument, 15 feet (4.6 m) taller than the Washington Monument, commemorates Texas's victory in its fight for independence. The 1,200-acre site, now owned by the Texas Historical Commission, preserves and interprets the legendary battleground where Texas Army troops under General Sam Houston defeated the Mexican Army in an 18-minute battle on April 21, 1836. The magnificent monument—topped by a 34-foot (10-m) star symbolizing the Lone Star Republic—is dedicated to the "Heroes of the Battle of San Jacinto and all others who contributed to the independence of Texas."

The ground level houses the San Jacinto Museum of History, containing 400,000 objects, documents, and books spanning 400 years of Texas

San Jacinto Battleground State Historic Site

history. The display case dedicated to Sam Houston is a highlight, containing personal artifacts and inspiring writings. Be sure to watch the fascinating 30-minute movie *Texas Forever!* The site's highlight is the observation deck, a 490-foot-tall (150-m) vantage point offering stunning sweeping views of the battlefield, ship channel, reflecting pool, and surrounding scenery. Don't be discouraged by the historic 1930s-era elevator—it's a quick ride to the top, where you'll be rewarded with an amazing panoramic view and enviable photo opportunities.

George Ranch Historical Park

A step back in time and away from the urban pace is George Ranch Historical Park (10215 FM 762, Richmond, 281/343-0218, www. georgeranch.org, Tues.-Fri. tours only, Sat. 9am-5pm, $15 adults, $12 seniors, $10 ages 5-15). About 30 miles (48 km) southwest of downtown near the community of Richmond, the 484-acre living-history site showcases four generations of the George family, settlers who began ranching operations here in the 1820s.

Visitors discover what life was like for Texans on a working cattle ranch through exhibits and displays at the pioneer farmstead, an 1890s Victorian mansion, and a 1930s ranch house. Nearby barns and working pens focus on 1930s-1940s ranching operations. Plan a few hours to explore this truly Texan locale, with daily demonstrations on tending to horses, pigs, and chickens, hands-on activities such as corn-grinding and weaving, and a chance to help harvest seasonal crops. You can even watch cowhands roping cattle. When it gets too hot outside, escape to the air-conditioned ranch house for exhibits, photographs, and artifacts about pioneer and farming life on the George Ranch.

RECREATION

Houston is home to several professional sports franchises, most notably the Texans football team, as well as myriad opportunities for outdoor activities such as golf, hiking, and cycling.

PARKS

Houston's showcase central park is Hermann Park, just outside downtown in the Museum District. Memorial Park is a haven for local hikers and bikers, a contrast to Hermann Park's strollers. The city operates dozens of neighborhood-oriented parks (visit www.houstontx.gov/parks). An outdoor experience near NASA is the Armand Bayou Nature Center.

Hermann Park

The huge green swath in the middle of the city map is Hermann Park (6001 Fannin St., 713/524-5876, www. houstontx.gov). In the heart of the Museum District just southwest of downtown, Hermann Park is a 400-acre magnet for joggers, dog walkers, bikers, and families, a rare green space in a city known for rampant development. Trails and trees are abundant, as are amenities and services, including a theater, a golf course, and a garden center. The park is filled with statues: Look for monuments to Sam Houston, Mahatma Gandhi, and the park's namesake George Hermann.

Memorial Park

Hugging the northwest corner of the city's inner loop is Memorial Park (6501 Memorial Dr., 713/845-1000, www.houstontx.gov), distinguished by its recreational facilities, primarily the hike and bike trails. Set on 1,400 acres that was once the World War I-era Camp Logan, Memorial Park is now a magnet for hiking and biking, and includes a full-service tennis center, a swimming pool, a golf course, a fitness center, baseball diamonds, a croquet field, and sand volleyball courts.

Armand Bayou Nature Center

Farther outside town but worth the 30-minute drive is Armand Bayou Nature Center (8500 Bay Area Blvd., Pasadena, 281/474-2551, www.abnc. org, Tues.-Sat. 9am-5pm, Sun. noon-5pm, $6 adults, $4 seniors and ages 4-12). Located near NASA on the west side of Galveston Bay, the nature center offers residents and visitors a chance to learn about native plant and animal species, hike on the discovery trails, or see the live animal displays featuring bison, hawks, and spiders. The main area of the park contains a boardwalk traversing the marshes and forests, providing a glimpse of the beautiful bayou region of East Texas. The best way to experience this natural wonder is by boat—consider taking a tour on the pontoon boat or signing up for a guided canoe tour.

HIKING

Despite reports claiming Houston and the South in general are the least-fit places in the nation, many residents are interested in exercise and health, although the city does not offer an abundance of hiking trails and coordinated recreational facilities.

The city's most popular outdoor destination for exercise is Buffalo Bayou, known as a biking destination. A slightly less-crowded area is nearby Seymour Lieberman Exercise Trail in Memorial Park. The 3-mile (4.8-km) trail is popular for daily workouts and has exercise stations and restrooms along the route. Dedicated runners use the nearby asphalt timing track to work on speed and develop skills, while the Memorial Park Picnic Loop offers a smooth surface for in-line skaters, traditional roller skate enthusiasts, and hikers. Dogs are welcome at the park—canine drinking fountains are at ground level along the jogging trails. Keep your pooch on a leash and bring waste bags.

A few miles outside town is the scenic tree-filled Houston Arboretum & Nature Center (4501 Woodway Dr. 713/681-8433, www.houstonarboretum.org, daily 7am-dusk). The arboretum's outer loop is a 2-mile (3.2-km) trail for hikers to combine exercise with bird and wildlife viewing. Its lush natural setting allows an escape from the concrete cityscape. For a topographically diverse alternative, consider a trek on the R. A. Vines Trail, offering up-close views of shallow wetlands, fish, and a boardwalk.

BIKING

Cyclists enjoy the challenging terrain along the city's Buffalo Bayou (1800 Allen Pkwy., 713/845-1000, www.buffalobayou.org), an urban greenbelt with the namesake waterway as its centerpiece. With the towering Houston skyline as a backdrop, the park draws bikers, joggers, art lovers, and walkers to its riverside trails and bustling activity. In addition to the smooth wide trails, the 124-acre park contains exercise stations, a recreation center, a disc golf course, a children's playground, and a popular dog recreation area. Public art abounds along the jogging trail, from stainless-steel objects representing tree roots on an overpass to the large stone block sculptures that remain from the city's demolished civic auditorium. Visit the park's website to download PDFs of trail maps. The southwest section of adjacent Memorial Park contains color-coded trails with maps at the trailheads, and Infantry Woods

provides an advanced trail for those with superior skills.

GOLF

Houston's Parks and Recreation Department (www.houstontx.gov) operates seven respectable municipal golf courses. Three of the most popular are within the loop, drawing golfers and hackers to well-maintained grounds and offering affordable greens fees.

The gem of the downtown-area municipal courses is Memorial Park Golf Course (1001 E. Memorial Loop Dr., 713/862-4033), a 600-acre oasis of rolling fairways and challenging greens. Originally a nine-hole sand green course for soldiers at Camp Logan (now Memorial Park), the links feature lush landscapes, putting and chipping greens, a golf museum, a contemporary clubhouse, and an always-packed driving range offering shade and lighting.

Adjacent to the city's Museum District, Hermann Park Golf Course (2155 Cambridge St., 713/526-0077) is another natural escape from the surrounding urban scenery. Lengthy fairways, snug out-of-bounds, and occasional water hazards make Hermann a favorite among serious golfers, who appreciate the shade of the ancient oaks and steady surface of the Bermuda grass greens. While at the turn, be sure to order a hot dog or two from the clubhouse kitchen.

Farther south of town is Gus Wortham Park Golf Course (7000 Capitol St., 713/928-4260), a former private course now operated by the city. The sportiest of the three downtown-area courses, Wortham Park features hilly terrain, tight turns, and several short par-fours. The course also offers a practice green and bunker, a chipping green, and a full driving range.

SPECTATOR SPORTS

Houston is a football town. Once home to the storied Houston Oilers, the city has hosted the NFL's Houston Texans (832/667-2000, www.houstontexans.com) since 2002. The Texans have become a formidable franchise that continues to draw substantial crowds to see defensive end J. J. Watt at NRG Stadium (1 NRG Pkwy.).

Minute Maid Park, home of the Houston Astros

Sports fans are also drawn to the venerable Houston Astros (713/259-8000, www.houston.astros.mlb.com). In 1965, the Astros became the primary occupants of the then-futuristic Astrodome, billed as the "Eighth Wonder of the World." It was a welcome respite from Houston's horrendous humidity, and the Astros assembled some worthy teams in the 1980s, most notably with hometown hero Nolan Ryan, and two decades later, local legend Roger Clemens, and a powerhouse offense in the "Killer B's"—Craig Biggio, Jeff Bagwell, and Lance Berkman. The Astros fled to their current home in downtown's Minute Maid Park (501 Crawford St.), a classic urban ball field with a modern retractable roof. The Astros gained national prominence in 2017 when they won the World Series, before their bright star was tarnished in 2019 by a cheating scandal.

Basketball isn't as big a draw in Texas as football, but the Houston Rockets (713/627-3865, www.nba.com/rockets) have always had a considerable following. Their successful 1990s teams, featuring top-notch talent such as Clyde "The Glide" Drexler and Hakeem "The Dream" Olajuwon, were the talk of the NBA during their glory years, when they won the NBA title in 1993 and 1994. The Rockets hold court at the downtown Toyota Center (1510 Polk St.).

ENTERTAINMENT AND EVENTS

The Urban Cowboy legend was born in Houston in the early 1980s, and in some parts of town, visitors can still get a feel for true honky-tonk nightlife. Houston has a healthy blues scene, and the downtown bars and dance clubs are reminders of the city's cosmopolitan culture. The performing arts in Houston truly befit the nation's fourth-largest city, particularly its internationally renowned opera and ballet companies and spectacular symphony.

NIGHTLIFE

With the fluid nature of clubs, instead of attempting to capture the moment's trendy venue, the following listings focus on established sites that have proven their venerability as the trends come and go.

Downtown

Surprisingly, pockets of downtown Houston are completely quiet at night, and the urban core doesn't tend to be a scene. Still, visitors can find notable clubs that boast a distinctive vibe.

Dean's Credit Clothing bar

An interesting spot to grab a cocktail is Dean's Credit Clothing (316 Main St., 713/227-3326, www.deansdowntown.com, Tues.-Sun. 5pm-2am). That's not a misprint: Inside a downtown 1930s clothing store, Dean's strives to maintain as much of its early charm as possible. Grab a spot at the low-lit bar, or sink into one of the comfy vintage couches. Original features from the 1893 building include the ornate flooring and exposed bricks. The craft cocktails are strong and well-made, with clever names referencing old-time department stores like Woolworth's and Penney's. On Sunday nights, Dean's hosts an acoustic lounge act or small jazz combo.

The energy picks up a few doors down at the hipper Nightingale Room (308 Main St., 832/968-3370, www.nightingaleroom.com, Tues.-Sat. 4pm-2am). Cocktails are a major draw, and the bourbon-based Godfather is a big hit. So is the booming sound system, evident when the 2nd-floor DJ helms the turntables and spins hip-hop from the impressive collection of vinyl behind the bar.

A few blocks away is the low-key and comfy Warren's Inn (307 Travis St., 713/247-9207, Mon.-Fri. 11am-2am, Sat. noon-2am, Sun. 2pm-2am). A longtime downtown lounge, Warren's is a dark and mellow place where the regulars look like they've occupied their spots at the bar for decades. Fortunately, the happy hour prices are similarly retro, with cans of brew offered for $2-3. Be sure to check out the jukebox with appropriate soundtrack music from the 1940s-1960s.

Warren's Inn in downtown Houston

If you're not interested in the latest trends or worried about specifically appropriate footwear, head to La Carafe (813 Congress St., 713/229-9399, daily 1pm-2am). Known for its laid-back vibe and legendary jukebox, La Carafe is in a historic brick building that exudes character. Order wine, punch in Otis Redding on the jukebox, and settle in for a cozy evening.

The Heights

Transcending its former trendy reputation is Max's Wine Dive (4720 Washington Ave., 713/880-8737, www.maxswinedive.com, Mon.-Thurs. 11am-midnight, Fri.-Sat. 10am-2am, Sun. 10am-midnight), just south of The Heights. "Dive" is a misnomer, since the dimly lit and comfortable locale caters to an upscale clientele, but the pairings of drink and food are down and dirty. You never realized a glass of red wine would complement a burger so well, or a flute of champagne with fried chicken. More than 150 wines are available by the glass or bottle, and many are available to go. An added bonus: Most of the beverages and food are Texas organic products.

If you'd rather dress down than up, The Heights is especially accommodating. Soak up a true Lone Star State experience at Alice's Tall Texan (4904 N. Main St., 713/862-0141, Sun.-Fri. 10am-midnight, Sat. 11am-1am), with no-frills cafeteria-style seating in a modest brick building and friendly folks chatting above the din of classic jukebox country music and cheap beer. For just $2.50 you can order a giant goblet of Lone Star or Shiner draft beer accompanied by a $1 bag of popcorn.

Another dive-ish option is Big Star Bar (1005 W. 19th St., 281/501-9560, www.bigstarbar.com, daily 4pm-2am). Dimly lit with a classic checkerboard floor, Big Star is a comfy place to kick back with a cheap bottle of beer and shoot a few rounds of pool while listening to Johnny Cash. An outdoor patio with a chain-link fence offers a friendly place to chat and hangout, and the vintage furniture and picnic tables were designed with chilling in mind.

Just north of The Heights in Garden Oaks-Oak Forest is the welcoming Petrol Station (985 Wakefield Dr., 713/957-2875, Mon. 5pm-midnight, Tues.-Fri. 2pm-midnight, Sat. noon-1am, Sun. noon-10pm). Petrol Station is known for an impressive selection of local beers and its burgers—some of the heartiest and tastiest in town. Choose from lamb, beef, or veggie, and top it with flavorful mushrooms and grilled onions.

Uptown

For a reliable cocktail and above-average bar food, check out the West End (5320 Westheimer Rd., 713/590-0616, www.westend-houston.com, Mon.-Fri. 3pm-2am, Sat.-Sun. 11am-2am). The West End is an ideal place to take things up a notch from typical bar fare. The margaritas are a bit stronger, with higher-quality ingredients, and the burgers and wings are extra flavorful.

For those in search of a classic British-style pub, head to Richmond Arms (5920 Richmond Ave., 713/784-7722, www.richmondarmspub-houston.com, daily 11am-2am). It's an ideal place to watch a soccer game on TV, and you can easily identify fellow fans at the outdoor picnic tables painted with team and national flags. Not surprisingly, there are plenty of fine British ales on tap, and the food is surprisingly good.

Montrose

One of the most colorful places to spend a late night is Poison Girl (1641 Westheimer Rd., 713/527-9929, daily 4pm-2am). The first thing you'll notice are the bright pink walls; next are the incredible selection of bourbons and pinball machines. Even if you're not a bourbon fan, chat with the bartender to help pick your, um, poison. Spend some time on the back patio, where you'll be in the presence of a fun-loving crowd and the largest statue of the Kool-Aid Man you'll ever see (or attempt to climb).

For the craft-beer crowd, it doesn't get much better than ✪ Hay Merchant (1100 Westheimer Rd., 713/528-9805, www.haymerchant. com, Mon.-Fri. 3pm-2am, Sat.-Sun. 11am-2am). Locals love the affordable sandwiches and rotating variety of beer. Bartenders will suggest brews based on specific preferences, and the food is always a step above normal bar fare. The Korean fried-chicken sandwich is a perfect example of a comfort food taken to the next level with a slightly spicy gochujang sauce and crispy exterior.

Far more refined is the cocktail-minded Anvil Bar & Refuge (1424 Westheimer Rd., 713/523-1622, www. anvilhouston.com, daily 4pm-2am), a place where steady crowds take their booze seriously. The bartenders shun the term "mixologists," but they're deft at concocting perfect cocktails. One of the bar's most popular is the Nitro Cuba Libre, the fanciest rum and Coke you'll ever experience, dispensed via a nitrogen tap. Also consider a First Growth, made with gin, pineapple juice, elderflower, and sage.

West University

Many Houstonians associate pub crawls with West University's Rice Village area, where a collection of English-style brewpubs has kept nearby students out of the libraries for decades. Two locales for a freshly poured pint, the jukebox of your dreams, and the freewheeling college scene are The Ginger Man (5607 Morningside Dr., 713/526-2770, www.gingermanpub.com, Mon.-Fri.

2pm-2am, Sat.-Sun. 1pm-2am) and nearby Little Woodrow's (5611 Morningside Dr., 713/522-4438, Mon.-Fri. 3pm-2am, Sat.-Sun. noon-2am).

GAY BARS

Houston has perhaps the largest gay scene in the South, centered on the city's Montrose district, west of downtown, where most of the gay bars are, both understated and overblown. One of the most popular clubs is JR's (808 Pacific St., 713/521-2519, www. jrsbarandgrill.com), drawing a semi-professional crowd for drink specials, karaoke, and male dancers. Parking is hard to find, so use the valet service across the street.

Next door is the popular South Beach (810 Pacific St., 713/521-0107, www.southbeachthenightclub.com, Thurs. 9pm-2am), a hot spot for dancing. South Beach attracts a primarily gay clientele, but everyone is welcome on the dance floor, where suspended jets spray liquid ice on the crowd to keep things cool. Nearby is Ripcord (715 Fairview St., 713/521-2792, daily 1pm-2am), reportedly the second-oldest gay bar in Texas. Pool is a popular draw, as are the cheap drinks.

LIVE MUSIC
Blues

Mention blues towns and most people think of Memphis or Chicago, but Houston belongs in the mix, with a long-standing tradition of swampy bayou blues. Some of the grittiest and most soulful players have emerged from the city's downtown African American neighborhoods.

The Continental Club (3700 Main St., 713/529-9899, www. continentalclub.com, Thurs. 6pm-2am, Fri. 7pm-2am, Sat. 8pm-2am) doesn't stage blues exclusively—roots and alternative rock acts are often on the bill—but the local and touring blues bands that play here are typically the best around. An offshoot of the legendary Austin venue, Houston's version of the Continental is appropriately more sprawling but still dedicated to soulful music.

Continental Club

Consistently topping Houston's annual "best blues club" lists is West University's The Big Easy Social and Pleasure Club (5731 Kirby Dr., 713/523-9999, www.thebigeasyblues. com, daily 7pm-2am). The quality musicianship is the epitome of integrity. Weekends are set aside for top-notch touring acts and Houston's premier local blues bands, while weeknights offer themes like open jams and dance parties. Sunday-night zydeco is another highlight.

Another local favorite is The Shakespeare Pub (14129 Memorial Dr., 281/497-4625, www. shakespearepub.net, daily 5pm-2am). Locals rule the stage here, including luminaries such as John McVey, Eugene Moody, and Texas Johnny Brown. If you get a chance, drop by at dinnertime on Sunday for Spare Time Murray's weekly Early Blues Jam.

Country and Western

Houston is the home of the Urban Cowboy, so grab those boots if you're fixin' to head out for some two-stepping at one of these fine dance halls, including the city's big-box country music venues. Near the Galleria among the trendy upscale dance clubs is the refreshingly unhip Firehouse Saloon (5930 Southwest Freeway, 713/977-1962, www.firehousesaloon.com, Sun.-Wed. 7pm-11pm, Fri.-Sat. 5pm-2am). There's some flashiness here—big ol' shiny belt buckles, fancy light machines, Vegas-style video games—but the crowd is genuinely friendly. Cover bands take the stage most nights, but you'll find the occasional worthy local band.

For an overwhelming dose of Lone Star State culture, drop by the Big Texas Dance Hall and Saloon (803 E. NASA Blvd., 281/461-4400, www. bigtexassaloon.com, Wed.-Sat. 7pm-2am). It's a bit hokey, with pseudo-rustic decor of cacti and Western "artifacts," but the scene is vibrant, especially for singles. Live music is the big draw on Thursday, when regional acts get boots scootin', but DJs fill the dance floor most weekends.

For drinking and country music without dancing, drop by Goode's Armadillo Palace (5015 Kirby Ave., 713/526-9700, www. thearmadillopalace.com, Tues.-Thurs. 11am-11pm, Fri. 11am-2am, Sat. 4pm-2am), among the cluster of Goode Company barbecue and Texas restaurants. The Armadillo has a huge bar in the middle and tiny stage in the corner, and fortunately the pure honky-tonk sounds from the bands are huge enough to fill the venue and get a few people two-stepping in the limited space near the stage.

Jazz

One of the many benefits of being a music fan in a big city is access to quality jazz clubs. Houston is a major player on the jazz circuit and a hotbed for the genre's rising stars. The stalwart on the scene is Sambuca (909 Texas Ave., 713/224-5299, www.sambucarestaurant.com, Mon.-Wed. 11am-11pm, Thurs. 11am-midnight, Fri. 11am-1am, Sat. 4pm-1am, Sun. 4pm-11pm). In the stunning historic Rice Hotel, Sambuca is a jazz fan's dream—a classy downtown venue offering nightly performances from local and national performers. Get a juicy steak from the acclaimed restaurant, and visit the cigar room after your meal or during the set break.

Intimate Cezanne (4100 Montrose Blvd., 713/522-9621, www.cezannejazz.com, Fri.-Sat. 9pm-midnight), a 40-seat venue in the trendy Montrose district, is considered Houston's premier jazz club, where aficionados get to sit feet from national acts. Every seat is a good one, and you'll feel every note being played.

Concert Venues

Since Houston is such a business and convention-oriented city, visitors often have expense accounts to afford the pricey tickets for familiar rock acts. Virtually every touring act makes a stop in Houston. Browse the online calendar for the downtown entertainment complex Bayou Place (500 Texas St., 713/227-0957, www.bayouplace.com).

Away from the hassle of downtown, head to folky Anderson Fair (2007 Grant St., 832/767-2785, www.andersonfair.net), tucked away in the Montrose area and hosting up-and-coming folk and roots rock acts for decades. It continues to stage some of Texas's most popular Americana acts. Note: Anderson Fair is only open on weekends.

PERFORMING ARTS
The Houston Grand Opera

A big city deserves a big-time opera company, and Houston has the Houston Grand Opera (713/228-6737, www.houstongrandopera.org). Performances are held at the downtown Wortham Theater Center (501 Texas Ave., 832/487-7000, www.houstonfirsttheaters.com). It's the only opera company on the planet to win a Tony, two Emmys, and two Grammy awards, and it has a reputation for commissioning and performing new works, with dozens of world premieres over 50 years. The company tours extensively, bringing productions to Europe, Japan, and Egypt, and has been lauded for accessibility: Tickets for some shows start at $15, and the casual dress series is popular among young people.

The Houston Ballet

World-class Houston Ballet (601 Preston St., 713/523-6300, www.houstonballet.org) also utilizes the beautiful Wortham Theater Center and has developed a national reputation for making stars of principal dancers as well as staging contemporary edgy ballets. In recent years, the company has taken its show to China, London, Canada, and Washington DC's Kennedy Center.

The Houston Symphony

Highly respected Houston Symphony (713/224-4240, www.

houstonsymphony.org) has been impressing audiences at the magnificent downtown Jones Hall (615 Louisiana St.) since 1966. Shows include a classical season, a pops series, *Messiah* performances at Christmas, and family concerts. In the summer, the symphony performs outdoor shows and stages children's performances throughout the region.

Theater

Houston boasts several high-quality theater companies, but two consistently emerge at the top. The Alley Theatre (615 Texas Ave., 713/220-5700, www.alleytheatre.org) stages productions in a Brutalist fortress in the heart of downtown that's separated into two stages. Classic and contemporary performances consistently draw diverse audiences.

Also drawing rave reviews is the Ensemble Theatre (3535 Main St., 713/520-0055, www.ensemblehouston. org). Billed as the largest African American professional theater company in the country with its own productions and facility, the Ensemble regularly stages acclaimed dramas, comedies, and musicals for enthusiastic crowds. The company also runs an educational touring program and a popular summer training program for youth.

EVENTS
Winter

Each year in mid-January, the Antioch Missionary Baptist Church of Christ is a gathering site for the Gardere Martin Luther King Jr. Oratory Competition (500 Clay St., 713/867-3286, www.gardere.com). Sponsored by the Gardere law firm for nearly two decades, the event is a highly anticipated contest for elementary school students, who research, write, and deliver inspiring speeches dedicated to Dr. King's legacy. The competition also includes a spirited performance by the Salvation Army Choir.

In mid-February, the Texas Home and Garden Show (8400 Kirby Dr., 800/654-1480, www. texashomeandgarden.com) offers interactive displays and more than 1,500 exhibitors at the Reliant Center to help with spring gardening plans.

Spring

Every March, the University of Texas Health Science Center presents the popular Brain Night for Kids (7000 Fannin St., 713/521-1515, www. thehealthmuseum.org), featuring presentations about how the brain works, a dissection of a sheep's brain, an informative video, and other brainy activities.

In April, don't miss the Bayou City Cajun Fest (7979 N. Eldridge Pkwy., 281/890-5500, www.tradersvillage. com) at Traders Village. Patrons enjoy crawfish, po'boys, zydeco bands, and all kinds of Cajun culture. Another popular annual springtime event is the AsiaFest (11903 Bellaire Blvd., 713/784-1112, www.asiasociety.org), featuring an impressive parade, food booths, and cultural activities at the Alief Community Park in southwest Houston each May.

Summer

It gets sweltering in Houston during the summer months, but that doesn't deter locals from celebrating. One of the best-known annual events is Juneteenth (7800 Airport Blvd., 713/558-2600, www.houstonculture. org), commemorating the day in June that enslaved Texans learned about their freedom via the Emancipation

Proclamation. Juneteenth activities include national gospel, blues, and jazz acts taking the stage at Hermann Park, along with plenty of good eats and revelry.

September is still the height of the summer in Houston, and residents celebrate by enjoying hot jazz at the Houston International Jazz Festival (520 Texas Ave., 713/839-7000, www.jazzeducation.org), with local and nationally known jazz artists at the Bayou Music Center.

Fall

Get your ghoul on with the city's annual Ghost Tour (www.houstonghosttour.com) throughout October. Hauntees gather in the scary suburb of Spring, where they can get freaked out by various urban legends and recreated historical death scenes.

People descend en masse on downtown neighborhoods on November 2 for the Dia de Los Muertos Festival (4912 Main St., 713/343-0218, www.hispanichouston.com). This Latin American cultural event includes parades and festivals honoring deceased family and friends.

SHOPPING

Mention "shopping" and "Houston" and most people immediately think of the Galleria, a sprawling community unto itself on the western edge of the city's outer loop. It's a glassy, bustling, commercial destination that inspires some and intimidates others. Plenty of shopping options run from exclusive high-end (Galleria) to funky bargain-basement (The Heights). Despite being associated with the Urban Cowboy mystique, Houston does not have an overabundance of specialty shops with Western gear, although you're likely to find flashy rhinestone-esque clothing.

DOWNTOWN

One of the most popular downtown shopping destinations is the pleasantly modest Shops at Houston Center (1200 McKinney St., 713/759-1442, www.shopsathc.com, hours vary), 50 specialty stores and boutiques beneath a canopy-style atrium. Look for jewelry, home decor, and quick bites in the two-block complex. The shops are connected to Houston's Downtown Tunnels (713/650-3022, tour info at 713/392-0867, www.houstonhistoricaltours.com), a 6-mile (9.7-km) system of air-conditioned subterranean walkways that links dozens of downtown buildings.

THE HEIGHTS

Shopping destinations in The Heights reflect the neighborhood's funky and trendy vibe. A good example is Casa Ramirez (241 W. 19th St., 713/880-2420), featuring Latin American folk art, clothing items, and traditional Latin American wares, from furniture to handbags and paintings. Look for Mr. or Mrs. Ramirez, who can provide suggestions and explain the shop's many interesting items.

See the culture of rural America at Wabash Antiques and Feedstore (4537 N. Shepherd Dr., 713/863-8322, www.wabashfeed.com), with high-end pet food and the sounds and sights of farms, including antique equipment, lawn art, and plenty of hens, turkeys, kittens, and rabbits.

Texas-style fashion boutique Hello Lucky (1025 Studewood St., 713/864-3556, www.hellolucky.com) is in a small historic home and filled with Texas-themed clothing and knickknacks. Featured items include jewelry, T-shirts, tote bags, and accessories like gold armadillo cufflinks.

UPTOWN

One of the city's most popular shopping destinations is the colossal Galleria (5085 Westheimer Rd., 713/622-0663, www.galleriahouston. com). This city within a city—the fourth-largest mall in the country—draws 30 million visitors annually. Noted for its remarkable glass atriums and suspended balconies, the Galleria contains a popular ice-skating rink, two high-rise hotels, and 400 shops, including high-end Nordstrom, Saks Fifth Avenue, Neiman Marcus, Cartier, Gucci, and Tiffany & Co. The best time to experience the Galleria is Saturday afternoon: It's an absolute madhouse, and you won't get much shopping done, but the people-watching is the best the city has to offer. Grab a latte and keep an eye out for the girls in flashy gowns celebrating their *quinceañera,* a Latin American rite of passage dedicated to a girl's 15th birthday.

WEST UNIVERSITY

Another of Houston's most popular shopping destinations is Rice Village (Rice Blvd. and Kirby Dr., 713/302-8918, www.ricevillagedistrict.com), just west of Rice University. This 16-block complex has been a favorite place for bargain hunting, browsing, and people-watching since the 1930s. The Village features scores of independent shops and eclectic boutiques along with local restaurants and services, some in historic homes, others in modest 1950s strip centers.

Independent Brazos Bookstore (2421 Bissonnet St., 713/523-0701, www.brazosbookstore.com) is fiercely loved by local book people—it was rescued from closure by a group of concerned citizens. Spend an afternoon out of the heat browsing, reading, and chatting with the knowledgeable and friendly staff.

GREATER HOUSTON

An eclectic mix of Asian shops and restaurants awaits on Harwin Drive, roughly between Gessner and Fondren Streets. The area offers an epic mash-up of the strip malls and gaudy signs of American suburban sprawl with the cultural diversity of Thai, Pakistani, Indian, and Chinese vendors and eateries. Spend an afternoon browsing for unexpected gems and bargain clothes, accessories, furniture, and knickknacks. Just a few miles west on Harwin is Chinatown, a concentrated collection of Chinese establishments, including a mall with bookstores, music, gifts, and cooking items.

FOOD

Houston has 11,000 restaurants, and recently the city's culinary scene has drawn the attention of national food critics and restaurateurs, regularly earning high marks. People here love eating out, so the array of options ranges from fast food to haute cuisine. The city's enormous international population means there is regional cuisine rarely seen elsewhere. Home-grown varieties include barbecue, Tex-Mex, and Southern cooking. The following suggestions don't represent the trends in Houston's always-evolving culinary scene but are examples of the impressive variety, with an emphasis on long-standing eateries.

DOWNTOWN
Steak

A steak house doesn't have to be stodgy, and the scene is downright comfortable at III Forks (1201 Fannin

St., 713/658-9457, www.3forks.com, Mon.-Thurs. 11am-10pm, Fri. 11am-11pm, Sat. 4pm-11pm, $16-49). Sumptuous steaks take center stage, with featured double-cut strip, filet mignon, and porterhouse. Sides cost extra but are ideal accompaniments, including the popular spinach and six-cheese potatoes. Save room for the Texas pecan cake.

Well-heeled nontraditional downtown steak house Vic & Anthony's (1510 Texas St., 713/228-1111, www.vicandanthonys.com, Mon.-Fri. 11am-10pm, Sat.-Sun. 5pm-10pm, $18-51) is chic, minimalist, and tightly packed. Vic & Anthony's sticks with the basics—a simple menu of high-quality cuts of meat and a few seafood and chicken options. Outstanding salads and appetizers include the pear salad and oysters, and the wine selection is impressive if pricey. Steaks are enormous, and the bone-in rib-eye is considered the best in town.

Cajun

With direct access to seafood, sauces, spices, and swamps, Houston is one of the few places in the country with authentic Cajun cuisine. It doesn't get much better than the legendary New Orleans establishment ✪ Brennan's (3300 Smith St., 713/522-9711, www.brennanshouston.com, Sun.-Fri. 11am-2pm and 5pm-10pm, Sat. 5:45pm-10pm, $13-41). In a historic brick mansion, Brennan's offers classic Louisiana flavors such as étouffée, lump crab cakes, and pecan-crusted amberjack. Breakfasts are legendary, and the eggs and delectable sauces taste even better paired with live jazz music during the weekend New Orleans Jazz Brunch.

Less formal is the popular downtown lunch chain Treebeard's (315

Travis St., 713/228-2622, www.treebeards.com, Mon.-Sat. 11am-2:30pm, $8-16). All the Creole classics are here—shrimp étouffée, jambalaya, gumbo, and a hearty dose of red beans and rice. Be sure to order a side of jalapeño cornbread, and save room for the bread pudding with whiskey sauce. Treebeard's isn't open for dinner.

Houston's famous Irma's Original

Tex-Mex

For true Tex-Mex, Irma's Original (22 N. Chenevert St., 713/222-0767, www.irmasoriginal.com, Mon.-Wed. 8am-3pm, Thurs.-Fri. 8am-10pm, Sat. 4pm-10pm, $13-28) was named for founder Irma Gonzalez Galvan, a Rio Grande Valley native who moved to Houston with her family in the 1940s and became one of the city's most famous chefs. Her authentic recipes are the ultimate Texas comfort food, including *caldo* (corn-based chicken soup), fajitas, and especially the enchiladas—try the mole sauce and green tomatillo options. The service may not be spectacular, but the food is supreme.

Breakfast

The Breakfast Klub (3711 Travis St., 713/528-8561, www.thebreakfastklub.com, Mon.-Fri. 7am-2pm, Sat.-Sun. 8am-2pm, $9-24) is known for its long line and its famous chicken and waffles, worth waiting up to an hour to experience. The line moves fairly quickly and is shorter if you arrive before 9am. The diversity of your fellow line-mates offers a refreshing perspective on this international city and its love for good food. The chicken and waffles are perfectly prepared, with tender and flavorful centers. The "biskuits" and gravy are flaky and flavorful.

THE HEIGHTS
Barbecue

Possibly Houston's best barbecue, ✪ Gatlin's Barbecue (3510 Ella Blvd., 713/869-4227, www.gatlinsbbq.com, Mon.-Thurs. 11am-8-pm, Fri.-Sat. 11am-9pm, $12-36) is in an uninspiring strip mall with perfectly smoked meat. Order a Gatlin sandwich just to taste the amazing bun, a buttery toasted delight. The meat is the main draw, with tender succulent brisket and savory smoked sausage.

UPTOWN
Steak

Although Uptown lacks the historical charm of downtown, it has a few of the city's most esteemed steak houses. A favorite is Pappas Brothers Steakhouse (5839 Westheimer Rd., 713/780-7352, www.pappasbros.com, Mon.-Thurs. 5pm-10pm, Fri.-Sat. 5pm-11pm, $17-53), where steak lovers gather for perfectly marbled cuts of top-notch beef. The filets are Pappas Brothers' specialty, and the somewhat lofty prices (upper $40s) feel like a wise investment once you're savoring each tender bite. The sides are also top-notch; suggested options include potatoes au gratin and asparagus.

Just down the street is Chama Gaucha (5865 Westheimer Rd., 713/244-9500, www.chamagaucha.

com, Mon.-Fri. 11:30am-2:30pm and 5pm-10pm, Sat. 4:30pm-10pm, Sun. 3pm-9pm, $13-44), a Brazilian-style steak house where the staff serves a plethora of meat options with sharp and shiny knives. The filet mignon and sirloin are excellent, but other styles to consider are the bacon-wrapped variety and a cut of lamb. The introductory salad bar may tempt you with its leafy goodness, colorful vegetables, and bread medallions, but don't overdo it at the expense of the magnificent meat.

Lebanese

Uptown contains several noteworthy informal lunch venues, the best among them serving savory Lebanese food. Mary'z Lebanese Cuisine (5825 Richmond Ave., 832/251-1955, www.maryzcuisine.com, daily 11am-midnight, $8-19) is tiny, but the tastes are huge, especially in freshly made kebabs, falafel, shawarma, and baba ghanoush. Complement your meal with a Lebanese beer like Almazo. At night, Mary'z becomes a hot spot for young adults who toke on hookahs.

American

One of the finest meals in town is at ✪ Lucille's (5512 La Branch St., 713/568-2505, www.lucilleshouston.com, Tues.-Thurs. 11am-9pm, Fri. 11am-10pm, Sat. 10am-3pm and 4pm-10pm, Sun. 10am-3pm, $13-39), in a cozy historic home run by chefs Chris Williams and Khang Hoang. Chris's great-grandmother Lucille was a local African American culinary pioneer, and Lucille's replicates some of her most famous recipes. This is Southern cooking at its best, with an emphasis on traditional dishes featuring exquisite sauces and sides. Order shrimp and grits, catfish and grits, or cheesy grits, or step it up and get the bone-in pork chop or smothered steak. One of the best items on the menu is the braised oxtail—the savory sauce makes this hearty dish a delectable meal.

Locals can't get enough of classy Cafe Annie (1800 Post Oak Blvd., 713/840-1111, www.cafeanniehouston. com, Mon.-Fri. 11:30am-10pm, Sat. 5pm-10:30pm, $12-43). Elegance exudes from the decor and the tantalizing appetizers of goat cheese crepes and entrées like the cinnamon-roasted pheasant and cocoa-roasted chicken. Haute Texas cuisine is represented in the cilantro-enhanced mussel soup and barbecued sweet potatoes. Reservations are strongly advised.

The enormous sandwich spot Kenny & Ziggy's (2327 Post Oak Blvd., 713/871-8883, www.kennyandziggys. com, Mon.-Fri. 7am-9pm, Sat.-Sun. 8am-9pm, $13-35) is a deli, a rarity in Texas. The corned beef and pastrami are favorites, especially piled high on a reuben. Portions are enormous, so consider splitting a plate. Save space for the potato salad and pickles.

Mexican

Molina's Cantina (7901 Westheimer Rd., 713/782-0861, www.molinas cantina.com, Tues.-Sat. 11am-9:30pm, Sun.-Mon. 11am-9pm, $9-20) is a traditional Mexican restaurant on the western edge of Uptown. A Houston institution since 1941, Molina's is the ultimate destination for old-school Tex-Mex, and the signature Mexico City Dinner captures it all: chili con queso, tamale, tostada, taco, and enchilada with rice and beans.

MONTROSE-KIRBY
Japanese

Houston's version of Uchi (904 Westheimer Rd., 713/522-4808, www.

Lucille's

uchirestaurants.com, Sun.-Thurs. 5pm-10pm, Fri.-Sat. 5pm-11pm, reservations strongly advised, $17-49) is as good as the original, with exquisite flavor combinations. Order a bottle of wine and the fried brussels sprouts to start—the smoky caramelized flavors are perfect with the leafy green vegetables. The sushi rolls are a delight, with disparate yet instantly perfect intertwined tastes. Examples include the salmon and Asian pear or yellowfin tuna and oranges. The *hamachi nabe* is tuna topped by a soy-based broth and an egg. Each of the uniquely crafted dishes are expertly explained by the waitstaff, who politely suggest menu items and recommend dishes based on your level of adventure and budget.

American

Close to the Rice University campus is contemporary, classy, and casual Local Foods (2424 Dunstan Rd., 713/521-7800, www.houstonlocalfoods.com, daily 10am-8:30pm, $13-35), an ideal spot for lunch in a welcoming environment. The restaurant is best known for its scrumptious Crunchy Chicken sandwich; the pretzel bun is worth ordering on its own. Pair it with the clean-tasting lemongrass soup and the flavorful kale.

Houstonians go berserk over Backstreet Café (1103 S. Shepherd Dr., 713/521-2239, www.backstreetcafe.net, Mon.-Fri. 11am-10pm, Sat. 10am-11pm, Sun. 10am-9pm, $12-30), a wildly popular two-story New American venue revered for its crafty chef, Hugo Ortega of Hugo's, who specializes in quality comfort food. Backstreet is known for its "crusted" dishes, including mustard-crusted salmon and sesame-crusted shrimp. The most popular entrée is the meat loaf tower, an aptly named stack of seasoned meat, garlic mashed potatoes, sautéed spinach, and mushroom gravy. Backstreet breakfasts are legendary, as is the Sunday jazz brunch (11am-3pm).

Popular with locals is ✪ Benjy's (2424 Dunstan Rd., 713/522-7602, www.benjys.com, Tues.-Thurs. 4pm-10pm, Fri.-Sat. 4pm-11pm, Sun.-Mon. 4pm-9pm, $13-33), a contemporary venue with outstanding food and service. Things change often, from the artwork to the menu, keeping things fresh. Seafood is the specialty (smoked salmon, seasoned shrimp), but Benjy's also serves comfort food with modern flair, including sandwiches and entrées such as the pecan- and pistachio-crusted chicken with mixed potato gratin. Locals flock to Benjy's for brunch, and the Bloody Marys are some of the best in the city, with wasabi instead of horseradish.

Mexican

A visit to this part of town is incomplete without a meal at the tremendous ✪ Hugo's (1600 Westheimer Rd., 713/524-7744, www.hugosrestaurant. net, Mon.-Thurs. 11am-10pm, Fri.-Sat. 11am-11pm, Sun. 10am-9pm, $15-39), a chic open-air hacienda serving trendy Mexican dishes. Start with Hugo's signature velvety margarita, paired with a tantalizing appetizer such as the squash-blossom quesadillas or one of four ceviches. Entrées range from savory pork *carnitas* to tender snapper Veracruzana. Desserts are legendary, especially the flan and Mexican hot chocolate, containing freshly roasted and ground cocoa beans.

Italian

Montrose residents can't get enough risotto, and several worthy Italian

Lua Viet Kitchen

options satisfy their craving, chief among them fresh, authentic, and homemade Divino Italian Restaurant (1830 W. Alabama St., 713/807-1123, www.divinoitalian.com, Tues.-Thurs. 5:30pm-10pm, Fri.-Sat. 5:30pm-10:30pm, $14-49). Locals love the Parma-style risotto, though the boar sausage-style is also commendable. In-house pasta specialties include Merlin's papardelle for mushroom lovers. The seasonal seafood dishes are consistently excellent.

Another notable destination is quaint and upscale DaMarco Cucina E Vino (1520 Westheimer Rd., 713/807-8857, www.damarcohouston. com, Tues.-Thurs. 11:30am-2pm and 5:30pm-10pm, Fri. 11:30am-2pm and 5:30pm-10pm, Sat. 5:30pm-10pm, $16-51), known for top-notch ingredients and the inventive flavor combos of renowned chef Marco Wiles. Diners choose Tuscany- and Texas-inspired dishes, including savory chianti-braised pork ribs, sea bass with grilled grapefruit, and roasted Texas quail.

Other suggested menu items include the flavorful lamb chops with a tasty cumin-based yogurt sauce, truffle pasta, served table-side, and the sweet corn lobster ravioli.

Vietnamese

Houston has an abundance of Vietnamese restaurants, some long-standing and consistently serving quality food.

For a modern fresh take, head to ✪ Lua Viet Kitchen (1540 W. Alabama St., 346/227-7047, www. luavietkicten.com, Sun.-Thurs. 11am-9pm, Fri.-Sat. 11am-10pm, $9-26), in contemporary space with suspended vertical lighting. Locally sourced ingredients (a list of contributing Houston-area farmers is on the menu) include the salt-and-pepper shrimp and shaking beef. Amazing rice-based dishes include the five-spiced hen. Lua's also has an extensive vegetarian menu.

Known for its late hours as much as its food, Mai's (3401 Milam St.,

713/520-5300, www.maishouston. com, Mon.-Thurs. 11am-3am, Fri.-Sat. 11am-4am, $8-27) draws enthusiastic revelers and foodies for dishes like *tom xao thap cam* (shrimp with mixed vegetables in a sumptuous sauce), *bun bo hue* (a flavorful soup with just the right amount of spice), and *mi xao don* (savory meats atop crispy noodles).

If you're craving tasty Vietnamese food and only have a few bucks to spare, head to Cali Sandwich and Pho (3030 Travis St., 713/520-0710, Mon.-Sat. 10am-9pm, $5-10). The *bánh mì* sandwiches are delicious and cost only $4. Fresh veggies and hearty pork, tofu, or chicken are packed in a perfect French roll. For a big bowl of flavorful soup, order a *bun bo hue,* which is on the spicy side. Lunchtime is especially busy; try to arrive before noon or after 1pm.

Lunch

Most restaurants in this traditionally trendy part of town have impressive lunch menus, but a few are noteworthy for their vibrant scenes, including Goode Co. Barbeque (5109 Kirby Dr., 713/522-2530, www. goodecompany.com, daily 11am-10pm, $11-29), a funky spot always packed with students, young professionals, and working-class carnivores. Goode's specializes in classic 'cue—sausage, ribs, chicken, and the signature tender and juicy brisket, all topped with succulent smoky sauce. The side items are better than average, including sweet coleslaw and jalapeño cornbread.

On the opposite end of the spectrum is the sleek Ra Sushi (3908 Westheimer Rd., 713/621-5800, www. rasushi.com, daily 11am-midnight, $7-22). Drawing a young crowd, Ra is known for its stylish social scene as much as its hip sushi rolls. Popular items include the spicy lobster roll, scallop dynamite, and Viva Las Vegas roll with light tempura, crab, tuna, and lotus root. Order a seaweed salad or a more substantial item from the Pacific Rim-themed full menu. Stick around for the happy hour scene at Ra's Flying Fish Lounge.

ACCOMMODATIONS

For all its cosmopolitan charm, Houston remains a business destination, reflected in its hotels. A few upscale independent options include the ZaZa and Derek, but most lodging is on the interstates, with easy access to business centers. Rooms are easy to book year-round and are mostly generic in their amenities.

Visitors can take advantage of the business orientation by booking upscale downtown rooms at affordable weekend rates (around $130). With the absence of work-related traffic on weekends, it's easy to drive to Museum District sites from a high-end historic downtown hotel like the Magnolia.

DOWNTOWN
$100-150

A worthwhile option just outside the inner loop is the clean and spacious Best Western Plus Downtown Inn and Suites (915 W. Dallas St., 713/571-7733, www.bestwestern.com, $119 d). Rooms and suites include microwaves, fridges, and free Wi-Fi, and the hotel offers a free full breakfast every morning, a fitness center, a spa, and an outdoor pool.

One of the best ways to experience Houston at an affordable rate is at the fabulous ✪ Magnolia Hotel (1100 Texas Ave., 713/221-0011, www. magnoliahotelhouston.com, $139 d), a historic downtown gem that hosts

Magnolia Hotel

business guests and events in a cosmopolitan 1926 building within walking distance of attractions and restaurants. Rooms are on the small side, and the Magnolia's complimentary services include Wi-Fi, downtown car transportation, and free milk and cookies at bedtime. The minibar is stocked with beverages and snacks, and the library and billiards room is stocked with an eclectic collection of books. There is a rooftop fitness center with a lap pool and a hot tub.

A deluxe downtown lodging experience is the Sam Houston (117 Prairie St., 832/200-8800, www.hilton.com, $149 d). "The Sam" offers near-luxury accommodations. Pamper yourself in this contemporary setting with amenities such as upscale baths (granite walls and glass-walled showers with plush robes and towels), quality bedding (down comforters and pillows, pillow-top mattresses), gourmet snacks, a minibar, and free Wi-Fi.

$150-200

Hotel Icon (220 Main St., 713/224-4266, www.hotelicon.com, $152 d) offers dynamic contemporary lodging in the heart of downtown. This 12-story hotel in a former bank is filled with bold colors and lavish details, including marble countertops, antique claw-foot tubs, luxury robes, and plush linens. Other amenities include free Wi-Fi, a stocked minibar, and fresh-cut flowers.

In the middle of the action is Hilton Americas (1600 Lamar St., 713/739-8000, www.hilton.com, $169 d), an enormous visually striking hotel with 1,200 rooms towering over downtown. A big-time business destination attached to the convention center, weekends are a cheaper time to stay, since the hotel's many amenities are more accessible. Highlights include three restaurants, several bars and lounges, and an impressive spa and health club with downtown views. Rooms feature free Wi-Fi, upscale linens, and an in-room refreshment center.

The comforts of home in a historical urban setting are at the Residence Inn Houston Downtown (904 Dallas St., 832/366-1000, www.marriott.com, $169 d), in the spectacular 1921 Humble Oil Building. Well-restored Classical Revival details include brass elevator doors, tall ceilings, and stately rose marble. Hotel amenities include free Wi-Fi, a large pool, a fitness center, and spacious suites with fully equipped kitchens and separate sleeping and living areas. An unexpected complimentary service: Leave a grocery list at the front desk and return in the evening to a stocked kitchen.

In a historic setting, the elegant yet comfortable ✪ Hotel Lancaster (701 Texas St., 713/228-9500, www.thelancaster.com, $199 d), one of Houston's original small luxury hotels, is in the heart of the Theater District. The lobby is decorated with large oil paintings and dramatic lighting, and

Hotel Lancaster

there's a sense of European opulence in the hotel's decor. Guest rooms capture this charm with dark-wood two-poster beds, feather pillows with the softest sheets imaginable, and brass furnishings. The breakfast buffet is cosmopolitan—muesli, salmon, and olives accompany sausage, eggs, and waffles. Guests notice the attention to detail and customer service. The Lancaster offers Wi-Fi, a bountiful breakfast, and car service to nearby attractions for a $15 service fee.

$200-250

Some of the most upscale lodging in town is at the Westin Houston Downtown (1520 Texas Ave., 713/228-1520, www.innattheballpark.com, $209 d), within earshot of Houston Astros games. The location is one of the prime amenities, since the other services are not overly inspiring. The Westin offers free transportation services around town and a fitness center, but there are fees for in-room internet access and breakfast.

The luxurious five-star Four Seasons (1300 Lamar St., 713/650-1300, www.fourseasons.com, $299 d) has skyline views and outstanding services, including the exquisite spa and salon, a spacious pool and fitness center, complimentary downtown car service, a tasty antipasti bar, and rooms featuring plush bathrobes, minibars, and Wi-Fi.

UPTOWN
$50-100

Some of the best bargains in the city are in the busy Uptown area west of downtown near the Galleria. Among them are La Quinta Inn & Suites (1625 W. Loop S., 713/355-3440, www.lq.com, $89 d), with a heated pool and spa, a fitness center, a free continental breakfast buffet, and rooms with free internet access.

Similarly priced and amenity packed is the adjacent Drury Inn and Suites (1615 W. Loop S., 713/963-0700, www.druryhotels.com, $99 d), offering a free hot breakfast, a fitness center, an indoor-outdoor pool, and a whirlpool. Guest rooms feature free Wi-Fi, microwaves, and fridges.

$100-150

Worth considering is Hotel Indigo at the Galleria (5160 Hidalgo St., 800/465-4329, www.ichotelsgroup.com, $116 d), featuring bold design and inspiring colors throughout, room options with separate sitting and work areas, free internet access and printing capacity, a fitness center, and an outdoor pool.

Unique and memorable ✪ Hotel Derek (2525 W. Loop S., 866/292-4100, www.hotelderek.com, $119 d) is an independent option with consistently reliable service. Hotel Derek's highlights include an outstanding pool with a gushing waterfall, day-spa treatments, and a chauffeured car providing free transportation to the

Galleria's nearby shopping locales. Rooms feature free Wi-Fi, minibars, bathrobes, and beds with goose-down duvets. The hotel's restaurant, Revolve Kitchen + Bar, is a destination itself.

Another worthy consideration is the impressive Hilton Post Oak (2001 Post Oak Blvd., 713/961-9300, www. hilton.com, $119 d). Each room includes a balcony offering impressive skyline views as well as Wi-Fi, minibars, and fridges. The hotel also offers complimentary shuttle service to destinations within a 3-mile (4.8-km) radius.

The reliable Doubletree Guest Suites (5353 Westheimer Rd., 713/961-9000, www.doubletree.com, $141 d) has an ideal location and spacious one- and two-bedroom suites with free Wi-Fi, an upscale fitness center, and a large outdoor pool area with a sundeck and a whirlpool.

$150-200

Galleria visitors enjoy Embassy Suites (2911 Sage Rd., 713/626-5444, www.embassysuites.com, $162 d). Hotel amenities include an impressive atrium, an indoor pool and whirlpool, a large fitness center, and an included cooked-to-order breakfast. Rooms offer a private bedroom and separate living area with a sofa bed, a minibar, a fridge, a microwave, and free Wi-Fi.

Another option favored by many Galleria shoppers is the JW Marriott Houston (5150 Westheimer Rd., 713/961-1500, www.marriott.com, $169 d), a stately 23-floor hotel featuring Wi-Fi, a fitness center, indoor and outdoor pools, and a whirlpool.

Connected to the country's fourth-largest mall, the Westin Galleria Houston (5060 W. Alabama St., 713/960-8100, www.marriott.com, $194 d) is in a prime location, allowing

guests to walk straight from the hotel to the massive shopping center. After shopping, unwind in a spacious room with internet access (for a fee) and attractive furnishings.

WEST UNIVERSITY

Downtown is quiet most nights, but the West University area is usually hopping. Visitors stay here for the abundant nearby nightlife and cultural attractions. One of the best deals is the Doubletree Greenway Plaza (6 Greenway Plaza E., 713/629-1200, www.marriott.com, $104 d), featuring spacious rooms with walk-in closets, luxury bedding, internet access, a fitness center, and an outdoor pool.

A similar bargain is Courtyard Houston West University (2929 Westpark Dr., 713/661-5669, www. marriott.com, $98 d), offering an outdoor pool and whirlpool, an exercise room, a book-filled library, and free Wi-Fi. Another worthy option is the enormous Hilton Houston Plaza (6633 Travis St., 713/313-4000, www. hilton.com, $149 d). The Hilton includes large suites, minibars, internet access, a fitness facility, a heated swimming pool, and free transportation within a 3-mile (4.8-km) radius of the hotel.

The lodging jewel of the city is ✪ Hotel ZaZa (5701 Main St., 713/526-1991, www.hotelzaza.com, from $219), just east of the university neighborhood on the edge of the Museum District. Billed as an "urban resort with a mix of glamour and warmth, high style, and creature comforts," the ZaZa is in a league of its own. Amenities include a poolside retreat and outdoor bar with private cabanas, the luxurious ZaSpa and fitness center, nightly turndown service, cordless phones, free Wi-Fi, ZaZa guest robes, upscale linens, fridges, and an in-room "grab and go gourmet refreshment bar."

GREATER HOUSTON

A 30-minute jaunt up I-45 is the luxurious and relaxing ✪ **Woodlands Resort** (2301 N. Millbend Dr., The Woodlands, 281/367-1100, www. woodlandsresort.com, from $229), contemporary accommodations with several pools, a tubing river, whirlpool tubs, a pampering spa, and tasty cuisine. Sheets and couches are incredibly soft and the bath is opulent in the modern rooms. The Forest Oasis Waterscape pool area has multiple swimming areas, waterslides, and the über-enjoyable lazy river tube ride. If you have kids in tow in summer, take advantage of the "dive-in" movies and poolside s'mores. Schedule a massage, facial, or manicure at the Woodlands Resort Spa. Two lush golf courses and an extensive tennis center with clay, hard, and indoor courts accompany the trail system, allowing guests to ride bikes (rentals are available) or hike and jog among in the pine and hardwood forest.

A resort getaway would be incomplete without a memorable meal at **Robard's Steakhouse** (281/364-6400, www.robardssteakhouse.com, Mon.-Thurs. 4pm-10pm, Fri.-Sat. 4pm-11pm, $16-53). Robard's mission is to offer "the perfect cut" of beef, and it's hard to argue with the results. Each steak is selected from the in-house butchery and prepared to order. The steaks are exquisite when paired with one of the hundreds of wine or craft beer options, flavorful sides, and delectable desserts.

Tech-minded **Element Houston Vintage Park** (14555 Vintage Preserve Pkwy., 281/379-7300, www.

elementhoustonvintagepark.com, $119 d) is an environmentally sustainable lodging option. Part of a "lifestyle center" in the bustling northwestern part of town, Element touts its environmentally friendly design and construction, as well as its provision of widespread Wi-Fi for computers, phones, and portable online devices. Other amenities include a hot breakfast, and open-flow guest rooms with fully equipped kitchens.

CAMPING

Houston's best camping is about 30 miles (48 km) southwest of the city at **Brazos Bend State Park** (21901 FM 762, 979/553-5102, www.tpwd.state. tx.us, $7 over age 12). Covering 5,000 acres, this popular park offers hiking, biking, equestrian trails, and fishing on six easily accessible lakes. Visitors are cautioned about alligators, which are numerous in some areas of the park. Facilities include restrooms with showers, campsites with water and electricity, screened shelters, primitive equestrian campsites, and a dining hall. Many visitors make Brazos Bend a weekend destination due to its abundant activities, including free interpretive programs and hikes. A nature center with informative displays contains a hands-on alligator discovery area, a model of the park, a freshwater aquarium, live native snake species, and the George Observatory.

INFORMATION AND SERVICES

TOURISM OFFICES

The **Greater Houston Convention and Visitors Bureau** (701 Avenida De Las Americas, 713/437-5200, www.visithoustontexas.com, daily 7am-10pm) office is of literature and knowledgeable staff members. Similar services are available southwest of town at Visit Bay Area Houston (604 Bradford Ave. in Kemah, 281/474-9700).

If you're entering East Texas by vehicle from Louisiana, look for the Texas Department of Transportation's Travel Information Center at two spots on the state border. The largest facility is in Orange (1708 E. I-10, 409/883-9416) on I-10 en route from New Orleans. The other is in Waskom (1255 N. I-20 E., 903/687-2547) on I-20 from Shreveport. Visit www.txdot.gov for road-related travel information.

PUBLICATIONS

The best source for news and information in Houston and southeast Texas is the *Houston Chronicle* (www.chron.com), with thorough coverage of city and state happenings as well as detailed listings of restaurants and entertainment venues. For specific information about local politics, touring shows, and movie listings, pick up a free copy of the *Houston Press* (www.houstonpress.com) at bars and coffee shops across town.

GETTING THERE
AIR

The major air hub in this part of the country is George Bush Intercontinental Airport (IAH, 2800 N. Terminal Rd., 281/230-3100, www.airport-houston.com), just north of the city. This is one of United's major hubs, with flights to 170 cities around the world, and it's typically bustling at all hours. The city's older airfield, William P. Hobby Airport (HOU, 7800 Airport Blvd., 713/640-3000, www.fly2houston.com) is now the center of activity for Southwest Airlines and several other carriers.

Located 10 miles (16 km) southeast of downtown, Hobby is more accessible than Bush and costs $20 less by taxi from downtown, but it's showing its age.

Super Shuttle (281/230-7275, www.supershuttle.com) offers shuttle service to and from area hotels and both airports. Look for the company's ticket counters in the lower-level baggage claim areas. Many downtown-area hotels offer free shuttle service to and from Bush Intercontinental Airport, but check first to make sure they're running.

TRAIN

Amtrak's *Sunset Limited* passenger train runs cross-country between Orlando and Los Angeles. Look for three weekly arrivals and departures at the Houston Amtrak station (902 Washington Ave., 713/224-1577 or 800/872-7245, www.amtrak.com).

BUS

Intercity buses are run by Houston Greyhound (2121 Main St., 713/759-6565 or 800/231-2222, www.greyhound.com).

GETTING AROUND
CAR

Rent a car at Bush Intercontinental Airport's Rental Car Center (281/230-3000, www.fly2houston.com). All the major rental companies are at this shared location about five minutes from the terminals. Shuttle buses, located outside the terminal, are marked "Rental Car Shuttle."

PUBLIC TRANSPORTATION

Houston has a decent public transportation system, but it can be confusing. A little homework can help to strategize plans to use the Metro, a.k.a. the

Metropolitan Transit Authority of Harris County (713/635-4000, www.ridemetro.org, $1.25), with light rail and bus lines. Tickets for trains are available in vending machines at each station. Metro's red line serves 17 stations near downtown's busiest commercial and recreational sites.

TAXI

Ground transportation employees outside each terminal of Bush Intercontinental Airport and near the lower-level baggage claim area (curb zone 1) of Hobby Airport will half-heartedly hail travelers a taxi. All destinations within Houston's city limits to or from Bush Airport are charged a flat zone rate or the meter rate, whichever is less. For more information on rates, see the Ground Transportation section at www.fly2houston.com. Arrange for cab pickup service within the city with Houston VIP Taxi (281/616-5838), Liberty Cab Company (713/236-1111), and Taxis Fiesta (713/225-2666).

Vicinity of Houston

BEAUMONT

Beaumont (population 118,428) isn't an average midsize Texas city. It's more connected to the eastern United States than the South, it has a working-class union element, and it has a denser historic downtown than sprawling West Texas cities. Its proximity to New Orleans and the Gulf Coast have earned it, along with nearby Port Arthur and Orange, the nickname "the Cajun Triangle."

The city's fate was forever changed on January 10, 1901, when the Lucas Gusher erupted from the Spindletop oil field. Tens of thousands of people flocked to Beaumont to capitalize on the oil boom and built an impressive collection of churches, civic buildings, and residences. Beaumont became an American melting pot, with Italian and Jewish influences combined with Cajun and African American inspirations. The city's architectural treasures give downtown its distinctive historical charm.

The corporate oil scene would eventually move to Houston, 80 miles (129 km) southwest, but Beaumont's petroleum legacy remains its true identity. In 1901, the first year of the boom, three major companies formed—the Gulf Oil Corporation, Humble (later Exxon), and the Texas Company (later Texaco). One year later, more than 500 corporations were doing business in Beaumont.

The boom soon went bust, as Spindletop fell victim to an overabundance of wells. Two decades later, new advancements in the oil industry allowed riggers to dig wells deeper, resulting in another Spindletop boom. In 1927, the oil field yielded its all-time annual high of 21 million barrels. Beaumont never experienced another major surge, but the city prospered during World War II as a shipbuilding center, and the petrochemical industry continued to sustain the economy for decades to come.

The nearby coastal communities of Port Arthur and Orange benefited from the oil money, opening art museums, forging a soulful music identity, and capitalizing on its Cajun culture by developing fabulous dining.

SIGHTS
Spindletop-Gladys City Boomtown Museum
To get a sense of the craziness that befell Beaumont on the discovery of the Spindletop oil field, visit the Spindletop-Gladys City Boomtown Museum (5550 Jimmy Simmons Blvd., 409/880-1750, www.lamar.edu, Tues.-Sat. 10am-5pm, Sun. 1pm-5pm, $5 adults, $3 seniors, $2 ages 6-12). Near the site of the famous Lucas Gusher, the museum offers a self-guided tour of 15 clapboard building replicas from the oil-boom era, including a general store, a saloon, a post office, a stable, and a blacksmith shop. The buildings and associated photos and interpretive panels tell the story of the massive and unprecedented boomtown saga, where Beaumont transformed from a village of several hundred to a city of 30,000 in a matter of weeks. The museum also features wooden oil derricks of the era, including a weekly water-spewing gusher that keeps families entertained and refreshed during the hot summer months.

McFaddin-Ward House
One of the city's top destinations is the remarkable 1906 McFaddin-Ward House (1906 Calder Ave., 409/832-2134, www.mcfaddin-ward.org, Tues.-Sat. 10am-3pm, Sun. 1pm-3pm, closed at lunch, over age 7 only, $5 guided tours). This impressive beaux arts mansion features decorative exterior detailing and opulent interior furnishings reflecting the lifestyle of William McFaddin, a Texas Army veteran who created a cattle and oil empire from the land he received for his military service. The guided tours of his home and adjacent carriage house provide anecdotal and architectural background information along with up-close views of furniture, artwork, and mementos.

Texas Energy Museum
Among Beaumont's best museums is the downtown Texas Energy Museum (600 Main St., 409/833-5100, www.texasenergymuseum.org, Tues.-Sat. 9am-5pm, Sun. 1pm-5pm, $3 adults, $2 seniors and ages 6-12), a spacious two-story facility that features a fascinating collection of exhibits dedicated to oil-based energy sources. Interactive displays highlight the history of oil and provide information about the global significance of this local commodity. The name is somewhat misleading—there aren't any power plants or lightbulbs here—but the museum educates visitors about the remarkable history and relevance of the petrochemical industry.

Fire Museum of Texas
The nearby Fire Museum of Texas (400 Walnut St., 409/880-3927, www.firemuseumoftexas.org, Mon.-Fri. 8am-4:30pm, free) is a small unexpected gem. In the 1927 Beaumont Fire Department Headquarters Station, it is dwarfed by the massive black-and-white-spotted "world's largest fire hydrant" out front. Now considered the third-largest in the world, this 24-foot-tall (7-m) hydrant was donated to the museum by Disney Studios on the release of the movie *101 Dalmatians*. Inside, the facility showcases the importance of firefighters in Texas and across the country through vintage fire engines and equipment, educational exhibits, and the Texas Firefighter Memorial.

Babe Didrikson Zaharias Museum

Babe who? You'll be telling everyone about her after experiencing the captivating Babe Didrikson Zaharias Museum (1750 I-10 E., 409/833-4622, www.babedidriksonzaharias.org, Mon.-Sat. 9am-5pm, free). Port Arthur native Zaharias was a pioneer in women's sports voted the world's greatest woman athlete in a poll by the Associated Press. Nicknamed "Babe" after swatting five home runs in one baseball game, Zaharias was an accomplished Olympic athlete, tennis player, basketball player, diver, bowler, and, most notably, golfer. She won every major professional golf championship at least once and is credited with single-handedly popularizing women's golf. The museum features trophies, golf clubs, photos, newspaper clippings, Olympic medals, and films representing her athletic career.

FOOD

American

For lively dinner-and-drinks atmosphere, go to Madison's (4020 Dowlen Rd., 409/924-9777, daily 11am-2am, $9-26). Classic American fare is the best option here, with reliable huge burgers, chicken, and fried food. Try the bacon-wrapped shrimp with jalapeño. Things pick up at Madison's after dark, when bands often take the stage and the bar gets busy.

More inspiring than its name implies is The Grill (6680 Calder Ave., 409/866-0039, www.theaspgrill.com, Tues.-Sat. 3pm-10pm, $11-34), with fine dining in Beaumont style: quality food with attentive service in a refined atmosphere. Recommended items include parmesan-crusted Chilean sea bass, grilled rack of lamb, and au poivre tournedos (beef tenderloin with a tasty cognac mushroom sauce). Save room for the amazing *tres leches* cake, topped with a velvety goat's milk caramel.

Cajun and Seafood

Beaumont is one of the best places in Texas to get authentic Cajun food, and the city's proximity to the Gulf of Mexico means the seafood is always fresh. A local favorite is no-frills Kajun Seafood and Wings (597 S. 11th St., 409/832-9988, Tues.-Sat. 10am-8:30pm, Sun. 10am-7pm, $10-25). Beaumonters love the succulent and slightly spicy shrimp and wings, an ideal representation of Beaumont's distinctive cuisine. Other popular items include the broiled seafood platter and fried, grilled, or blackened catfish.

Locals line up at consistently delectable Vautrot's Cajun Cuisine (13350 Hwy. 105, 409/753-2015, Tues.-Fri. 11am-2pm and 5pm-9pm, Sat. 11am-9pm, $9-12). Start with the tasty crawfish étouffée or jam-packed gumbo, or proceed directly to the ridiculously large and flavorful Uncle Emrick's Seafood Sampler, containing the gumbo and étouffée along with fried crawfish, fried catfish, fried shrimp, fried oysters, onion rings or french fries, and a salad.

Floyd's Cajun Seafood (2290 I-10 S., 409/842-0686, www.floyds beaumont.com, Sun.-Thurs. 11am-10pm, Fri.-Sat. 11am-11pm, $10-22) is a small regional chain that's huge on authentic flavor. Reliable standards include crawfish, shrimp, oysters, and catfish. Floyd's specializes in southern Louisiana home-style cooking, with regional favorites like po'boys (go for the shrimp or crawfish), gumbo, and étouffée.

ACCOMMODATIONS

Beaumont lacks downtown hotels within walking distance of its many museums and cultural attractions. A popular and reliable option is Econo Lodge Inn & Suites (2030 N. 11th St., 409/892-6700, www.choicehotels.com, $69 d), featuring free Wi-Fi, a free deluxe continental breakfast, a fitness center, and an outdoor pool.

The best bang for the buck is ✪ Holiday Inn Beaumont-Plaza (3950 I-10 S., 409/842-5995 or 800/465-4329, www.holidayinn.com, $99 d). An enormous three-story cascading waterfall greets guests in the spacious garden atrium, and the renovated rooms provide clean and comfortable accommodations. The Plaza location (not to be confused with Holiday Inn Midtown) features free Wi-Fi, an indoor pool and whirlpool, a full fitness center, and free meals for kids under age 13.

Regional chain MCM Elegante (2355 I-10 S., 409/842-3600, www.mcmelegantebeaumont.com, $115 d) features a tropical outdoor pool, an upscale fitness center, free Wi-Fi, fridges, and microwaves.

Another consistently solid choice is Homewood Suites by Hilton (3745 I-10 S., 409/842-9990, www.homewoodsuites3.hilton.com, $149 d), 4 miles (6.4 km) from downtown. The suites feature separate living and sleeping areas, fully equipped kitchens with full-size fridges, and free Wi-Fi. Accommodations include a full breakfast each morning and a complimentary grocery shopping service. Homewood Suites is a dog-friendly hotel.

INFORMATION AND SERVICES

To get a handle on the layout of the city, contact the friendly folks at the Beaumont Convention & Visitors Bureau (505 Willow St., 409/880-3749 or 800/392-4401, www.beaumontcvb.com, Mon.-Fri. 8am-5pm).

GETTING THERE AND AROUND

The 75-minute drive on I-10 to Houston is considered by some a suburban commute. The cities have completely different identities, and the proximity makes Beaumont an easy day trip.

The closest airports are in Houston: George Bush Intercontinental Airport (IAH, 2800 N. Terminal Rd., 281/230-3100, www.airport-houston.com), just north of Houston, is one of the major hubs for United Airlines. Houston's old airport, William P. Hobby Airport (HOU, 7800 Airport Blvd., 713/640-3000, www.fly2houston.com), is the center of activity for Southwest Airlines.

In Beaumont, it's easy to get anywhere in about 15 minutes. If you don't have a car, cab companies include Royal Taxi (409/289-9950) and King Cab (409/242-8136). If you're feeling adventurous, you may even consider tackling the Beaumont Municipal Transit System (409/835-7895, www.beaumonttransit.com) buses.

PORT ARTHUR

It's worth the 20-mile (32-km) drive from Beaumont to Port Arthur (population 55,018) to spend an afternoon at a museum or sample some seafood. With several major oil refineries, Port Arthur's economy remains petroleum-centered. Named for Arthur Stillwell, a Kansas City businessperson who brought the railroad to town, this low-key community has been tied to the shipping industry since a navigable canal was dredged in the early 1900s.

Aside from oil and shipping, Port Arthur is known for churning out music stars (Janis Joplin, the Big Bopper, Johnny Winter, and Tex Ritter) as well as Cajun food, fishing, and a legendary Mardi Gras celebration, drawing tens of thousands of people each February.

SIGHTS

Get a grasp on the region's illustrious history at the Museum of the Gulf Coast (700 Proctor St., 409/982-7000, www.museumofthegulfcoast.org, Mon.-Sat. 9am-5pm, $8 adults, $6 seniors, $4 ages 4-18). In a large downtown building that was once a bank, the two-story museum covers prehistory to the Texas Revolution artifacts to the modern era, and a comprehensive representation of cultural events in the region.

Check out the replica of Janis Joplin's painted psychedelic Porsche in the museum's music exhibit, where visitors can play songs on a jukebox for free and browse displays dedicated to the surprising number of musicians from the area, including Joplin, George Jones, the Big Bopper, Tex Ritter, and members of ZZ Top. Nearby, a large number of sports legends and celebrities feature in the pop-culture exhibit, including Jimmy Johnson, Bum and Wade Phillips, and, head-scratchingly, two stars of the *Police Academy* film, G. W. Bailey and Charles "Bubba" Smith.

The Sabine Pass Battleground State Historic Site (6100 Dick Dowling Rd., 512/463-7948, www. visitsabinepassbattleground.com, free), 12 miles (19.3 km) south of town, is worth visiting even if you aren't a history buff. Owned and operated by the Texas Historical Commission, this 58-acre site tells the story of a fierce Civil War battle where severely outnumbered Confederate troops prevailed over a formidable Union fleet. Interpretive panels in a large concrete kiosk, historical markers, and a bronze statue help portray the conflict. Visitors have access to walking trails and camping facilities overlooking the Sabine Ship Channel.

The Buu Mon Buddhist Temple (2701 Procter St., 409/982-9319, www. buumon.org) was the first Buddhist center in Beaumont (inspiration for its name) and moved to Port Arthur into a former Baptist and Vietnamese Catholic church. A stupa replaced the steeple, and a 7-foot-tall (2-m) gilt bronze Buddha rests on the altar. The temple's annual spring garden tour attracts hundreds to the lotus garden. Monks are always on hand to guide visitors through the temple and the garden and even offer a cup of freshly brewed green tea.

FOOD

Port Arthur is known for seafood and Cajun restaurants. One of the best spots in town is the bland-looking yet consistently tasty Bruce's Seafood Deli (6801 9th Ave., 409/727-3184, Mon.-Sat. 10am-9pm, $9-21). You can't go wrong with the basics—shrimp, crawfish, and catfish. Just about everything is deep-fried and incredibly flavorful and fresh. The uninspiring decor (it was once a fast-food chain restaurant) allows you to focus on the fine seafood.

Another favorite Bayou-style eatery is Larry's French Market and Cajun Cafeteria (3701 Atlantic Hwy., Groves, 409/962-3381, www. larrysfrenchmarket.com, Mon.-Wed. 11am-2pm, Thurs. 11am-9pm, Fri. 11am-2pm and 5pm-10pm, Sat. 5pm-11pm, $9-24), offering an all-inclusive combo in the Captain's Platter, featuring fresh and flavorful shrimp, catfish, oysters, barbecue crabs, fried crawfish, seafood gumbo, and Cajun fries. Alternate menu options include the "boiled water critters" (crawfish and crab) served with corn, potatoes, and a dipping sauce, as well as fried critters (alligator, frog legs). Larry's often hosts live music, so check the website for showtimes.

Locals tend to loiter at the traditionally minded and classically decorated (a.k.a. dated) The Schooner (1507 S. Hwy. 69, 409/722-2323, www. theschoonerrestaurant.com, Mon.-Sat. 11am-10pm, $9-27). Seafood is the main catch, from fresh fillets to fried platters. Popular menu items include broiled fillet of snapper, stuffed crab, and oysters.

Piney Woods

The Piney Woods are the natural heart of East Texas, comprising several national forests and not much else. Most of this vast area remains as it was centuries ago, when Native Americans and pioneers hunted wild game in the dense woods by day and slept under the pine canopy by night.

The name Piney Woods is a Texas colloquialism describing this forested region, not typically associated with the wide-open landscape of the Lone Star State. These aren't dense lush groves of evergreens but rather shortleaf and loblolly pines, sprinkled with hardwoods such as oak, elm, ash, and maple. The combination is appealing in autumn, when bursts of changing color offer a pleasant outdoor escape.

Nearly 750,000 acres of East Texas pine forests remain standing due to federal protection. The trees were mostly clear-cut during the zealous timber harvesting of the early 1900s, but the U.S. Forest Service eventually became administrator of the vast woodlands, allowing them to be responsibly harvested and replenished. Several of the forests, Angelina in particular, feature logging-related trails and historical exhibits. A highlight is

the abandoned and ghostly Aldridge Sawmill in Angelina National Forest.

The four national forests of East Texas make a natural weekend getaway for camping, hiking, and mountain biking, and there are rivers and lakes for canoeing and fishing, drawing tens of thousands. Texans frequent the forests year-round, but out-of-staters will most enjoy the temperate months of spring and late fall.

These wooded areas provided shelter and sustenance for the region's earliest inhabitants, the Native Americans displaced by westward frontier expansion. The legacy of the Caddo people is evident in Piney Woods communities like Nacogdoches, and the Alabama-Coushatta Tribe is a vital cultural presence on its land in the Big Thicket National Preserve.

✪ BIG THICKET NATIONAL PRESERVE

The Big Thicket National Preserve's name is misleading: There are dense, seemingly impenetrable forests, but this National Park Service preserve is mostly woodsy, with pines, oaks, and swamplands dominating the landscape. The tremendous variety of habitats and the thicket's geographic location result in a unique destination for nature lovers and wildlife enthusiasts.

Species from the Gulf Coast, Central Plains, and Southeastern forests coexist with critters from the deserts, bayous, woods, and swamps. Birds from all regions of the country share airspace as they pass through on migration. There are 85 tree species, 186 kinds of birds, and 50 reptile species, including a small and rarely seen population of alligators.

SIGHTS

A good place to start is the **Big Thicket visitors center** (6102 FM 420, 409/951-6725, daily 9am-5pm), 7 miles (11.3 km) north of Kountze at the intersection of U.S. 69 and FM 420, with brochures, maps, and a discovery room with interactive educational exhibits. The Big Thicket consists of nine separate land units over an expanse of East Texas. View the visitors center's 30-minute orientation film and talk to an NPS nature guide about taking a short excursion to several of the ecosystems found in the preserve.

Lake Tombigbee

Lake Tombigbee is in one of only three Native American reservations in Texas, the **Alabama-Coushatta reservation** (936/563-1100, www. alabama-coushatta.com). The tribe no longer runs its museum or tourism activities, but visitors can use the reservation's **Lake Tombigbee Campground** (936/563-1221 or 800/926-9038), with cabins, tent sites, primitive camping sites, full-capacity RV stations, restrooms with bathhouses, swimming areas, and hiking and nature trails. Fishing is popular on

Big Thicket National Preserve

the historic Aldridge Sawmill ruins

From the 1880s until the 1920s, East Texas's Piney Woods saw a "lumber bonanza" with 18 million acres of timber being cut. Lumber production started with small owner-operated sawmills and eventually evolved into large operations that dominated the East Texas economy. These corporations built their own railroads into the forests and connected their isolated sawmills with major cities and shipping points.

FACTORY TOWN

The men who worked in the sawmills and on cutting crews were encouraged to remain with a company long-term, with the incentive that their wives and children could live in the lumber company towns. The companies would choose a location on a rail line and construct a makeshift town, complete with homes, schools, churches, stores, and hospitals. Workers were often paid with credits they could use for food, merchandise, and services in the company town facilities. Learn about this phenomenon at Diboll's **History Center** (102 N. Temple St., Diboll, 936/829-3543, www.thehistorycenteronline.com, Mon.-Fri. 8am-5pm, Sat. 9am-1pm, free).

Sometimes the towns would pick up and move with the ever-changing frontier of virgin forest. Homes in railcars allowed for easy mobility, leaving behind a ghost town of clapboard buildings and dirt roads. By the 1920s, the depletion of the East Texas timber resources and the subsequent Great Depression caused the decline of the lumber bonanza. Some of the companies went bankrupt, while the larger timber corporations moved to the Pacific Northwest.

the lake; bring your own equipment as rental operations are scarce.

RECREATION
Hiking

Eight trails offer 45 miles (72 km) of mild hiking terrain through the muggy forest. The ideal time to hike in Big Thicket is late fall-early winter or spring, since the summer is brutally hot. The trails include wheelchair-accessible half-mile loops to an 18-mile (29-km) cross-forest trek. The best slices of Big Thicket life:

- **Beaver Slide Trail:** In the southeast corner of the preserve's Big Sandy Creek Unit, this 1.5-mile (2.4-km) trail encircles several ponds formed by old beaver dams. The towering shaggy-barked cypress trees are a main attraction.
- **Kirby Nature Trail System:** This group of trails offers a lot of flexibility with distance and environments.

A printed guide at the trailhead is handy to have in your back pocket, providing basic maps and information about the ecosystems and trails, ranging from a half-mile loop through a cypress slough to a 2.4-mile (3.9-km) hike traversing the southern edge of the Turkey Creek Unit.

- **Pitcher Plant Trail:** For a distinctive trek through diverse ecosystems, take this 1-mile (1.6-km) trail through a mixed pine forest to a wetland savanna to a mixed hardwood-pine forest. Watch for the sundews and pitcher plants along the wooden boardwalk.
- **Turkey Creek Trail:** Environmental highlights of the preserve's Turkey Creek Unit and its namesake creek along this lengthy 15-mile (24-km) trail include baygalls, floodplains, sandhill pine uplands, and mixed forests.

Biking

Big Thicket is remote, and cyclists should bring their own bikes, as you won't find bike rentals. Bikes are only allowed on the Big Sandy Creek Horse/Bike Trail in the southern portion of the Big Sandy Creek Unit. It is the Big Thicket's longest trail, offering 18 miles (29 km) of beautiful natural scenery. Highlights include a diverse hardwood forest of sweetgum, basket oak, and hornbeam; dense and fragrant upland pine forests; and a mixed area with loblolly pines and beech-magnolia trees. Be sure to check ahead about trail access, as it's occasionally closed during hunting season, and keep an eye out for horses.

Bird-Watching

Several popular trails, including the Big Thicket Loop and Sundew Trail, offer opportunities for birders, with 185 species in the park either year-round or on two migratory flyways. Bird migration peaks March-May, and the most sought-after species include the red cockaded woodpecker and the Bachman's sparrow. In the spring, bird and wildflower enthusiasts flock to the Sundew Trail in the park's Hickory Creek Savannah Unit to see the rare brown-headed nuthatch or an eye-catching pitcher plant.

Paddling

The Big Thicket is gaining a reputation for its paddling opportunities. Canoeists and kayakers are fond of the Village Creek area, where they can explore the lush waterway and find camping opportunities. Another popular area is the Lower Neches River Corridor, a larger body of water with East Texas-style bayous and swamps leading south to the Gulf of Mexico. Equipment rentals and shuttles are available—check with the visitors center for a list of companies.

Backcountry Camping

The Big Thicket is a hard-core camping destination. There are no developed sites with water and electricity; campers are required to procure a Backcountry Use Permit for a primitive site. The permit is available for free at the visitors center or headquarters office (409/951-6725, visit www.nps.gov/bith). Naturalist activities are available with reservations or on selected weekends. Call to find out more about making reservations.

FOOD AND ACCOMMODATIONS

Since the Big Thicket is spread across a large geographic area, there is no specific town for food or lodging. The preserve's sections range 80 miles (129 km) west-to-east from Livingston to Kirbyville, with dozens of small communities between, and 70 miles (113 km) north-to-south from Jasper to Beaumont. Nearby communities with services include Woodville and Kountze. Beaumont is less than an hour from most of the Big Thicket's nine areas, so consider budgeting time to drive to this comparatively big city for food and lodging.

INFORMATION AND SERVICES

Get trail maps, boating conditions, and information on nearby restaurants at the Big Thicket visitors center (409/951-6725, www.nps.gov/bith, daily 9am-5pm). It's 7 miles (11.3 km) north of Kountze at the intersection of U.S. 69 and FM 420.

For fishing or camping on the Alabama-Coushatta reservation (936/563-1100, www.alabama-coushatta.com), call 936/563-1221 or 800/926-9038.

SAM HOUSTON NATIONAL FOREST

Approximately 40 miles (64 km) north of Texas's largest city, Sam Houston National Forest comprises 162,984 acres of shortleaf and longleaf pine, hardwood forests, and abundant recreational opportunities. Camping is the main draw, complemented by daytime activities on Double Lake and Lake Conroe and the 140-mile-long (225-km) Lone Star Hiking Trail.

RECREATION

The Lone Star Hiking Trail is 140 miles (225 km) of walkways open to foot travel only. The trail traverses the Sam Houston National Forest through woodlands, swamps, and meadows via five loops to accommodate various starting points and parking for day hikers or overnight backpackers. Trail maps and brochures are available at the park headquarters in New Waverly.

Cyclists will enjoy the 8-mile (12.9-km) trail on the east side of the forest custom-built by mountain bikers. Most East Texas forests are devoid of significant slopes, but this hilly trek offers terrain-filled passages winding through the pine forests.

The 22,000-acre Lake Conroe is a big draw in Sam Houston Forest for swimming, boating, fishing, and sailing. The lake is stocked with bass and bluegill, and boats are available for rent at several marinas along the lakeshore.

FOOD

When in East Texas, stick with what the locals know best: Southern food.

When it comes to burgers, one of the most popular spots is in the small town of Coldspring: The Hop (14801 Hwy. 150 W., Coldspring, 936/653-4889, Mon.-Sat. 10:30am-9pm, $9-17). This down-home, charmingly cluttered local establishment is a classic 1950s-style burger joint, so you can't go wrong with a big ol' burger, fries, and chocolate milk shake. Pop a few dollars in the corner jukebox to complete your classic Americana experience.

Just up the road from Coldspring in the slightly larger town of Livingston is Courthouse Whistlestop Cafe (318 N. Washington Ave., Livingston, 936/327-3222, www.courthousewhistlestop.com, daily 6am-2pm, $8-16). Across from the

DOWN-HOME SOUTHERN COOKING

Texas is in a geographically undefined region—it isn't really the South, and it doesn't quite qualify as the Southwest. Although Southern cooking is on the menu in most Texas cities, it's especially prevalent in East Texas, with geographical proximity to the South. Like everything else, Texas puts its own spin on down-home country cuisine.

a traditional plate of chicken-fried steak

- **Chicken-Fried Steak:** One of the best examples of Southern cooking in Texas is chicken-fried steak, a thin cut of cube steak that's tenderized, breaded in a seasoned flour mixture or egg batter, pan fried in lard or vegetable oil, and served smothered in peppered cream gravy. The term "chicken-fried" refers to the similar process used in frying chicken. Where to try it: **Dolli's Diner** (116 S. Pecan St., Nacogdoches, 936/305-5007, Mon.-Wed. and Thurs.-Sat. 7am-5pm, Sun.9am-4pm, $7-19)

- **Catfish:** Another East Texas fried favorite is catfish. Near the Gulf Coast, some chefs take a Cajun-style approach by dipping the fillet in hot sauce and milk before dredging it in a traditional blend of cornmeal, salt, pepper, paprika, and cayenne and frying it in a cast-iron skillet until golden brown. Where to try it: **Vautrot's Cajun Cuisine** (13350 Hwy. 105, Beaumont, 409/753-2015, Tues.-Fri. 11am-2pm and 5pm-9pm, Sat. 11am-9pm, $9-12)

- **Fried Okra:** A cornmeal-based covering is common for fried okra. A basic batter starts with whisked egg and buttermilk with a covering of cornmeal, flour, brown sugar, salt, peppers, and seasoning before frying in a skillet. Where to try it: **Courthouse Whistlestop Cafe** (318 N. Washington Ave., Livingston, 936/327-3222, www.courthousewhistlestop.com, daily 6am-2pm, $8-16)

Another Southern cooking tendency is to include **meat in veggie dishes.** Texans spruce up their beans, greens, and black-eyed peas with ham hock or bacon. Lard or bacon grease can add an extra dimension of flavor to just about any vegetable or bread recipe.

One more Southern-tinged trait: If you order tea in a Texas restaurant, you'll get **iced tea** (usually unsweetened, but East Texans often prefer the sweetened variety). Finally, never skip an opportunity to order a **fruit cobbler** or **pecan pie** for dessert.

stately Polk County Courthouse in the historic downtown district, the Whistlestop is an ideal place to grab a hearty breakfast before a hike or a paddle. Start with a mug of strong coffee and a meaty omelet or stack of buttermilk pancakes. For lunch, opt for a big deli sandwich (the reuben is a local favorite) or a bowl of chili. Order a side of fried okra.

CAMPING

Sam Houston National Forest contains three developed campgrounds. Cagle Recreation Area (936/344-6205, $20-30) is a campground with 48 sites with electricity, water, and sewer; hot showers; lakeshore hiking, biking, and equestrian trails; fishing; and swimming. Double Lake Recreation Area (936/653-3448, $20-30), constructed in 1937 by the Civilian Conservation Corps, surrounds a 24-acre lake with campsites that have a tent pad, parking, and a picnic table; some have water, sewer, and electrical hookups. There is a swimming area and a beach, a concession stand, and a bathhouse. Stubblefield Recreation Area (936/344-6205, $8-15) has 28 campsites, hot showers, and access to fishing and hiking.

Double Lake is by reservation, while Cagle and Stubblefield are first-come, first-served only. Call ahead for availability and fee information.

INFORMATION AND SERVICES

For more information about recreational opportunities at the forest, including maps, contact the Sam Houston National Forest headquarters (394 FM 1375, 936/344-6205 or 888/361-6908, www.fs.usda.gov/texas, Mon.-Fri. 8am-4:30pm), 2 miles (3.2 km) west of I-45 and New Waverly. For campground reservations, call 877/444-6777 or go to www.recreation.gov.

GETTING THERE

Since the national forests are in rural areas of East Texas, the only way to access them is by car. From Houston, take I-45 north for 40 miles (64 km) to the small town of New Waverly. The forest's visitors center is a few miles west of the I-45 at New Waverly. Drivers can also take U.S. 59 northeast from Houston. When you reach Cleveland or Shepherd, look for signs directing you to county roads heading west into the forest.

DAVY CROCKETT NATIONAL FOREST

For hikers, the Davy Crockett National Forest is a wild frontier, with 160,000 acres of scenic woodlands just west of Lufkin and some of the region's best opportunities for hiking and horseback riding.

RECREATION

The most popular hiking trail in the forest is the Four C National Recreation Trail, named after the Central Coal and Coke Company, which logged the forest's trees 1902-1920. The 20-mile (32-km) trail traverses moderate terrain amid lofty pines, swampy bogs, and hardwood forests. Horses and hikers share the woodsy, mossy, and boggy 50-mile (80-km) Piney Creek Horse Trail.

The Ratcliff Lake Recreation Area was built in 1936 by the Civilian Conservation Corps around a 45-acre lake that was once a log pond and source of water for the Central Coal and Coke Company Sawmill. The area offers camping, a swimming beach and a bathhouse, an interpretive trail, showers, boating, and fishing.

The forest's abundant wildlife includes deer, turkeys, doves, quail, and various waterfowl. The endangered red-cockaded woodpecker also lives in a managed habitat within the forest.

FOOD

Since Lufkin is just 10 miles (16 km) east of the forest's boundaries, it's worth heading to there for the better restaurant options than in the small towns around the forest's perimeter.

CAMPING

Some of the forest's most scenic camping sites are along the Four C Trail at the Walnut Creek campsite (5 tent pads, a shelter, and a pit toilet) and at another small campsite, farther north, with two tent pads. Another option is the Ratcliff Lake Recreation Area. For primitive sites, head to the nearby Neches Bluff Overlook at the north end of the trail, with a panoramic view of pine-hardwood forest in the Neches River bottomlands. Call the forest headquarters (936/655-2299) for availability and fee information.

INFORMATION AND SERVICES

To obtain a trail map of the forest or to learn more about camping and boat accessibility, contact the Davy Crockett National Forest headquarters near Kennard (Route 1, Box 55 FS, 936/655-2299, www.fs.usda. gov). The ranger district office is near Ratcliff on Highway 7, about a quarter mile west of FM 227.

GETTING THERE

By car from Houston, take I-45 north to Highway 19 in the town of Crockett. Turn right onto Highway 7, and in a few miles you'll find the main visitors center in Ratcliff. You can also take U.S. 59 northeast from Houston. When you reach Lufkin, take a left onto Highway 103, which turns into Highway 7 and leads to the visitors center.

ANGELINA NATIONAL FOREST

Just east of Lufkin, the 153,179-acre Angelina National Forest is popular for fishing and boating. Angelina encapsulates most of massive 114,500-acre Lake Sam Rayburn, formed on the Angelina River by Sam Rayburn Dam in the early 1960s.

The forest is gently rolling landscapes covered with shortleaf and loblolly pine, hardwoods, and a swath of longleaf pine in the southern portion. When the federal government took on its management in 1935, Angelina was in bad shape—most of the land had been clear-cut. The Texas Forest Service's fire prevention efforts resulted in much of the land naturally seeding in, a practice that continues to this day.

ALDRIDGE SAWMILL

Angelina is about water-based activities, but the most memorable experience in the forest is a surreal and spooky abandoned sawmill. All that's left of the Aldridge Sawmill are huge concrete structures. A century ago, thousands of people thrived in a busy logging community called Aldridge, bustling with several saloons, hotels, and churches, before abandoning the site practically overnight. Aldridge workers logged East Texas's largest longleaf pines, some more than 30 inches in diameter. When the trees were depleted by 1920, the residents and their families moved on to the next woodland, leaving behind several large-scale mill facilities.

The enormous stark concrete walls of these buildings offer an eerie juxtaposition to the surrounding natural beauty of the second-growth forest. Similarly intriguing are the remnants from local teenagers—graffiti, beer bottles, and flip-flops—who frequent the ghost town. A U.S. Forest Service guide noted, "A lot of innocence has been lost here."

National Forest Service sign in East Texas

Forest officials discourage publicizing Aldridge's location to deter even more teenagers from discovering and destroying it, but legitimate visitors can get a map and directions (look for the Sawmill Hiking Trail) from the visitors center.

RECREATION

Lake Sam Rayburn is a popular destination for anglers seeking the lake's abundant largemouth bass, crappie, and catfish. Recreational boating is a major activity, with water-skiers, sailboats, and personal watercraft dotting the surface. Even if you don't have a boat, drive across Lake Sam Rayburn on the long Highway 147 bridge. On the east side of the bridge, an access road leads to Jackson Hill Park, where you can explore the lakeside and catch a picturesque sunset.

Wildlife in the Angelina Forest includes deer, wild turkey, woodcock, quail, and a year-round resident population of wood ducks. In winter, bald eagles live near the reservoir, and the forest is also home to the endangered red-cockaded woodpecker, a small black-and-white bird that is difficult to locate.

FOOD

Nearby food options are minimal, so make the 15-mile (24-km) drive to Lufkin for quality regional cuisine. In the Zavalla area, basic Carlene's Place (594 E. Main St., 936/897-2900, daily 6am-8:30pm, $8-14) features a buffet of fried food and a salad bar along with standard American fare like burgers, chicken-fried steaks, and sandwiches.

CAMPING AND LODGING

The park's two main recreation areas, Caney Creek and Sandy Creek, offer camping, boating, and fishing on the shores of Lake Sam Rayburn. Also popular are Bouton Lake Recreation Area and Boykin Springs Recreation Area, including historic structures built by the Civilian Conservation Corps, and offering camping, swimming, fishing, and canoeing. Call the park office (936/897-1068) for campsite availability and fee information.

INFORMATION AND SERVICES

To learn more about the campsite availability and fees, lake access points, and trail maps, contact the Angelina National Forest park office (111 Walnut Ridge Rd., Zavalla, 936/897-1068, www.fs.usda.gov, Mon.-Fri. 8am-4:30pm).

GETTING THERE

Take U.S. 59 northeast from Houston. At Lufkin, turn right onto Highway 103. To reach the visitors center, head southeast from Lufkin on U.S. 69 to Zavalla.

SABINE NATIONAL FOREST

The 160,656-acre Sabine National Forest is the easternmost of Texas's four national forests, dominated by the massive Toledo Bend Reservoir along the Louisiana border. The second-largest lake in Texas and the fifth-largest reservoir in the United States, Toledo Bend offers extensive recreation, from boating and fishing to swimming and lakeshore camping.

RECREATION

Outdoor recreation includes fishing, hunting, camping, hiking, horseback riding, and mountain biking. A popular destination is the 12,369-acre Indian Mounds Wilderness Area, designated by Congress as a site "to allow the Earth's natural processes to shape and influence the area." Unfortunately it was misnamed, since the mounds are actually just natural hills that host beautiful flora, including American beech, southern

magnolia, yellow lady's slipper orchids, and broad beech ferns.

Hike the 28-mile (45-km) Trail Between the Lakes, extending from the Toledo Bend Reservoir's Lakeview Recreation Area to U.S. 96 near Lake Sam Rayburn. Contact park headquarters for a map showing the many miles of roads throughout the forest that are open to mountain bikers and horseback riders.

Fishing draws people to the Lake Sam Rayburn reservoir, ideal for catching striped bass. The forest's rivers and creeks teem with crappie, bass, and bluegill.

Birders flock to the area during spring and fall to glimpse of migratory waterfowl and other neotropical migratory songbirds, hawks, and shorebirds. As in the other East Texas forests, the red-cockaded woodpecker, an endangered species, receives special habitat management.

FOOD

One of the best food options is 15 miles (24 km) east of the state line in Leesville, Louisiana, at a homey spot called Mustard Seed (1152 Entrance Rd., Leesville, 337/537-1933, Mon.-Fri. 11am-8pm, Sat. 11am-3pm, $9-21). Go for the local specialty, crispy and tender fried catfish and savory chicken or sausage gumbo. Side dishes include Louisiana-style collard greens and brown gravy.

One of the only recommended barbecue options is Hemphill BBQ (3285 S. Bayou Rd., Hemphill, 409/787-1814, Mon.-Sat. 11am-8pm, $9-21) in the small town of Hemphill. In East Texas the specialties tend to shift away from beef toward pork, so order the baby back ribs or a pulled pork sandwich. The sides tend to be sweeter in this part of the state, which works well for Hemphill's coleslaw and potato salad. Locals come for the homemade desserts, so save room for a pie or pastry.

CAMPING
Get a primitive camping spot at Indian Mounds Wilderness Area. Less primitive is the Ragtown Recreation Area, offering opportunities for hiking, fishing, and bird-watching atop a bluff that faces the lake. Camping with electrical hookups is available at Red Hills Lake and Boles Field. Call the forest headquarters (409/787-3870) for availability and fee information.

INFORMATION AND SERVICES
For a comprehensive list of Toledo Bend Reservoir services—fishing guides, private resorts, and boat launch sites—visit www.toledo-bend.com. To learn more about Sabine Forest's campsites and fees, lake access points, and trail maps, contact the Sabine National Forest headquarters (201 S. Palm St., Hemphill, 409/787-3870). To learn more about the park's recreational opportunities and seasonal news, visit www.fs.usda.gov.

GETTING THERE
Take U.S. 59 northeast from Houston. At Lufkin, turn right onto Highway 103. To reach the park's visitors center, head south on Highway 87 in Milam for 3 miles (4.8 km).

LUFKIN
Lufkin (population 35,510) played a unique role as a major logging town. Founded in 1882 as a stop on the Houston, East & West Texas Railway, the town was named for Abraham P. Lufkin, a Galveston cotton merchant

and close friend of the railroad company president.

The construction of railroad lines in the early 1880s allowed access to the forests' interiors, and the lumber industry and regional economy began to boom. Between 1890 and 1900 the forest industry contributed more to Texas's economy than any other industry, including cattle and cotton. As a result, lumber company towns sprang up in the Lufkin area. The corporations provided jobs for men and prioritized family life by building schools, churches, and medical facilities. Workers were often paid in credits redeemable for merchandise and services in company town facilities. Although some sawmill workers were later drawn to the oil fields for higher wages, many chose to stay with their families in the lumber company towns for the community environment.

The lumber industry continues to play a significant role in Lufkin's economy. Each year, the region produces more than a million board feet of saw timber as well as a significant manufacturing of pulpwood from the nearby pine and hardwood forests.

Antiques shoppers and history buffs are drawn to downtown Lufkin's quaint mix of restaurants and retail shops. A walking tour showcases several remarkable historic buildings, including the 1925 Pines Theater and the location of the first Brookshire Brothers grocery store. Along the way, look for the five colorful murals by artist Lance Hunter that depict historic area businesses and stories.

SIGHTS
Texas Forestry Museum
An essential stop in Lufkin is the Texas Forestry Museum (1905 Atkinson Dr., 936/632-9535, www.

treetexas.com, Mon.-Sat. 10am-5pm, free), offering a look at the region's lumber industry in a forest history wing and the resource and management wing.

Highlights include a compelling exhibit about life in a lumber company town, complete with model buildings and a collection of artifacts from early logging camps. Historic equipment, a fire lookout tower cab, a paper mill room, and an educational exhibit detail the natural succession of a forest. The scenic Urban Wildscape Trail runs behind the main building.

Museum of East Texas

The Museum of East Texas (503 N. 2nd St., 936/639-4434, www.metlufkin.org, Tues.-Fri. 10am-5pm, Sat.-Sun. 1pm-5pm, free) isn't as grand as it sounds. Built in 1976, it showcases regional artists as well as occasional traveling shows and science or children's exhibits. The museum hosts occasional lectures, performances, classes, kids art camps, and publications on the character and heritage of East Texas.

Ellen Trout Zoo

Expectations are exceeded at the large and impressive Ellen Trout Zoo (402 Zoo Circle, 936/633-0399, www.cityoflufkin.com/zoo, daily 9am-5pm, $7 adults, $3.50 ages 4-11), home to 700 animals from all over the planet. The zoo contains a surprising variety of rainforest beasts, tropical birds, and swamp creatures in a well-organized and spacious setting. Spend 3-4 hours to fully appreciate animals typically seen only in big-city zoos, including monkeys, a giraffe, rhinos, and hippos. Keep an eye out for alligators, seals, and birds around every corner.

downtown Lufkin

A highlight for families is the miniature train that circles the zoo and then makes an unexpected detour across Ellen Trout Lake (look for the elusive gators), followed by a loop through the nearby forest.

The History Center

Just 11 miles (17.7 km) outside Lufkin in the small town of Diboll is a fascinating attraction known simply as The History Center (102 N. Temple St., Diboll, 936/829-3543, www. thehistorycenteronline.com, Mon.-Fri. 8am-5pm, Sat. 9am-1pm, free). Diboll is one of the oldest continually operated forest company sites in Texas, and the 12,000-square-foot History Center is technically a public archives dedicated to East Texas history. That makes it sound boring, which it's not.

The History Center in Diboll

The vaguely named History Center did not get a more specific moniker because organizers did not want it to be classified as just a museum or a library. Although it contains many reference materials, it's more than a research center. It features artifacts but it's not really a museum. It's best described as a public history and archive center that collects, preserves, and explores the heritage of East Texas.

Visitors are drawn to the exquisite woodwork, consisting of cypress walls preserved from the 1950s along with floors of locally harvested yellow pine. Exhibit panels feature century-old photos showcasing Diboll's dynamic past as a lumber company town along with an impressive collection of archives, including 70,000 photos, decades of community newspapers, and lumber company log books.

For children, the History Center's highlight is parked behind the building: an authentic 1920 Baldwin 10-wheel, 68-ton steam locomotive, which visitors can explore by climbing in, on, and around it. Pull on a rope to hear the engine's steam whistle blast across the courtyard.

RECREATION

With its proximity to four national forests, Lufkin is surrounded by boating, hiking, camping, and biking. In town, the city manages 16 municipal parks through Lufkin Parks and Recreation (936/633-0250, www. lufkinparks.com) to jog or walk your dog. Check the website for hours and accessibility to swimming pools, jogging trails, playgrounds, and picnic areas.

FOOD
Barbecue

Lufkin Bar B Q (203 S. Chestnut St., 936/634-4744, www.lufkinbbq.com, Mon.-Sat. 10am-9pm, $10-21) is in an unassuming 1950s-era strip mall. The lightly fried rolls served before the meal are so tasty you'll be tempted to make a meal of them. Save space for the main event: succulent brisket and spicy sausage barbecue, or try a chipped beef sandwich for a smaller quantity.

American

Lufkin has many generic chains and a few admirable local eateries. Mingle with the locals at Mar Teres Tea Room (3157 Ted Trout Dr., 936/875-6200, Tues.-Fri. 11am-2pm, reservations suggested, $10-23), a classic luncheon spot filled with antiques and pink decor. This tightly packed home is the ultimate destination for quality cuisine in Lufkin. The almond tea is the talk of the town, and entrées like chicken spaghetti, chicken salad, and French onion soup are outstanding. Desserts are top-notch, especially the lemon cake, coconut pie, and old-fashioned chocolate cake.

More down-home and low-key is Mom's Diner (900 W. Frank Ave., 936/637-6410, Mon.-Fri. 11am-7pm, $7-16) with the best chicken-fried steaks in the area as well as juicy burgers, fried chicken, and outstanding peppered cream gravy.

For old-time greasy and tasty burgers, locals love the classic 1950s feel and fare of Ray's Drive In Cafe (420 N. Timberland Dr., 936/634-3262, Mon.-Sat. 10am-10pm, $7-12), including the mouthwatering bacon cheeseburger with onion rings, mushroom burger, chili dog, and chocolate milk shake. Classic oldies music completes the nostalgic scene.

Tex-Mex

Lufkin is known more for barbecue than Tex-Mex, but a couple places in town draw sizable lunch crowds. Consistently reliable Cafe Del Rio (1901 S. 1st St., 936/639-4471, daily 11am-10pm, $9-19) has crispy chips, spicy salsa, loaded nachos, and sizzling fajitas. Also recommended is Casa Ole (2109 S. 1st St., 936/632-2653, daily 11am-10pm, $8-17), offering tasty tacos and hearty enchiladas.

ACCOMMODATIONS

Lufkin's lodging options are limited, but several chains offer reliable rooms and amenities. An affordable commendable hotel is La Quinta (2119 S. 1st St., 936/634-3351, www.lq.com, $53 d). Features include an outdoor pool, free continental breakfast, and free Wi-Fi. Also worthwhile is Hampton Inn & Suites (4400 S. 1st St., 936/699-2500, www.hamptoninn.com, $92 d), featuring a free hot breakfast, to-go breakfast bags on weekdays, and free Wi-Fi. A step up is Best Western Crown Colony Inn & Suites (3211 S. 1st St., 936/634-3481, www.bestwesterntexas.com, $119 d), offering spacious rooms with microwaves and fridges, free Wi-Fi, deluxe continental breakfast, an outdoor pool, and a fitness room.

INFORMATION AND SERVICES

To get the scoop on lodging and dining options or to pick up a map or brochure, stop by the Lufkin Convention & Visitors Bureau (1615 S. Chestnut St., 936/633-0349 or 800/409-5659, www.visitlufkin.com, Mon.-Fri. 8:30am-5pm).

NACOGDOCHES AND VICINITY

Nacogdoches (population 33,542) claims to be Texas's oldest town, and there's no denying the wealth and breadth of its heritage and culture. Named for the Nacogdoche Caddo people that live in the area, Nacogdoches was an active Native American settlement until 1716, when Spain established a mission at the site. In 1779 Nacogdoches received official designation from Spain as a pueblo, prompting locals to deem it Texas's first official "town."

Nacogdoches became a center of trading activity, much of it illicit, primarily among the French and Americans, centered around the Old Stone Fort. With the town's strategic location on major trade routes, Nacogdoches was prominent in early military and political activities.

By the mid-1800s Nacogdoches lost its distinction in these areas due to its lack of modern steamboat and railroad transportation. Growth remained stagnant until the 1920s, when the Stephen F. Austin State Teachers College (now Stephen F. Austin State University) opened, bringing jobs and cultural activities. With a current enrollment of 13,000, the university remains the lifeblood of Nacogdoches.

SIGHTS
Old Stone Fort Museum

The Old Stone Fort Museum (1936 North St., 936/468-2408, www.sfasu.edu/stonefort, Tues.-Sat. 9am-5pm, Sun. 1pm-5pm, free) on the Stephen F. Austin State University campus is a 1936 replica of the home of Don Antonio Gil Y'Barbo, the founder of present-day Nacogdoches. The original building, dating to the 1700s, was the oldest stone structure in Texas before it was torn down amid much protest in 1902. Now historic itself, this replica is a Nacogdoches landmark, featuring a permanent exhibit on the history of the building that served as a trading post, church, jail, private home, and saloon, but never an official fort. The Old Stone Fort Museum contains artifacts related to the early history of East Texas, with a special focus on the Spanish and Mexican periods (1690-1836).

Sterne-Hoya House

One of the oldest homes in East Texas is the 1830 Sterne-Hoya House (211 S. Lanana St., 936/560-5426, www.ci.nacogdoches.tx.us, Tues.-Sat. 10am-4pm, free admission and tours). Built by Adolphus Sterne, a leader of the Texas Revolution, the home stands on its original site, which is rare for the era, as most were moved or demolished. Prominent figures of the time, including Davy Crockett, Sam Houston, and Cherokee chief Bowles, visited the Sterne home in the mid-1800s. Tour guides explain the significance of the period antiques and the prominent families who occupied the home, now listed on the National Register of Historic Places.

✪ Texas State Railroad

All aboard the Texas State Railroad (Hwy. 84 W., Rusk, 877/726-7245, www.texasstaterr.com, $40-75 adults, $25-45 ages 2-12). The depot is in Rusk, 30 miles (48 km) northwest of Nacogdoches, where passengers board for a historic journey through the East Texas Piney Woods. Trains have plied these 25 miles (40 km) from Rusk to Palestine since 1881, when the state prison system began constructing the railway to transport iron ore and timber.

The 90-minute trek is an enjoyable and relaxing journey into the past, with gently rolling train cars clickety-clacking over bridges and through the dense green forest. Sit back while the steam locomotive's whistle bellows and the genial conductor checks your ticket. Before you know it, you'll be at the Victorian-style depot at the end of the line, where you'll find historical exhibits, gift shops, and food service.

Round-trip excursions depart Saturday-Sunday at 11am year-round

Most of East Texas was originally occupied by the **Caddo people,** a large nation comprising dozens of distinct groups or "families" in modern-day Texas, Oklahoma, Arkansas, and Louisiana. To learn all about their heritage and culture, go to **Caddo Mounds State Historic Site** (1649 Hwy. 21 W., 936/858-3218, www.visitcaddomounds.com).

When Europeans arrived in the 1500s and 1600s, they encountered Caddo communities along streams and rivers. The Caddo were farmers who grew corn, beans, squash, sunflowers, and other crops that flourished in the humid and rainy East Texas environment.

Although the Caddo people lived in remote river and stream valleys, their leaders usually lived in larger villages, where tall temples built of poles and thatched grass often stood atop earthen mounds. These centers were where community members gathered for festivities or during times of crisis.

The vast lands of the Caddo provided them much protection, but they also had a reputation as fierce and skilled warriors. When threatened, groups would band together. The Caddo were known for their pottery skills. Caddo women made everything from 3-foot-tall (1-m) storage jars to tiny bowls as well as smoking pipes and earspools. The Caddo traded bison hides and horses for French guns and merchandise.

Today, descendants of this great nation make up the Caddo Nation of Oklahoma, with nearly 4,000 members. The nation's headquarters is 45 miles (72 km) west of Oklahoma City in the town of Binger.

from both the Rusk and Palestine depots, and return to their point of origin by 3:30pm. Yes, the tickets are pricey, but the experience is one-of-a-kind. A 90-minute layover is scheduled at the opposite train depot, where a variety of lunch options are available. Snacks, beverages, and restrooms are available on the train.

Caddo Mounds State Historic Site

Just south of Rusk near the small town of Alto is the Caddo Mounds State Historic Site (1649 Hwy. 21 W., 936/858-3218, www.visitcaddomounds.com, Tues.-Sun. 8:30am-4:30pm, $2 adults, $1 students). Caddo-speaking farmers built these ceremonial burial mounds more than 1,200 years ago, and historians now say they are the southwesternmost structures of the legendary Mound Builders of the eastern North American woodlands. Three of these earthen mounds, used for burials, temples, and religious ceremonies, still rise from the East Texas forests. Visitors can walk among the gently sloping structures and explore the interpretive center's exhibits and displays. Note that a devastating tornado struck the site in 2019, so a temporary visitors center is in operation while the permanent museum is built.

The Fredonia Brewery

Not historic but drawing a large number of heritage travelers is the Fredonia Brewery (138 N. Mound St., 936/305-5125, www.fredoniabrewry.com, Thurs. 5pm-9pm, Fri. 4pm-9pm, Sat. 2pm-10pm), just a block north of downtown. The founders,

Fredonia Brewery

both Nacogdoches natives, opened the 15-barrel brew house in 2017. Their shared love of beer and local history is evident in the pine taproom and the beers, including the tasty Nine Flags Amber Ale and Pine Cove Porter. Even the brewery's name and logo reference local history: the Fredonia Republic (1826-1827), "Brewed with the independent spirit that created Texas."

RECREATION
Hiking

For a quiet retreat to the surrounding woodlands, hoof it to the Stephen F. Austin Experimental Forest (6598 FM 2782, 936/564-8924, www.srs. fs.usda.gov), 8 miles (12.9 km) southwest of Nacogdoches. Not as compelling as its name implies, the forest is dubbed "experimental" for its crazy variety of tree species planted in the 1940s. A century ago, the area was logged and abandoned for use as cotton fields, but the U.S. government's purchase of more than 600,000 acres of East Texas land—eventually becoming the region's national forests—allowed for the reforestation of hardwoods and pines that would eventually populate the area. The Experimental Forest contains 3 miles (4.8 km) of trails with interpretive signs. Walk the wooded trails to glimpse 150 species of birds and 80 kinds of butterflies at this peaceful site.

Biking

A scenic and pleasant hour's ride is the campus of Stephen F. Austin State University (1936 North St., 936/468-3200, www.sfasu.edu). Enjoy the tree-lined streets and classic collegiate structures while keeping an eye out for the thousands of meandering-while-texting students.

For a lengthy ride with cyclists knowledgeable about the area, consider meeting up with the Nacogdoches Bicycle Club (www. bikenacogdoches.org). The group meets several times a month for a 30-mile (48-km) ride on the rolling rural roadways outside town. Membership is not required, and visitors are welcome to drop in. The group meets Saturday morning near the SFASU campus at Java Jack's (1122 North St., 936/560-3975, www.javajacks.com).

FOOD
American

If you're downtown at lunch, drop by the wonderful Dolli's Diner (116 S. Pecan St., 936/305-5007, Mon.-Wed. and Thurs.-Sat. 7am-5pm, Sun. 9am-4pm, $7-19), a classic lunch spot on the square with everything you'd expect from a small-town diner, including the best chicken-fried steak in the region, hearty sandwiches, healthy salads, big burgers, and friendly waitstaff.

Another popular lunch spot is the campus-area NacBurger (3205 N. University Dr., 936/564-3588, Mon.-Sat. 11am-7pm, $5-10). Students and professors line up at this shopping-center deli for tasty burgers and

Dolli's Diner in downtown Nacogdoches

chicken sandwiches accompanied by bacon cheddar fries and a large iced tea.

Locals also love the regional chain Clear Springs Cafe (211 Old Tyler Rd., 936/569-0489, www. clearspringsrestaurant.com, Mon.-Thurs. 11am-9pm, Fri.-Sat. 11am-10pm, $7-21). Seafood is the main draw, including popular dishes such as the pan-seared tilapia, salmon or crawfish salad, and catfish étouffée.

Barbecue

CC's Smokehouse (2709 Westward Dr., 936/462-8880, Mon.-Sat. 11am-8:30pm, $10-21) is classic East Texas-style barbecue done right: delicious brisket, savory sausage, and meaty pork ribs. Not quite as reliable is The Barbeque House (704 N. Stallings Dr., 936/569-9004, daily 11am-8:30pm, $9-22). The brisket and chicken are popular, and the sausage is a bit spicy but worth ordering.

Mexican

Nacogdoches isn't known for quality Mexican restaurants, but a couple options include Tacos Dona Pancha (112 W. Seale St., 936/559-9995, daily 6am-7pm, $8-18), with authentic tacos in tasty tortillas—opt for the beef with cilantro and onions. Don't be concerned by the surrounding iron gates and possibility that you'll have to order by pointing at menu items.

Another option is Restaurant El Ranchero (123 King St., 936/569-2256, daily 10:30am-9pm, $8-18), featuring some of the hottest and heartiest salsa in town, along with traditional favorites such as quesadillas, fajitas, and flautas. Call in advance to see if El Ranchero is offering its semi-regular "two free margaritas" special.

ACCOMMODATIONS

Nacogdoches's lodging options are primarily chains, with most located near the Stephen F. Austin campus. The best budget choice is Best Western Inn of Nacogdoches (3428 South St., 936/560-4900, www.bestwestern. com, $74 d), offering rooms with free internet access along with microwaves and fridges, a free continental breakfast, and an outdoor pool.

One of Nacogdoches's few locally run establishments is the wonderful downtown six-story ✪ Fredonia Hotel (200 N. Fredonia St., 936/564-1234, www.thefredonia.com, $99 d). Deemed "as modern as an atomic submarine" when it opened in 1955, the Fredonia's contemporary architectural style has French-inspired details in its decorative ironwork. This mid-century modern masterpiece is within walking distance of restaurants, coffee shops, and bars. The Fredonia features free Wi-Fi, a large and stylish outdoor pool, a good on-site restaurant, and a fitness center.

Moving into the slightly-more-expensive range is the clean and comfortable Hampton Inn & Suites

the historic Fredonia Hotel

(3625 South St., 936/560-9901, www.hamptoninn.com, $116 d), offering free internet access, a complimentary hot breakfast buffet, an outdoor pool, and a fitness center.

A popular option with business travelers is the nearby Holiday Inn Express Hotel & Suites (3807 South St., 936/564-0100, www.hiexpress.com, $126 d), with amenities such as free Wi-Fi, an upscale fitness center, and an outdoor pool.

INFORMATION AND SERVICES

While strolling historic downtown Nacogdoches, drop by the town's two main tourism offices. The Nacogdoches Convention & Visitors Bureau (200 E. Main St., 888/653-3788, www.visitnacogdoches.org, Mon.-Fri. 9am-5pm, Sat. 10am-4pm, Sun. 1pm-4pm) has information about the city's history and local sites of interest. Just around the corner is the headquarters of the Texas Forest Trail Region (202 E. Pilar St., 936/560-3699, www.texasforesttrail.com, Mon.-Fri. 8:30am-5pm). Operated by the Texas Historical Commission, the Forest Trail Region oversees heritage travel destinations and cultural activities in Nacogdoches and the East Texas Piney Woods region. Drop by to pick up brochures and maps, and to talk to the friendly and knowledgeable staff.

INFORMATION AND SERVICES

While strolling historic downtown Nacogdoches, drop by the town's two main tourism offices. The Nacogdoches Convention & Visitors Bureau (200 E. Main St., 888/653-3788, www.visitnacogdoches.org, Mon.-Fri. 9am-5pm, Sat.

10am-4pm, Sun. 1pm-4pm) has information about the city's history and local sites of interest.

Just around the corner is the office headquarters of the Texas Forest Trail Region (202 E. Pilar St., 936/560-3699, www.texasforesttrail.com, Mon.-Fri. 8:30am-5pm). Operated by the Texas Historical Commission, the Forest Trail Region oversees heritage travel destinations and cultural activities in Nacogdoches and the entire East Texas Piney Woods region. Drop by to pick up brochures and maps, and to talk to the friendly and knowledgeable staff.

TYLER

Slow-moving Tyler will never be confused with fast-paced Austin, but this large town or small city (population 105,729) certainly has a distinctive feel: Southern. From stately plantations to hospitable residents to deep-fried cooking, Tyler has a strong cultural connection to the Deep South.

One of the city's big draws is its roses. Tyler now provides nearly 20 percent of the roses in the United States. The Tyler Municipal Rose Garden contains tens of thousands of rose bushes representing hundreds of varieties. The gardens attract bees, butterflies, and thousands of people annually from around the world. Many visitors come for the Texas Rose Festival, held each October since 1933, featuring the queen's coronation, the rose parade, the queen's tea, and the rose show.

Tyler changed dramatically in 1930, when the discovery of the nearby East Texas oil field turned this small agricultural and railroad city into a major destination for workers and corporations. The town received an added

In the early 1900s, East Texas was a land of opportunity, with prospectors speculating about the location of the next big oil field. More often than not, their efforts were unsuccessful, but when they guessed correctly and tapped into a fertile patch of petroleum, the fortunes of everyone associated with the discovery exploded like the gusher of oil.

These stories, along with photos and artifacts, are on display at local history museums in East Texas. For a full look at the region's oil boomtown years, visit Kilgore's comprehensive **East Texas Oil Museum** (1301 S. Henderson Blvd., Kilgore, 903/983-8295, www.easttexasoilmuseum.com), at the intersection of U.S. 259 and Ross Street.

After Beaumont, another East Texas boomtown was Kilgore, 30 miles (48 km) east of Tyler. Kilgore's glory years began in 1930, when the first oil gusher arrived; within weeks, the town's population surged from 500 to more than 10,000. Before well-spacing regulations were adopted, Kilgore boasted a small section of downtown that became known as the "World's Richest Acre," where 24 oil wells once stood.

At the height of Kilgore's boom, residents woke up to find their yards filled with strangers covered with boxes, sacks, and newspapers. People installed iron doors on their homes for protection from the influx of newcomers, and they stopped hanging their clothes out to dry since they'd be stolen off the line.

Not surprisingly, the oil boom brought con artists, criminals, and prostitutes to these small East Texas towns. The Texas Rangers were assigned to clean up the area, and they often had to resort to unorthodox means—like the time they "remodeled" an old church into a makeshift prison, with padlocked prisoners lining the interior walls—to address the newfound population of ne'er-do-wells.

boost in the 1940s when Camp Fannin was established nearby, including a troop capacity of 19,000 at the height of World War II.

In the following decades, Tyler's economic base shifted from agriculture to industry. Most were petroleum related, but other manufacturing plants soon followed, including metal and fabricating companies, railroad and machine shops, furniture and woodwork manufacturers, aluminum foundries, and air-conditioning and refrigeration plants.

In the 1970s-1980s, Tyler was best known as the hometown of football legend Earl Campbell, who earned the Heisman Trophy at the University of Texas and went on to become a Hall of Fame running back in the National Football League. Campbell's nickname, "The Tyler Rose," forever linked him with his hometown.

SIGHTS
Tyler Municipal Rose Garden and Museum

The region's most popular attraction is the Tyler Municipal Rose Garden and Museum (420 Rose Park Dr., 903/597-3130, www.parksandrec. cityoftyler.org, Mon.-Fri. 8am-5pm, Sat. 9am-5pm, Sun. 1pm-5pm, free), with numerous displays showcasing the elaborately jeweled, hand-sewn gowns worn by rose queens dating back to 1935. Check out the scrapbook pages from each rose queen, including memorabilia, personal recollections, and photos, including one with a queen and her freshly killed deer. Visitors can also view videos about the history of Tyler's rose industry and rose festival, and experience an interactive "attic" exhibit with an eclectic collection of antiques from Tyler's past.

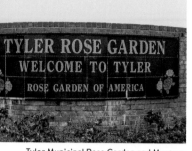

Tyler Municipal Rose Garden and Museum

The municipal garden is the primary draw, however, with its sea of colorful roses—35,000 bushes representing 500 varieties. The blooming period is May-November, and early May is the peak of the flowers' natural growing cycle. This is when the garden's 14 acres burst with the bright sight and sweet scent of fresh roses.

Plantation Museums

Tyler's heritage is on full display at Tyler's three plantation museums, where the Old South comes to life through historic furniture, artifacts, and photos. This lifestyle, typically associated with the Deep South, wasn't prevalent in most of Texas, and these sites provide a feel for the ornate homes and luxurious grounds. If you're lucky, the docents and tour guides may be dressed in period costume.

The Goodman-LeGrand House Museum (624 N. Broadway Ave., 903/531-1286, www.cityoftyler.org, Tues.-Sat. 10am-4pm, free) was the home of Dr. W. J. Goodman, a local doctor and Civil War surgeon. His son, also named Dr. William Jeffries Goodman, was a Civil War Major and chief surgeon, who bought the house from his father. The family lived in the home for 73 years and four generations. Originally built in 1859,

the house is Tyler's first property to be listed on the National Register of Historic Places. The museum features original furnishings, including hand-carved tables and chairs, a grandfather clock from the colonial era, surgical tools and medical cases, and fine silver and china. It's open for walk-in tours.

Just as impressive is the 1854 Dewberry Plantation (14007 FM 346 W., 903/825-9000, www. dewberryplantation.com, by appointment, tours $8 adults and seniors, $5 ages 6-18). The plantation site served as a campground for the officers of the Army of the Republic of Texas prior to their final battle with the Cherokee people. The home, billed as the only original two-story pre-Civil War house still standing in Smith County, was built for War of 1812 hero Colonel John Dewberry, who moved to Tyler in 1835.

Also noteworthy is the grand 1878 McClendon House (806 W. Houston St., 903/592-3533, www. mcclendonhouse.net, Fri.-Sat. 10am-4pm, tours $7). Once a hub for Tyler's elegant Victorian society, the home was eventually purchased by the McClendon family, whose youngest daughter, Sarah, became a noted Washington DC journalist with a presidential-coverage career spanning Franklin D. Roosevelt to George W. Bush. The home is now primarily used as a wedding and events site but is open for tours.

Caldwell Zoo

One of the best-run and most highly acclaimed zoos in the state is Tyler's Caldwell Zoo (2203 W. Martin Luther King Jr. Blvd., 903/593-0121, www. caldwellzoo.org, Mar.-Labor Day daily 9am-5pm, Labor Day-Feb. daily 9am-4pm, $11.60 ages 13-54, $10 seniors,

$8.40 ages 3-12). What started in 1938 as a backyard menagerie of squirrels and parrots for schoolchildren has evolved into an 85-acre zoo containing 2,000 animals from East Africa and North and South America. Animals on display in naturalistic habitats include monkeys, rhinos, elephants, giraffes, cheetahs, and mountain lions.

Tyler Museum of Art

For a dose of traditional culture, visit the respectable Tyler Museum of Art (1300 S. Mahon Ave., 903/595-1001, www.tylermuseum.org, Tues.-Sat. 10am-5pm, Sun. 1pm-5pm, $5 adults, $3 students), on the east side of the Tyler Junior College campus. The museum showcases local and regional artists with an emphasis on contemporary works; occasional traveling exhibits feature centuries-old European paintings, Japanese artwork, and Native American pottery and ceramics. It contains three galleries on the main level, a smaller gallery for special exhibits upstairs, and a children's gallery.

Discovery Science Place

With the family in tow, this is the place to go: Discovery Science Place (308 N. Broadway, 903/533-8011, www.discoveryscienceplace.org, Mon.-Sat. 10am-5pm, Sun. 1pm-5pm, $8 adults, $6 children and seniors) offers three large exhibit halls with fun interactive features like the earthquake shake, a cavern crawl, a dinosaur exhibit, and a bat cave.

ENTERTAINMENT AND EVENTS

For a city of 100,000, Tyler has a surprising number of entertainment options, perhaps due to the increasing number of Dallas-area retirees moving to Tyler for its slower-paced lifestyle. The quality of the local arts scene has grown over the past decade, resulting in top-notch ballet, symphony, and cultural offerings.

Ballet Tyler

An organization drawing plenty of local attention is Ballet Tyler (4703 D. C. Dr., Suite 105, 903/596-0224, www.artandseek.org). A convergence of two programs, the School of Ballet Tyler and the Tyler Junior College dance program, has helped raise the group's profile. Dancers range in age 11-20, and the company stages several performances throughout the year. Visit the website for schedules and tickets.

East Texas Symphony Orchestra

One of Tyler's enduring cultural entities is the East Texas Symphony Orchestra (522 S. Broadway Ave., Suite 101, 903/526-3876, www.etso.org). Newly named to encompass the larger region, the orchestra has also bumped up its mission to bring classical music to a larger segment of the community. The organization offers a wide range of concerts, from contemporary to Renaissance.

Cowan Center

For big-name touring acts, Tyler residents and visitors head to the University of Texas-Tyler's Cowan Center (3900 University Blvd., 903/566-7424, www.cowancenter.org), the stage for international and touring stars in comedy, jazz, and Broadway shows. Past performers and performances include Bill Cosby, David Copperfield, Lyle Lovett, *Cats, Stomp*, and Larry Hagman.

SHOPPING

East Texas Fresh Farmer's Market

Tyler isn't a major shopping destination, but locals spend time and money at the East Texas Fresh Farmer's Market (2112 W. Front St., May-Aug. Tues. and Sat. 7am-1pm). The market features regional vendors offering fresh produce, flowers, and wares. Soak up the local scene and support the local farming community.

FOOD

Tyler's quality restaurant options are better than you'd expect in a smallish city in a rural part of the state.

American

A stalwart on the scene is ✪ Rick's on the Square (104 W. Erwin St., 903/531-2415, www.rix.com, Mon.-Fri. 11am-10pm, Sat. 4pm-1am, $13-39), a swanky lunch and dinner joint and rowdy blues bar by night. In the heart of downtown in an old saloon and theater, Rick's has tempting shrimp and oyster appetizers, gigantic juicy burgers with chunks of fried potatoes on the side, and exquisite entrées ranging from chicken dumplings to the recommended crawfish-stuffed filet mignon.

The popular Potpourri House (3200 Troup Hwy., 903/592-4171, www.potpourrihouse.com, Mon.-Sat. 10am-3pm, $11-32) is a welcoming spot combined with a retail establishment offering candles, antiques, jewelry, more candles, and potpourri. The restaurant's offerings range from club sandwiches to baked fish, chicken, and prime rib.

A local legend and a must-experience for barbecue fans is ✪ Stanley's Famous Pit Bar-B-Q (525 S. Beckham Ave., 903/593-0311, www.stanleysfamous.com, Mon.-Fri.

7am-7pm, Sat. 11am-8pm, $7-19). The smoked ribs are atop "best of" barbecue lists across Texas—their tender, succulent taste will have you thinking about them for days. Try the smoked turkey and sausage, or sample a sliced brisket sandwich. Better yet, tackle the Brother-in-Law sandwich, teeming with sausage, chopped beef, and cheese.

Tex-Mex

Tyler is far from the border but has a few worthy Mexican restaurants, including popular homegrown regional chains.

If you're downtown, drop by Posado's (2500 E. 5th St., 903/597-2573, daily 11am-9:30pm, $9-19). Mission-style decor adds to the authentic Mexican-inspired taste, including interior-style dishes such as marinated quail fajitas and shrimp or fish platters. The classics include chicken enchiladas and spicy beef tacos.

Locals also love Taqueria El Lugar (1726 E. Gentry Pkwy., 903/597-4717, Mon.-Thurs. 9am-9pm, Fri.-Sat. 9am-10pm, $10-20). As the name implies, tacos are the specialty, listed on the menu by number. Order anything with the amazing guacamole and tasty beef (the cabbage isn't quite as recommendable), and be sure to ask for it on a corn tortilla.

ACCOMMODATIONS

Chain hotels are the only choice in Tyler. The available options are safe, reliable, and relatively affordable. On the lower end of the price spectrum is La Quinta (1601 W. Southwest Loop 323, 903/561-2223, www.lq.com, $69 d), featuring free Wi-Fi, a free continental breakfast, and an outdoor pool.

Perhaps the best deal in town is the

Comfort Suites at South Broadway Mall (303 E. Rieck Rd., 903/534-0999, www.choicehotels.com, $99 d), offering rooms with free Wi-Fi, microwaves, and fridges, and hotel amenities such as an exercise room, free continental breakfast, and an indoor heated pool and whirlpool. The only drawback is its location, far from the downtown activity.

On Broadway, about 10 minutes from downtown, is the recommendable Country Inn & Suites (6702 S. Broadway Ave., 903/561-0863, www.countryinns.com, $105 d). There's plenty of space to spread out, with a mini kitchen (fridge, microwave) and rooms offering free Wi-Fi. The free breakfast includes meat, eggs, bagels, and cereals.

Nearby is the city's largest hotel—the comfortable Holiday Inn Select (5701 S. Broadway Ave., 903/561-5800 or 800/465-4329, www.holidayinn.com, $109 d), which features free Wi-Fi service, an outdoor pool, a full-feature fitness center, and free meals for kids under age 13.

INFORMATION AND SERVICES

The Tyler Convention & Visitors Bureau (315 N. Broadway Ave., 903/592-1661 or 800/235-5712, www.visittyler.com) is just a few blocks north of the downtown square on the 1st floor of the historic Blackstone building. The friendly staffers provide brochures, maps, and general information to help you get around the Rose Capital.

GETTING THERE

American Airlines flies regional jets to Tyler Pounds Regional Airport (TYR, 700 Skyway Blvd., 903/531-9825, www.cityoftyler.org) several times a day from Dallas-Fort Worth. Most visitors opt to drive, which takes 3.5 hours from Houston.

JEFFERSON

Set aside a few hours to explore Jefferson (population 1,967). This quaint Deep South community is nestled in the forest, offering a pleasant escape to the Piney Woods's past. In its glory days of the mid-19th century, Jefferson was a burgeoning boomtown containing a kaleidoscope of cultures, including entrepreneurial East Coast shop merchants, newly freed enslaved people, and westward-moving pioneers. For more than a decade, Jefferson welcomed a steady flow of steamboats bringing worldly influences and people.

In 1870, Jefferson had a population of 4,180 and was the sixth-largest city in Texas, and 1867-1870, steamboats became important in the town's commercial trade, which grew from $3 million to $8 million. By 1870, only the port of Galveston exceeded Jefferson in volume. In 1873, things changed dramatically for Jefferson. The destruction of the Red River raft, a natural dam on the river, lowered the water level of the surrounding lakes and streams, making navigation to Jefferson via steamboat impossible. Also that year, the Texas and Pacific Railway, which bypassed Jefferson, was completed. Without steamboat or railroad access, Jefferson shrank.

In the mid-1900s, locals began looking at Jefferson's distinctive past as a way to preserve and promote the town's heritage, particularly its remarkable 100-plus recognized historic structures. Known as the "Bed and Breakfast Capital of Texas," tourism is now Jefferson's economic base.

SIGHTS
Historic Buildings

With so much Southern heritage in such a small town, it's necessary to visit some of the sites that make Jefferson historically significant. One of its crown jewels is the House of the Seasons (409 S. Alley St., 903/665-8000, www.houseoftheseasons.com, tours Mon.-Sat. 11am, $10). Built in 1872 by Colonel Benjamin Epperson, a prominent businessperson and friend of Sam Houston, this magnificent home contains Greek Revival, Italianate, and Victorian architectural elements. The name is from the glass encasement on top of the house, with colored glass representing each of the seasons.

A visit to Jefferson is incomplete without a stop at the Jefferson General Store (113 E. Austin St., 903/665-8481, www.jeffersongeneralstore.com, Sun.-Thurs. 9am-6pm, Fri.-Sat. 9am-10pm). Walking through the creaky screen doors offers a step back in time, with vintage trinkets and current-day souvenirs mingling in a historic 1870s mercantile setting. Touches of bygone days are everywhere, in the signature five-cent cup of coffee, the homemade pecan pralines, and the soda fountain. Jams, salsas, T-shirts, and candy round out the experience.

Also worth a visit is The Grove (405 Moseley St., 903/665-8018, www.thegrove-jefferson.com, call for tour information, $6). Referred to as "the most haunted house in Jefferson," The Grove is a private residence built in 1861 and listed on the National Register of Historic Places. An hour-long tour offers a fascinating glimpse into the home, along with stories about the supernatural experiences of the owners, including a woman in a white dress who always takes the same path through the house. Its paranormal activity is so legendary, *This Old House* placed it on its list of Top 12 Haunted Homes, and it graces the cover of the book *A Texas Guide to Haunted Restaurants, Taverns, and Inns.*

The Atalanta Railroad Car

The Atalanta (210 W. Austin St., 903/665-2513, daily 10am-3pm) was a private railcar used by railroad tycoon Jay Gould. It's rather odd that this elaborately designed and elegantly furnished car ended up in Jefferson, since the city rejected Gould's plans to bring a railroad through the town. Upon being spurned, he left, predicting Jefferson's demise; he was partly right, since the town never regained its steamboat-era splendor of the 1860s. *The Atalanta* features a dozen rooms containing opulent mahogany, crystal light fixtures, and silver bath accessories. Across from the Excelsior House downtown, it remains a major attraction of Jefferson's heritage tourism. Tours are $5, and guides are available at the adjacent Excelsior House Hotel.

Scarlett O'Hardy's Gone with the Wind Museum

The campy and somewhat strange Scarlett O'Hardy's Gone with the Wind Museum (408 Taylor St., 903/665-1939, www.scarlettohardy.com, Thurs.-Sat. 10am-4pm, $3 adults, $1 under age 13) is jam-packed with everything imaginable related to the classic film *Gone with the Wind,* including posters, photos, costume reproductions, dolls, and seats from the Atlanta theater where the movie premiered in 1939. Perhaps most interesting is the collection of autographs from the movie's stars, most notably Clark Gable, Vivien Leigh, Leslie Howard, Hattie McDaniel, and Butterfly McQueen.

Lake o' the Pines

Nearby Lake o' the Pines (903/755-2597, www.lakeothepines.com) is as charming as its name implies. The popular destination is known for bass, catfish, and crappie fishing as well as boating for waterskiing, sailing, pontoon boats, party boats, and "floating cabins," all available at several lakeside marinas. Campers flock to Lake o' the Pines, pitching tents and parking RVs at four U.S. Army Corps of Engineers parks and privately owned campgrounds. Other options include guesthouses, cabins, and motels.

✪ Caddo Lake

For the area's premier recreational destination, head just downriver from Jefferson to Caddo Lake, the only natural lake in Texas (all the others were created by dams). Stringy Spanish moss and outstretched cypress trees surround this mysteriously beautiful and sometimes marshy lake. The Caddo people say a massive flood formed the lake, but scientists believe logjams blocked the Red River, causing it to back up into the Cypress Bayou watershed, which formed the lake. Popular lake activities include camping, hiking, swimming, fishing, and boating. Among the many attractions at Caddo Lake is the Texas Parks and Wildlife-operated Caddo Lake State Park (FM 2198, via Hwy. 43, 903/679-3351, www.tpwd.state.tx.us). The park offers access to diverse fishing, canoe rentals, and quaint cabins built by the Civilian Conservation Corps in the 1930s.

FOOD

Because of its modest size, most restaurants in Jefferson are within walking distance of the historic downtown shopping and lodging attractions. One of the stalwarts is the tremendous Joseph's Riverport Barbecue (201 N. Polk St., 903/665-2341, Tues.-Sun. 11am-6pm, $10-22). This is traditional East Texas-style 'cue, with sweet spicy sauce covering savory smoked meats, including pork ribs, brisket, and chicken. The turkey and chopped beef sandwiches are amazing, and the potato salad, coleslaw, and beans as sides are way better than average. Drop by Friday night for a catfish feast.

For a fancier dining experience, make reservations at the top-notch Stillwater Inn (203 E. Broadway St., 903/665-8415, www.stillwaterinn.com, Tues.-Sat. 5:30pm-9pm, $12-35). In an 1890s Victorian house, this busy upscale restaurant is famous for its grilled seafood and steak, veal specials, and roasted rack of lamb.

ACCOMMODATIONS
Bed-and-Breakfasts

Jefferson claims to be the "Bed and Breakfast Capital of Texas." The dozens of B&Bs far outnumber the few hotel options, and the town is a Victorian-era playground.

Among the popular choices is the Claiborne House Bed & Breakfast (312 S. Alley, 903/665-8800, www.claibornehousebnb.com, $109-199), a stately Greek Revival home built in 1872 and offering six rooms—four in the main house and two in the carriage house, each named after romantic poets (Yeats, Wilde, Dickinson). All rooms have a framed poem, a book of the poet's work, free Wi-Fi, private baths, and TVs. A full Southern gourmet breakfast is served at 9am, and a day spa is available for massages, body wraps, hot rock treatments, and salt scrubs.

The Old Mulberry Inn and Cottages (209 Jefferson St., 903/665-1945, www.oldmulberryinn.com, $89-189) is recommended by *Southern Living* magazine and even the *New York Times*. The antebellum home contains five guest rooms and two cottages with private baths that feature claw-foot tubs, family heirlooms, cable TV, and free Wi-Fi. The three-course gourmet breakfasts include delectable items such as artichoke quiche, baked pears with cranberries, Rocky Mountain grits, and mulberry almond coffee cake.

Hotels

For those who insist on staying in a normal plush-free hotel in the B&B Capital of Texas, there's really only one option: the Executive Inn & Suites (200S. Walcott St., 903/665-3700, www.executiveinnjefferson.com, $85 d). There's nothing fancy here, but it's new and pleasant, with a free hot breakfast, suites with jetted tubs, and free Wi-Fi. A word of caution: The whistles from the trains across the highway can be loud in the night.

The historic Excelsior House (211 W. Austin St., 903/665-2513, www.theexcelsiorhouse.com, $129 d) is technically a hotel but feels like a B&B. It's rich in history and ghosts and has hosted guests since the 1850s. Fans of paranormal activity claim this is one of the most haunted locations in town. During Jefferson's prosperous days, guests included Ulysses S. Grant, Rutherford B. Hayes, and Oscar Wilde, and its 150-plus years of operation make it one of the oldest establishments of its kind still in business in Texas.

INFORMATION AND SERVICES

To find out more about the dozens of available B&Bs or other area attractions, pick up a map or brochure from the kind folks at the Marion County Chamber of Commerce (101 N. Polk St., 903/665-2672, www.jefferson-texas.com).

GETTING THERE

Like the other destinations in the Piney Woods region, Jefferson is accessed via U.S. 59, which runs north-south to Houston, passing through Lufkin, Nacogdoches, and Marshall. The drive can take four hours if you're doing things right—making time to soak up the forest views, stopping for a bite to eat, and waiting patiently to pass the logging trucks. From Dallas, the drive is two hours eastbound on I-20 before heading north on U.S. 59 for Marshall and Jefferson or south for Nacogdoches and Lufkin.

THE GULF COAST

Stretching more than 350 miles (560 km) along the Gulf of Mexico, this region of sun, sea, and sand offers the ultimate escape. Moderate beaches and waves don't attract crowds the way Florida's mighty surf does, but draws casual beachcombers, anglers, and families.

Occasionally referred to as the country's "Third Coast," the gulf region offers quiet natural seashores, crazy spring break parties, and world-class museums. The constant breeze off the ocean keeps sailors and windsurfers cruising, and temperatures are a few degrees cooler than inland,

HIGHLIGHTS

✪ **WINDOW SHOP ON THE STRAND.** Galveston's thriving historic district hosts hotels, restaurants, art galleries, and boutiques amid 19th-century splendor (page 103).

✪ **GET A FEEL FOR SEAFARING LIFE.** Walk the sturdy wooden decks of **THE *ELISSA*,** one of the oldest operational sailing vessels in the world (page 104).

✪ **EXPERIENCE THE DEPTHS OF THE TEXAS GULF.** Start with birds and gators at sea level before descending to oil-rig depths with menacing sharks and hundreds of other slippery species at the **TEXAS STATE AQUARIUM** (page 125).

✪ **TOUR A 33,000-TON FLOATING MUSEUM.** The decommissioned aircraft carrier **USS *LEXINGTON* MUSEUM** transports you back to World War II with vintage aircraft and an impressive collection of historic memorabilia (page 127).

✪ **WATCH SEA TURTLES HATCH.** You can also witness the migrations of thousands of birds along **PADRE ISLAND NATIONAL SEASHORE,** the longest undeveloped barrier island in the world (page 140).

✪ **EXPERIENCE COWBOY CULTURE.** At 825,000-acre **KING RANCH,** genuine cowboys herd longhorn cattle in wide-open spaces, evoking the Texas mystique (page 146).

✪ **TAKE IN VIEWS FROM PORT ISABEL LIGHTHOUSE.** It's well worth climbing the 74-step spiral staircase for the sight of the gorgeous Laguna Madre stretching to Port Isabel (page 152).

although the humidity is always hair-curling. The ocean is warm and inviting, sometimes uncomfortably warm in summer, and is technically responsible for stirring up the horrific hurricanes far out at sea. Hurricanes Ike (2008) and Harvey (2017) wreaked havoc on the Gulf Coast, and the Deepwater Horizon oil spill (2010) caused visitors to avoid the beaches.

All along the Gulf Coast are anglers of different stripes, from solo artists casting lines off a pier or at surf's edge to groups on charter deep-sea boats with professional guides. The promise of fresh flounder, trout, bull reds, snapper, and even shark and tuna is one of the region's main draws.

Naturalists come for the abundant birding opportunities. The Great Texas Coastal Birding Trail links 300-plus miles (480 km) of shoreline, from hummingbird sighting near Galveston to whooping cranes and tropical species on Padre Island. Two major migratory flyways intersect along the Gulf Coast, allowing birders to photograph elusive species.

In addition to the recreational opportunities along the shore, the cool air-conditioning at numerous Gulf Coast museums offers a welcome

The Gulf Coast

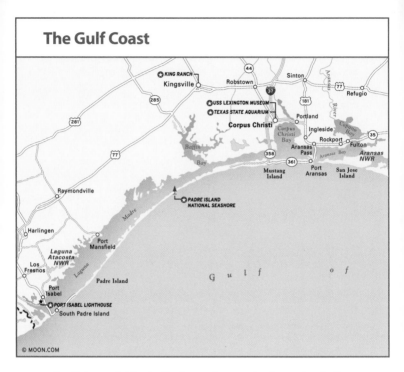

© MOON.COM

respite. Galveston's Moody Gardens and several Corpus Christi attractions are world-class facilities for learning about regional history, wildlife, and art. Top your day off with a fresh catch from a seaside restaurant.

Aside from Galveston's festive springtime Mardi Gras and South Padre's spring break, most of the Gulf Coast is a slow-moving year-round vacationland, where the biggest challenge is determining the day's activities—swimming, fishing, shell collecting, sunbathing, surfing, boating, or building sand castles. Visitors responding to the call of the sea find the region to be as low-key as the gulf's lightly lapping waves.

ORIENTATION

With 350 miles (560 km) of shoreline, Texas's Gulf Coast is challenging to

characterize but uniquely Texan—from oil refineries to spring break beach parties, the coastline stretches from urban playgrounds to a national seashore.

The northern part of Texas's coast is dominated by Galveston Island, just 45 minutes from Houston. It can be crowded with urban escapees on weekends, but Galveston has small-town charm with a fascinating past and impressive historic buildings. Just an hour down the coast is the Brazosport Area (that's its actual name), a collection of communities known for oil refineries and chemical plants balanced by welcoming beaches and fishing.

Three hours farther south, Corpus Christi offers a less urban vibe. Visitors flock here for birding, fishing, seafood, and recreation. The

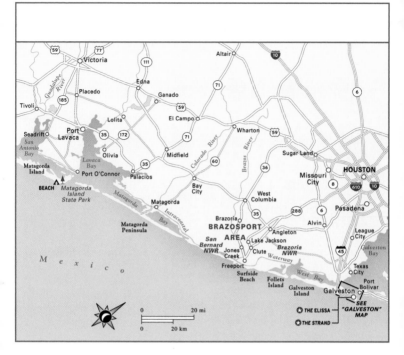

final stretch of coastline is three hours' drive from Corpus to South Padre along an uninspiring inland highway through the enormous King Ranch. The drive culminates at gorgeous South Padre Island, with pristine beaches and tasty waves.

PLANNING YOUR TIME

Coast-bound travelers tend to stay for a weekend in one area—Galveston, Brazosport, Corpus Christi, or South Padre—at a beach condo or fishing village, as opposed to roaming the entire region. If you have time and money to spare, you can cruise along the coast in a rented boat.

The two main types of Gulf Coast travelers are busy families on a getaway from the burbs, and anglers on a getaway from the family. The South Padre Island beaches are the nicest, so if quality sand and surf are priorities, that's the place to start. Spend at least two or three days in the sun, soft white sand, and gentle surf.

Farther up the coast, the beaches tend to be less scenic—the sand is darker and civilization is more apparent in the oil rigs, tankers, and commercial buildings. The lure of the sea is just as strong, but there is more traffic and crowds. Spend a long weekend in Corpus Christi on pleasant Mustang Island or nearby Padre Island National Seashore. Corpus's USS *Lexington,* Texas State Aquarium, and Museum of Science and History are a family-friendly, air-conditioned change of pace.

The Brazosport Area offers fewer cultural amenities, and anglers spend quiet weekends here sans water parks and booming car stereos. Things are more laid-back and less commercial here, where retirees, anglers, and professional beachcombers peacefully coexist.

Galveston is where Houston folk go to spend money to get their beach and seafood fix. It's the least pristine of all the Gulf Coast beaches, but the waves are welcoming, and the shopping and restaurant scene in the historic Strand district are deserving of two travel days.

INFORMATION AND SERVICES

Most communities along the Gulf Coast have visitors bureaus to inquire about directions, equipment rental, and other travel-related assistance. Contact the following entities before your trip with questions about logistics or scheduling. Their physical addresses and hours of operation are included at the end of each destination section in this chapter.

Brazosport Area Chamber of Commerce (979/285-2501, www. brazosport.org), Corpus Christi Area Convention & Visitors Bureau (361/881-1800 or 800/766-2322, www. visitcorpuschristitx.org), Galveston Island Convention & Visitors Bureau (409/763-4311 or 888/425-4753, www.galveston.com), and South Padre Island Convention & Visitors Bureau (956/761-6433 or 800/767-2373, www.sopadre.com).

GETTING THERE AND AROUND

Most travelers arrive on the Gulf Coast by car. Commercial flights are available to Corpus Christi International Airport and at Brownsville South Padre Island International Airport.

Since most of the coastline is undeveloped, no major freeways link the coastal cities. Highway 35 is primarily a rural road between Houston and Corpus Christi, passing through dozens of small towns along the way. The lengthy Padre Island National Seashore is only accessible via the park road near Corpus Christi. Otherwise, the trek to South Padre beaches is 20 miles (32 km) inland via U.S. 77 through Kingsville, Harlingen, and Brownsville.

Corpus Christi International Airport (CRP, 1000 International Blvd., 361/289-0171, www. corpuschristiairport.com) has flights on American Eagle, United, and Southwest. South Padre is accessible via the Brownsville South Padre Island International Airport (BRO, 700 Amelia Earhart Dr., 956/542-4373, www.flybrownsville.com), served by United and American Eagle. Galveston is an hour's drive from Houston's George Bush Intercontinental Airport (IAH, 2800 N. Terminal Rd., 281/230-3100, www.airport-houston. com) or William P. Hobby Airport (HOU, 7800 Airport Blvd., 713/640-3000, www.fly2houston.com). Rental cars are available at each airport.

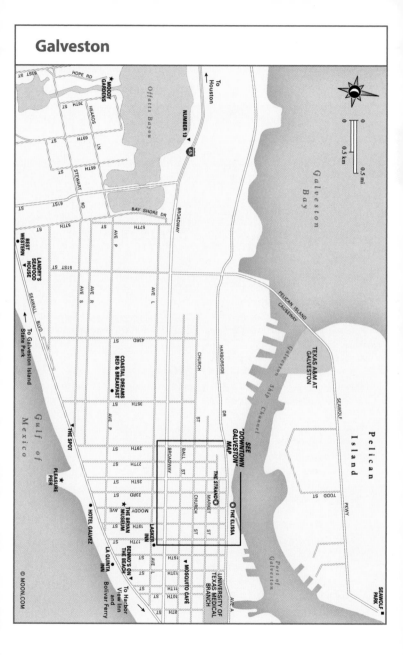

Galveston

HOPE RD
61ST ST
MOODY GARDENS
76TH ST
HEARDS LN
69TH ST
65TH ST
STEWART RD
61ST ST
Offats Bayou
NUMBER 13
To Houston
45

BAY SHORE DR
57TH ST
BROADWAY
AVE P
AVE L

BEST WESTERN
LANDRY'S SEAFOOD HOUSE
61ST ST
AVE S
AVE R
43RD ST
CHURCH ST
HARBORSIDE DR

SEAWALL BLVD
To Galveston Island State Park
COASTAL DREAMS BED & BREAKFAST
36TH ST
AVE P

THE SPOT
29TH ST
27TH ST
BROADWAY
BALL ST

PLEASURE PIER
26TH ST
23RD ST
THE STRAND
MARKET
CHURCH ST

HOTEL GALVEZ
20TH ST
19TH ST
MOODY AVE
THE BRYAN MUSEUM
THE ELISSA

LA QUINTA INN
17TH ST
LASKER INN
BENNO'S ON THE BEACH

To Harbor View Inn and Bolivar Ferry
AVE L
15TH ST
MOSQUITO CAFÉ
14TH ST
13TH ST
11TH ST
10TH ST
8TH ST
UNIVERSITY OF TEXAS MEDICAL BRANCH
AVE A

Gulf of Mexico

Galveston Bay

PELICAN ISLAND CAUSEWAY
TEXAS A&M AT GALVESTON
Galveston Ship Channel
SEAWOLF
Pelican Island
TODD ST
PKWY
Port of Galveston
SEAWOLF PARK

SEE "DOWNTOWN GALVESTON" MAP

© MOON.COM

0 0.5 km
0 0.5 mi

Galveston

On an island 50 miles (80 km) southeast of Houston, Galveston (population 50,457) is a hotbed of Texas history. Most people remember the Alamo, but they don't realize Galveston was once Texas's largest city and busiest port, with thousands of immigrants arriving each year. Devastating hurricanes have destroyed property and driven some residents permanently out of town.

Galveston was founded in 1839 and a burgeoning commercial center until the Civil War slowed its growth. On January 1, 1863, Confederate troops recaptured the city, the same day Abraham Lincoln signed the final Emancipation Proclamation. Word didn't make it to Galveston until June 19, 1865, when enslaved Texans finally received their freedom. Afterward, Galveston became the birthplace of the now nationwide Juneteenth celebration, which commemorates the announcement.

After the Civil War, Galveston grew steadily with hundreds of immigrants, primarily Germans, disembarking from ocean liners each day. Trade was prosperous, especially cotton exports, and for a while Galveston was known as the "Wall Street of the South" due to its robust economy and cosmopolitan amenities, such as electric light, telephones, and modern streetcars. The stately mansions and downtown commercial buildings of this era still stand as the heart of Galveston's historic district. Most of these ornate homes are now museums that draw visitors from around the globe.

Galveston was forever altered in 1900 when a massive hurricane destroyed a third of the island's buildings. The torrential 120-mph (190-km/h) windstorm caused an estimated 6,000 deaths. As a result of the devastation, Galveston's industries and residential population shifted to Houston.

Thanks in part to the construction of a massive seawall to protect the northern part of the island, Galveston eventually recovered to become one of the state's top destinations. Hurricane Ike caused widespread flooding damage in 2008, but most of the island's cultural and historical attractions survived and reopened. The beach remains the island's main draw, especially for Houstonians, and its pleasant slice of Victorian life attracts international visitors.

SIGHTS

Many of Galveston's attractions are heritage-related. The historic commercial buildings along The Strand and the century-old mansions showcase a distinctive time not seen inland.

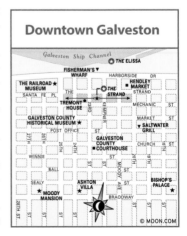

✪ THE STRAND

The heart of Galveston's thriving business district in the late 1800s and early 1900s, The Strand (Strand St. and Mechanic St. between 20th St. and 25th St.) still captures the essence of the city's "Wall Street of the South" era. This 36-block National Historic Landmark District features New Orleans-style hotels, restaurants, art galleries, and boutiques, most of which escaped the devastation of the 1900 hurricane. Today, visitors are drawn to antiques and clothing shops, art studios, and seasonal festivals, including the popular Dickens on the Strand and Mardi Gras celebrations.

Pleasure Pier

PLEASURE PIER

The smile-inducing amusement park Pleasure Pier (2501 Seawall Blvd., 855/789-7437, www.pleasurepier.com, hours vary, $20-27 day pass, $4 individual rides) harks back to a 1940s facility with the same name, although the gangsters of yore have been replaced with families and couples. The current Pleasure Pier is the third iteration—two earlier sites were knocked out by hurricanes.

Spend a few hours exploring 16 rides, midway games, boardwalk-style shopping, food vendors that include a Bubba Gump Shrimp restaurant, and the gulf view from a bench on the deck. The bumper cars are a blast, and the Rock-n-Roll ride has unforgettable thrills. There aren't many other places to enjoy a roller coaster, giant swing, or Ferris wheel with ocean water beneath you.

THE BRYAN MUSEUM

Galveston's newest attraction, The Bryan Museum (1315 21st St., 409/632-7685, www.thebryanmuseum.com, Tues.-Sun. 10am-5pm, $14 adults, $10 seniors and students, $4 ages 6-12) is the realized dream of J. P. Bryan, an oilman with a passion for Texas history—this museum reportedly houses the world's largest collection of Southwestern artifacts.

The building itself has a storied past, dating to 1895 as the Galveston Children's Home. Three floors of rare and fascinating objects and documents include original correspondence from infamous Gulf Coast pirate Jean Lafitte, a sword used to help capture Mexican general Santa Anna, historic guns used in significant Texas battles, and an amazing collection of decorative saddles.

Visitors view these objects in dramatically lit exhibit cases along with accompanying artwork that highlights the artifacts. The exhibits begin with Native American history and progress chronologically to the Spanish and French colonial eras and the Texas Revolution.

HURRICANES: DEADLY TROPICAL CYCLONES

Hurricane season is tumultuous for Gulf Coast residents. These devastating tropical cyclones can come ashore anytime June-November, though most strike in the hot summer months of **August-September.**

Hurricanes originate when ocean waters reach their highest temperatures, leading to thunderstorms with winds of up to 40 mph (64 km/h), officially a tropical storm. At this point, the National Hurricane Center names the storm, working from a predetermined alphabetical list of names. Tropical storms get their energy from warm humid air over the ocean, and they release this energy as powerful winds.

Traditionally the probability of a hurricane hitting Texas hasn't been high, but the past decade or so has been a different story. In September 2005, Hurricane Rita, a category 5 storm with intense 120 mph (190 km/h) winds, made landfall near Sabine Pass on the Texas-Louisiana border and caused $11 billion in damage and seven deaths. Even more devastating was Hurricane Ike, which slammed into Galveston Island in September 2008, leaving an enormous swath of destruction. Ike leveled several communities, and its 110 mph (175 km/h) winds ripped apart hotels, office buildings, and countless homes in Galveston, Houston, and the surrounding area. Devastation struck again in 2017, when Hurricane Harvey walloped Rockport, near Corpus Christi, with 130mph (210 km/h) winds. The associated storms resulted in unprecedented flooding in Houston.

WALLOPING WINDS

The statistical possibility of Texas being hit by a hurricane is once every six years along any 50-mile (80-km) stretch of the coast. The recent incidents, plus the memory of 2005's devastating Hurricane Katrina in New Orleans, have residents tuning in to the weather whenever the words *"tropical depression"* surface. Annual probabilities of a hurricane striking a 50-mile (80-km) segment of the coast range from 30 percent near Port Arthur to 40 percent at Matagorda Bay, northeast of Corpus Christi.

Some of the strongest hurricanes to hit the U.S. coast have come ashore in Texas historically typically in uninhabited areas. In 1970, meteorologists recorded wind gusts of 180 mph (290 km/h) near Aransas Pass, and in 1961, Hurricane Carla brought 175 mph (280 km/h) winds to Port Lavaca. By comparison, Katrina's wind speeds were 140 mph (225 km/h) at landfall, but Katrina's extremely low barometric pressure made it unusually intense.

In the wake of the devastating losses with Hurricanes Ike and Harvey, officials have organized emergency plans and evacuation routes for coastal cities. Public awareness campaigns focus on the importance of being informed and prepared. The unpredictable nature of these storms makes evacuation planning a challenge, but an increasing number of Gulf Coast residents pack up and move inland when an intensifying tropical storm is on the horizon.

SCHLITTERBAHN WATERPARK

Creating waves of excitement for families is Schlitterbahn Waterpark (2026 Lockheed St., 409/770-9283, www.schlitterbahn.com, hours vary, $53 adults, $41 ages 3-11), more a water amusement park than a swimming destination. The ocean can't compete with Schlitterbahn's "uphill water coasters" in a convertible facility that can be opened or closed for indoor or outdoor recreation year-round to keep the water and air temperatures in the 80s (27-31°C). Other attractions include traditional twisty waterslides, white-water rapids, a wave pool, playgrounds, hot tubs, a vertical plunge tower, and a surf ride.

✪ THE *ELISSA* AND TEXAS SEAPORT MUSEUM

One of the city's most treasured landmarks is the 1877 ship *Elissa* (Pier 21, 2200 Harborside Dr., 409/763-1877, www.galvestonhistory.org, daily

10am-5pm, self-guided tours $8 adults, $6 ages 6-18). This remarkable historic vessel is one of the only ships of its kind restored to full sailing capacity and one of the oldest merchant boats still afloat. Get a feel for seafaring life by walking across the sturdy wooden decks under the massive masts and 19 square sails. Head below to explore the sleeping quarters and mechanical room. The ship serves as the Official Tall Ship of Texas and is a National Historic Landmark.

Elissa's origins are a shipyard in Aberdeen, Scotland, where she was constructed in 1877 as an iron-hulled, three-masted boat. For a century she traveled the world, including stops at Galveston for cotton shipments in the 1880s. This local connection prompted the Galveston Historical Foundation to purchase the ship in 1975 and undertake its painstaking restoration.

The *Elissa*

In April you can arrange for the unique and unforgettable experience of an *Elissa* "day sail." Participants can grasp the weathered lines and assist with raising the massive sails while enjoying a day at sea. A hard-working crew of volunteers serves guests a hearty lunch. Visit the Galveston Historical Foundation's website for dates and prices.

To learn more about the *Elissa*'s history and restoration, visit the adjacent Texas Seaport Museum (daily 10am-5pm) The portside facility features informative exhibits about maritime culture and a movie about Galveston's port-based heritage as the "Ellis Island of the West." The museum's database contains the names of more than 133,000 immigrants who entered the United States through Galveston. Admission to the museum is included in tickets for the *Elissa*.

The Bishop's Palace

THE BISHOP'S PALACE
Grand. Stately. Ginormous. However you choose to describe it, the spectacular 1886 Bishop's Palace (1402 Broadway St., 409/762-2475, www.galvestonhistory.org, daily 11am-6pm, guided tours hourly, $14 adults, $9 students) is the centerpiece of Galveston's historic Broadway Street. The American Institute of Architects designated Bishop's Palace as one of 100 outstanding buildings in the

country. This Victorian castle exudes elegance, with ornate fireplaces (one is lined with pure silver), grand stairway, stained-glass windows, and intricately carved furnishings and details. Galveston's most visited historical attraction, it transports visitors to another era. For a behind-the-scenes tour of the inner workings and rare views of the marvelous mansion, ask about the monthly Basement-to-Attic tour.

THE MOODY MANSION

Galveston entrepreneur W. L. Moody Jr. purchased the four-story, 32-room, 28,000-square-foot limestone and brick Moody Mansion (2618 Broadway St., 409/762-7668, www.moodymansion.org, daily 10am-5pm, $15 adults, $7 students) a week after the 1900 hurricane. The impressive and opulent home features rare hand-carved wood, coffered ceilings, stained glass, and heirlooms from the Moody family, whose financial empire was built on banking, ranching, and insurance. Marvel at the manicured grounds, exquisite furnishings, expansive ballroom, and the dining room's gold-leaf ceiling. Behind-the-scenes tours (Fri.-Sun. 4pm, $35 pp) are available.

MOODY GARDENS

Natural wonders await beneath three enormous glass pyramids at Moody Gardens (1 Hope Blvd., 409/744-4673, www.moodygardens.com, daily 10am-6pm, $65 day pass, $26-33 individual pyramid tickets), an elaborate collection of plants, animals, and educational exhibits inside the 100-foot-tall (30-m) structures. If you only have time to explore one area, go with the Rainforest Pyramid. The Aquarium Pyramid has more animals

and features, but in the rainforest environment you'll find yourself face-to-face with African animals, tropical birds, and colorful reptiles, along with massive plants, cascading waterfalls, and the constant chatter of birds and insects. Check out the bat cave, with various species of bats hanging upside-

Aquarium Pyramid at Moody Gardens

down and nibbling on fresh fruit.

The Aquarium Pyramid displays the world's oceans, viewed at the surface and underwater. Marvel at penguins as they waddle and dive, and catch an up-close view of sea lions as they glide and play. Sharks, sea turtles, rays, and tropical fish await below the surface, viewable in a traditional aquarium tank setting or from the underwater tunnel, surrounded by a million gallons of water.

The Discovery Pyramid features science and nature exhibits, and there are a ropes course, a zip line with a bird's-eye view of the pyramids, three IMAX theaters, kids' activities aboard a paddle-wheel boat, seasonal recreation at Palm Beach (swimming lagoons, whirlpools, volleyball, and paddleboats), formal gardens, a golf course, nature trails, and the Moody Gardens conference center, hotel, and spa.

One of the newest attractions is "animal experiences," offering guests the chance to interact one-on-one with river otters, seals, and adorable penguins in a secluded environment. Check the website for prices and timing.

GALVESTON TREE SCULPTURES TOUR

Check out the East End Historical District's offbeat Galveston Tree Sculptures Tour (information and maps 409/797-5144, www.galveston. com). Hurricane Ike devastated Galveston in 2008 with a tidal surge that led to the demise of thousands of oak trees. Local artists honored the former foliage by creating carvings from the remains. Highlights include a large live oak containing a dozen carved birds called *Birds of Galveston,* and a carving named *Tin Man and Toto* at the birth home of *Wizard of Oz* director King Vidor.

ASHTON VILLA

Also of historical interest is the 1859 Ashton Villa (2328 Broadway St., 409/762-3933, www.galvestonhistory. org, call ahead for guided tours), built as the residence of wealthy businessman James Moreau Brown. It set the standard for the exquisite Galveston homes that followed. Experience the Victorian lifestyle through the home's grand entryway, life-size paintings, and beautifully landscaped grounds. The house contains artworks, furniture, and mementos the family acquired during travels to Asia. Ashton Villa's carriage house now houses a Galveston Island Visitors Center, open

daily, but tours of the mansion are by appointment only.

THE RAILROAD MUSEUM

Anchoring Galveston's historic downtown Strand district is the former Santa Fe Union Station, home to The Railroad Museum (2602 Santa Fe Place, 409/765-5700, www. galvestonrrmuseum.org, daily 10am-5pm, $10 adults, $8 seniors, $5 students). More than 20,000 railroad items and several dozen vintage passenger, dining, and kitchen cars provide views of railroad life in the late 19th-early 20th centuries. The main terminal, at the heart of this impressive art deco building, contains interactive exhibits and a collection of unique plaster sculptures depicting "ghosts of travelers past." Kids will love the miniature model trains and the historic railcars behind the depot.

OCEAN STAR OFFSHORE DRILLING RIG AND MUSEUM

The Ocean Star Offshore Drilling Rig and Museum (1900 Harborside Dr., 409/766-7827, www.oceanstaroec. com, summer daily 10am-5pm, winter daily 10am-4pm, $10 adults, $8 students and seniors), just a block from the Strand historic district, is a distinctive small museum that educates visitors about the offshore oil and gas industry via a refurbished drilling rig. Visitors can take a self-guided tour through three levels of the retired rig to learn about oil exploration, drilling, and production through informative exhibits and videos.

THE GALVESTON NAVAL MUSEUM

The Galveston Naval Museum (100 Seawolf Park Blvd, 409/797-5114, www.galvestonnavalmuseum.com, daily 9am-6pm, $10 adults, $5 students) features historic World War II vessels on a guided or self-guided tour, allowing visitors to experience what it was like to patrol underwater in the Pacific or assist Allied forces in the Atlantic. Hop aboard the USS *Cavalla,* a submarine that sank a Japanese aircraft carrier involved in the Pearl Harbor attacks, or the USS *Stewart,* the only battleship of its kind preserved in the United States.

BEACHES

There are a few different kinds of beaches in Galveston—the touristy stretches near hotels and attractions, quiet areas frequented by locals, and the party spots. The Galveston Park Board recently helped organize an expansion project that widened existing beaches and added a significant amount of new beach, the largest restoration project of its kind in Texas history.

One of the most family-friendly spots is Stewart Beach (6th St. and Seawall Blvd., 409/765-5023, Mar.-mid-Oct., $12-15 per car), where you'll find parents and kids building sand castles, playing volleyball, and bodysurfing. Nearby amenities include a children's playground with waterslides, umbrella and chair rentals, a concession area, a souvenir shop, restrooms, and a bathhouse.

Things get a bit crazier at East Beach (1923 Boddeker Dr., 409/762-3278, $12-15 per car), where Houston's young crowd comes to party and one of the few places where drinking is legal on the beach. As a result, there are more concerts, promotions, and festivals than at other beaches. Up to 7,000 cars pack the beach for drinking and sunbathing, and the bar area is a magnet for partiers. East Beach

has restrooms with showers, volleyball courts, chair and umbrella rentals, and a souvenir shop.

RECREATION

Recreational opportunities abound in Galveston. Outdoor-based activities have expanded in recent years as visitors increasingly search for physical challenges and workout opportunities on the coast.

GALVESTON ISLAND STATE PARK

A popular place to enjoy the outdoors is Galveston Island State Park (14901 FM 3005, 409/737-1222, www.tpwd.state.tx.us, $7 over age 12), with camping, hiking, biking, fishing, swimming, and birding, followed by a dip in the ocean or the simple pleasure of beachcombing. There are 4 miles (6.4 km) of trails through bayside salt marshes and prairie grassland. There are no lifeguards on the beach, but there are restrooms and rinse showers.

BIKING

Bike rentals have become a popular way to experience Galveston, with no freeways or traffic jams. To rent a bike and learn about Galveston's best cycling areas, head to Island Bicycle Company (1808 Seawall Blvd., 409/762-2453, www.islandbicyclecompany.com). The shop claims to have the largest selection of rental bikes in the city and offers hotel pickup service. For $60, you can take a bike for a full-day self-guided tour that includes a ferry ride. The package includes a lock and a map.

PADDLING

A slightly more adventurous way to explore Galveston Island is to rent a kayak, paddleboard, or canoe. Start at

Galveston Island State Park, with convenient established put-ins and take-outs. Paddlers have three different water "trails": the 2.6-mile (4.2-km) Dana Cove Trail, beginning at Lake Como and meandering through shallow seagrass; the Oak Bayou Trail, a 4.8-mile (7.7-km) course beginning near the boardwalk and following the inlets and breakwaters of Galveston Bay; and the Jenikins Bayou Trail, a 2.8-mile (4.5-km) trail traversing a freshwater pond and a small inlet.

A worthy outfit for kayak rental and excursion info is Gulf Coast Kayak Adventures (979/215-6319, www. gulfcoastkayakadventures.com), offering shuttle service to specified locations, full-day rentals ($65 single kayak, $80 tandem). Guided kayak tours ($150 plus $60 pp) range from beginner trips exploring birding opportunities to advanced tours offering potential porpoise sightings.

BIRD-WATCHING

The Gulf Coast is a birder's paradise, with ample opportunity to catch glimpses of flying species during migrations in spring and fall. Galveston Island offers a few incentives to stay for a while: The natural barrier island habitat provides protection and food-rich bayous and marshes.

Galveston Island State Park is an ideal perch for bird-watching opportunities. Keep an eye out for great blue herons, white ibis, great egrets, and white spoonbills as well as hawks, gulls, and terns.

SURFING

"Galveston" and "surfing" don't usually go together, but there are places where surfing exceeds expectations. Steady coastal winds allow for windsurfing, and there are often decent surfing conditions along the Seawall (between 21st St. and 51st St.). Waves are most consistent in spring, and their gentle nature offers an opportunity for beginners to hone their skills. Watch for the beach patrol's red-flag warnings on gusty days. The Galveston Beach Patrol (409/763-4769, www. galvestonislandbeachpatrol.com) provides current weather conditions. For information about surf equipment rental, contact one of the city's surf shops, like Ohana Surf & Skate (2814 Ave. R, 409/763-2700, www. ohanasurfandskate.com).

FISHING

Fishing opportunities abound, and a fishing license ($40 nonresidents, $20 residents) is required. Obtain one at the Super Wal-Mart (6702 Seawall Blvd.), or the Texas Parks and Wildlife Office (800/895-4248) to purchase by credit card.

Spotted sea trout, black drum, and flounder can be caught along the shore at Galveston Island State Park, and a fish-cleaning station is at the end of the park road near the camping area. For information about conditions, contact the park's administrative office (409/737-1222).

One of the most popular fishing spots on the island is the Galveston Fishing Pier (90th St. and Seawall Blvd., 409/974-4383, www. galvestonfishingpier.com, $12 adults, $8 under age 12). The 300-foot-long (90-m) T-head is an ideal spot to view the shoreline while casting a line for redfish, jackfish, and sea trout. The pier offers equipment rental, bait, chairs, and mobile carts.

ENTERTAINMENT AND EVENTS

NIGHTLIFE

Like most beach towns, Galveston's nightlife scene is a mix of surfside venues (often the most fun and memorable options) and standard beer joints or restaurant-bar combos. Unlike other travel destinations, the bar scene tends to shut down early—10pm at many locations—so be sure to call ahead if you're planning a pub crawl.

During hot summer months, touristy and genuinely fun **Float** (2828 Seawall Blvd., 409/765-7946) has an outdoor pool where customers are encouraged to enjoy a cold beverage while floating. The atmosphere is like a supersize backyard pool party, with a full bar and views of the Gulf of Mexico. If you didn't bring a bathing suit or are visiting when temperatures are below 80°F (27°C), there's indoor seating and standard pub grub.

For those who take their drinking slightly more seriously, head directly to **Brews Brothers Brew Pub** (2404 Strand St., 417/230-6644). You won't find any commercial light beers here, and that's undeniably refreshing. The brewpub specializes in craft beers, and the staff is extremely knowledgeable and will gladly make recommendations.

To grab a meal followed by some drinks, people-watching, and a steady ocean breeze, drop by **Yaga's Café and Bar** (2314 Strand St., 409/762-6676, www.yagaspresents.com), in the heart of the Strand district adjacent to Saengerfest Park. Yaga's is known for its large outdoor patio and dance parties to live music on weekends.

PERFORMING ARTS

Nighttime entertainment tends to be bars rather than theaters, but Galveston has a few notable venues. Foremost is the **Grand 1894 Opera House** (2020 Post Office St., 409/765-1894, www.thegrand.com), which survived the devastating storms of 1900 and 1915 as well as more recent Hurricanes Carla, Alicia, and Ike. Listed on the National Register of Historic Places, the Grand was proclaimed "The Official Opera House of Texas" by the state legislature in 1993.

Grand 1894 Opera House

The building's rich history is apparent, with a grand staircase, wooden walls, and turn-of-the-20th-century furnishings. Friendly ushers offer stories to crowds who regularly pack the house for Texas legends (Lyle Lovett, Robert Earl Keen) and classic artists (Oak Ridge Boys, Kingston Trio).

Island Etc. (2317 Mechanic St., 409/771-0165, www.islandetc.org) is billed as Galveston County's only professional repertory theater company, staging up to six productions a year, mostly traditional shows such as *Cat on a Hot Tin Roof, Avenue Q,* and *Harvey.* The venue also screens classic movies, including *The Wizard of Oz,*

Rocky Horror Picture Show, and *Back to the Future.*

EVENTS

The biggest annual event in Galveston, and one of the biggest in Texas, is Mardi Gras (888/425-4753, www. mardigrasgalveston.com), held in February or early March. This all-out party draws a quarter million people (that's not a misprint). Held on the island for more than a century, the crazy days-long party features extravagant parades, exhibits, live entertainment, and galas. One of the biggest attractions is the three million beads thrown from floats and balconies.

Many beachside communities host sand castle competitions, but most aren't like Galveston's. The builders at Galveston's annual sand castle competition on East Beach in August are actual architects. Hosted by the Houston chapter of the American Institute of Architects since 1986, Galveston's event is a sight to behold. The imaginative and professionally designed sand structures have to be seen to be believed.

Aside from Mardi Gras, Galveston's most venerable event is Dickens on the Strand (502 20th St., 409/765-7834, www.galvestonhistory.org), held the first weekend of December to transports participants to the past for a weekend of 19th-century high society, Galveston style. Costumed revelers, carolers, entertainers, and attendees recreate the festive atmosphere of 1800s Galveston, then Texas's largest and richest city.

The city's other major holiday-related event is the Moody Gardens Ice Land (1 Hope Blvd., 800/582-4673, www.moodygardens.com), with a winter wonderland throughout the site's signature pyramid structures. The festival features a rarity in Texas: an outdoor ice-skating rink and Ice Slide ride.

SHOPPING

Shopping is among Galveston's main draws, with abundant fashion boutiques and knickknack shops throughout in the historic downtown area. Keep in mind that this is where wealthy Houstonians come to play, so prices reflect this clientele.

THE STRAND

The gaslit street lamps, ornate architectural detailing, and lofty display windows along the 36-block Strand district attract even non-shoppers with their Victorian-era charm. Start at the eclectic Hendley Market (2010 Strand St., 409/762-2610, www. hendleymarket.com), a fascinating emporium with Mexican imports, vintage jewelry, kitschy knickknacks, and antique medical instruments. Kids will love the baskets filled with handcrafted toys and plastic novelty trinkets. Not quite as charming yet equally beguiling in its array of objects is Big House Antiques (2212 Mechanic St., 409/762-0559). Shoppers will find many estate-sale pieces, including furniture, jewelry, decorative items, and books.

For something shiny and tasteful, head to The Jewel Garden (2326 Strand St., 409/766-7837), a fancy-yet-casual shop with a range of quality gifts, including silver jewelry, home decor objects, wind chimes, and hand-carved woodwork.

If you forgot your flip-flops or lost your sunglasses on the beach, drop by Jammin Sportswear (2314 Strand St., 409/763-4005). Every beach town needs T-shirt shops, and Jammin is one of the most popular on

"Jellies" on Texas's Gulf Coast refers to jellyfish, and despite their iridescent wiggly appearance, they cause much more pain than pleasure. One of the most common to wash up on the shore isn't technically a jellyfish, despite its translucent air bubble and blue tentacles. The Portuguese man-of-war (a.k.a. the blue bubble, blue bottom, or man-of-war) is actually a colony of organisms, each with its own distinct function. Its name comes from the air bubble's resemblance to the sails of a historical Portuguese war vessel. The man-of-war floats on ocean currents and is deposited on beaches during spring-late summer. These crafty carnivores feed on small fish and other small animals that get caught in their venom-filled tentacles.

The other washed-up organisms visitors may encounter are traditional jellyfish—gelatinous invertebrates with varying-size tentacles hanging from the main "body" of the organism (technically referred to as the mollusk). You won't find an abundance of these animals on a typical beach stroll, but watch for them, as their stings pack a wallop. They're much harder to see in the water, but a good indication of their presence is the appearance of washed-up organisms on the beach. The man-of-war is especially difficult to see since it's translucent and often blends in with sea foam.

Aside from avoiding areas of the ocean where you see beached jellies, make sure you don't step anywhere near the washed-up variety, since their stinging cells remain toxic even when the body has died. The tentacles are often nearly invisible, though you'll definitely feel the sharp shot of pain up your leg. If you step on one, scrape the tentacles off with a credit card. If a jellyfish stings you, place the affected area under hot water and apply hydrocortisone cream to relieve the itching. For a man-of-war sting, splash the area with saltwater, then apply vinegar or a diluted bleach solution (1 part bleach to 10 parts water) to the sting site without pressing too hard on the skin. The pain should go away within an hour.

the island. Pick up towels, caps, sunscreen, or one of those bitey alligator toys. A step up is Surf Styles (2119 Strand St., 409/763-0147), where you can get a T-shirt for the beach and some stylish cruise wear for a night on the town. Brands include Stüssy, Miss Me Denim, Converse, and Lucky Brand.

A mandatory stop on The Strand is the venerable Old Strand Emporium (2016 Strand St., 409/515-0715). The longest-running spot in the district, it offers fresh fudge, ice cream, deli sandwiches, and cold drinks, including beers and wine. Texas foods are the specialty, including salsa, pecan pralines, and tangy barbecue sauce.

FOOD

There's no excuse not to eat seafood in Galveston, and the city is brimming with quality restaurants. After you've had your fill of shrimp, oysters, and snapper, try the Southern-style comfort food at one of the island's tremendous neighborhood joints.

SEAWALL AND VICINITY
Seafood

If you're staying in a hotel on Seawall Boulevard, your inaugural meal should be at ✪ Gaido's Seafood Restaurant (3800 Seawall Blvd., 409/762-9625, www.gaidos.com, Sun.-Thurs. 11am-9pm, Fri.-Sat. 11am-10pm, $12-39), a venerable institution serving memorable meals since 1911. Its legendary reputation is evident in the time-honored trimmings, traditional menu, and attentive service. The shrimp bisque is amazing, the garlic snapper is succulent, and the crab cakes are outstanding. If it's on the menu, order the full snapper—head and bones and all, exquisitely prepared with complementary seasoning. A wide variety of local specialties are on the combination platter, including charcoal-grilled gulf shrimp, deep sea scallops, and catfish or snapper. Save room for a fun after-dinner cocktail by sharing a unique treat known as the Old Shoe (vanilla ice cream, coconut, and chocolate liqueurs).

Exceptional dining awaits at Galvez Bar & Grill (2024 Seawall Blvd., 409/765-7721, www.hotelgalvez.com, daily 6:30am-11am, 11:30am-2pm, and 5pm-10pm, $13-49), inside the historic Hotel Galvez and offering some of the highest-quality cuisine on the island. Menu highlights include fresh-caught seafood from nearby Pier 19, a sublime shrimp and polenta dish, and a grilled seafood platter with oysters, crawfish, and shrimp.

For an awesome lunch with an outstanding view, hit The Spot (3204 Seawall Blvd., 409/621-5237, www. thespotgalveston.com, Sun.-Thurs. 11am-10pm, Fri.-Sat. 11am-11pm, $9-23). After beachcombing, this is the place for a shrimp po'boy, fish-and-chips, or even a big ol' burger. The crunchy breading and homemade rolls are what set this spot apart, with crispy fresh-flavored seafood and sandwiches. The 2nd-floor deck offers panoramic views of the gulf.

A welcoming contemporary option on the island's East End is Porch Café (1625 E. Beach Dr., 409/762-0808, www.porchcafe.com, Thurs. 5pm-10pm, Fri. 11:30am-3pm and 5pm-10pm, Sat. 9am-2pm and 5pm-10pm, Sun. 9am-2pm and 5pm-8pm, $12-33). Open and bright, Porch Café is an ideal place to linger for weekend brunch or an early dinner. Start with a light local lager paired with gulf white ceviche (shrimp and scallops) or seafood au gratin. Follow it with a crab cake-topped salad or a sumptuous plate of seafood linguini. A postmeal stroll on the adjacent beach is a necessity.

Although it's a regional chain, Landry's Seafood House (5310 Seawall Blvd., 409/744-1010, www. landrysseafoodhouse.com, Sun.-Thurs. 11am-10pm, Fri.-Sat. 11am-11pm, $9-31) is a respected eatery, even in a Gulf Coast town known for its local legends. Opt for the fresh catch Lafitte, gulf flounder, or broiled flounder. Landry's also does shrimp well, including a fried option stuffed with seafood.

Specializing in Cajun seafood is Benno's on the Beach (1200 Seawall Blvd., 409/762-4621, www. bennosofgalveston.com, Sun.-Thurs. 11am-10pm, Fri.-Sat. 11am-11pm, $9-20). This is an unassuming place until the food arrives, and it's apparent where Benno's focuses its resources. The shrimp dishes are perfectly seasoned with Cajun spices, and you can't go wrong with Benno's crawfish étouffée, jambalaya, spicy crab, or oysters.

For an ocean-side dining experience, have a meal at Jimmy's on the Pier (9001 Seawall Blvd., 409/974-4726, www.galvestonfishingpier.com, Mon.-Thurs. 11am-9pm, Fri.-Sat. 11am-11pm, Sun. 11am-9pm, $9-30). At the base of the popular T-head fishing pier, Jimmy's is a step above other pier restaurants, offering a variety of menu items, not just beach grub. Grab a table near the edge of the deck for optimal viewing of surfside activity and sunset. Jimmy's food ranges includes standard burgers, pizza, blackened fish, and broiled oysters. Everything on the menu is above average, especially paired with a St. Arnold's lager on tap.

Fresh and contemporary ✪ BLVD Seafood (2804 Ave. R½, 409/762-2583, www.blvdseafood.com, Sun.-Thurs. 11am-9pm, Fri.-Sat. 11am-10pm, $9-36) serves a perfect lunch order: fish

fish tacos at BLVD Seafood

tacos topped with a red bell-pepper sauce and avocado, paired with a Galveston Island Brewery pale ale. You can't go wrong with a diversified seafood sampler for dinner, including the catch of the day, shrimp, scallops, and garlic butter sauce.

American

A few minutes from the shore is popular Mosquito Café (628 14th St., 409/763-1010, www.mosquitocafe. com, Tues.-Sat. 8am-9pm, Sun. 8am-3pm, $9-27). Have breakfast here at least once—the flavor-packed creative healthy food makes an impression. Grab a coffee and try to decide among the delectable options, such as Mosquito Benedict (a fresh-baked scone covered with portabella mushrooms, sautéed shrimp, sun-dried tomatoes, artichoke hearts, asparagus, and poached eggs topped with serrano hollandaise sauce), cinnamon-tinged french toast, fluffy pancakes, or bagels and lox. Lunch items include bowls of pasta with homemade pesto,

olives, and feta cheese, or tasty sandwiches on delicious fresh-baked bread with hickory-smoked bacon, avocado salsa, and goat cheese.

For simple low-key fare, neighborhood stalwart Sunflower Bakery and Cafe (512 14th St., 409/763-5500, www.thesunflowerbakeryandcafe. com, daily 7am-5pm, $6-17) has fresh-made breads, pastries, and desserts as well as flavor-packed sandwiches (the turkey, bacon, and avocado on honey wheat bread is especially tasty), along with healthy salads and eclectic daily specials. The tomato basil soup is a local favorite. Family-owned Sunflower has a full menu complete with crab cakes, burgers, and po'boys, and this is the perfect place to order a to-go lunch for the beach—don't forget to include brownies and the legendary strawberry lemonade.

STRAND AREA
Seafood

What else are you going to eat in Galveston? Fresh seafood is everywhere, and several of the best places are on the bay just a few blocks from The Strand.

Satisfy this urge for a plate of shrimp, oysters, snapper while overlooking the water downtown at Willie G's (2100 Harborside, 409/762-3030, www.williegs.com, daily 11am-9pm, $10-33). Opt for bayside seating and order some peel-and-eat shrimp to start—squeeze fresh lemon on top and dip them in tangy cocktail sauce—and proceed to the fresh catch of the day, from blackened snapper to grilled flounder to fried trout.

Next door is the larger and consistently dependable Fisherman's Wharf (Pier 22 and Harborside Dr., 409/765-5708, daily 11am-9pm, $9-33). Red snapper is the specialty, but shrimp kisses, oysters on the half shell, calamari, and even the steak and pasta are tasty. Ask for a table with a view of the bay, where you can sit on the deck and watch the shrimp boats glide by.

About a half mile inland is one of the finest restaurants in town. The fabulous ✪ Saltwater Grill (2017 Post Office St., 409/762-3474, Mon.-Fri. 11am-2pm and 5pm-10pm, Sat. 4pm-10pm, Sun. 5pm-9pm, $14-42) feels urban and spare like Houston but tastes fresh and flavorful like a Gulf Coast restaurant should. Fresh is a genuine approach to food preparation: The restaurant utilizes a bizarre steam-kettle device that's linked to a large heater, pipes, and steel buckets that cause water to boil in three minutes. The result is rapidly cooked fresh seafood as opposed to reheated or perpetually boiled fare. Enjoy a plate of mussels, clams, or shrimp, and order the grand gumbo. Another must-taste is the appetizer with fried asparagus topped with crabmeat, and entrées such as the grilled yellowfin tuna, flounder, and seafood linguini. Reservations are recommended.

Enjoy a unique twist on island fare at Rudy and Paco (2028 Postoffice St., 409/762-3696, www.rudyandpaco. com, Mon.-Thurs. 11am-2pm and 5pm-9pm, Fri.-Sat. 11am-2pm and 5pm-10pm, $11-39). The seafood and meat dishes have a Central and South American flair, with distinctive seasonings and ingredients like *yuca* and roasted pork (the tacos de puerco are *fabuloso*). For dinner, order house specialty red snapper, crusted in plantains and topped with savory crab meat sauce. Rudy and Paco's has a low-key dress code for dinner; shorts are not allowed.

For old-school, affordable, flavorful seafood, head to Shrimp n' Stuff (3901 Ave. O, 409/763-2805, www. shrimpnstuff.com, daily 10:30am-8:30pm, $7-14). Skip the "stuff" and head for the shrimp—fried, boiled, or grilled. At this classic local joint, you order at the counter, get your food in a Styrofoam box, and sit in lively packed quarters.

American

Step back in time at the charming and moderately priced Star Drug Store (510 23rd St., 409/766-7719, www. galvestonstardrug.com, daily 8:30am-3pm, $7-13). The historic neon and porcelain Coca-Cola sign out front sets the tone, featuring an a century-old horseshoe-shaped lunch counter with a soda fountain. Menu options are typical old-time lunch fare: burgers, reubens, pimiento cheese sandwiches, chicken salad, dilled pasta salad, and ice-cream floats. The drugstore's signature item is a tasty tomato-basil soup.

Despite its location on the Gulf Coast, Galveston doesn't have a strong Cajun flavor. That's not the case at Little Daddy's Gumbo Bar (2105 Post Office St., 409/744-8626, daily 11am-10pm, $9-21). The tasty seafood gumbo, packed with oysters, shrimp, and crab, is worth the trip. For something heartier, feast on the meaty Mumbo Gumbo, a concoction of sausage, prime rib, and chicken. *Bon temps!*

Waterman's Restaurant

Italian

For one of the finest meals on Galveston Island, head to ✪ Riondo's Ristorante (2328 Strand St., 409/621-9595, www.riondos.com, Sun.-Thurs. 11am-9pm, Fri.-Sat. 11am-10pm, $14-52), with a delicious combination of Italian and seafood. Some of the best items include the gulf shrimp spaghetti carbonara, seafood ravioli pillows, and the cioppino, including clams, mussels, sea scallops, gulf coast shrimp, and homemade fettuccine.

OUTSIDE DOWNTOWN

It's worth making the 5-mile (8-km) drive west of downtown for the food and views at Number 13 Prime Steak and Seafood (7809 Broadway Ave., 409/572-2650, www.number13steak.com, Tues.-Thurs. 4pm-9pm, Fri. 4pm-10pm, Sat. 11am-10pm, Sun. 11am-9pm, $13-51). Number 13 elevates the traditional surf-and-turf concept to haute cuisine. Steaks are available in wet-aged and dry-aged variety (the bone-in rib-eye rivals Houston's best steak houses), and the seafood ranges from iron-seared salmon to oak-grilled snapper. The wine list is top-notch, and the baked Alaska dessert is simply sublime.

For a step up from the standard touristy seafood joints, head to Waterman's Restaurant (14302 Stewart Rd., 409/632-0233, Tues.-Thurs. 4pm-9pm, Fri.-Sat. 11am-10pm, Sun. 11am-9pm, $12-35). There isn't anything too out of the ordinary, but the quality is noteworthy. Waterman's specializes in snapper; go with the Texas option, pecan and crabmeat. If you're not in the mood for fish, the flame-kissed Waterman Burger is ideal.

ACCOMMODATIONS

Galveston's popularity as a tourism destination means there's no shortage of lodging options, from cheap beachside motels to luxurious historic resorts.

SEAWALL BOULEVARD

For most visitors, the best way to experience an island vacation is on the shore. The following hotels aren't technically on the beach—you'll have to cross busy Seawall Boulevard to get your toes in the sand—but are close enough to smell the salty air and see the sailboats and barges.

At the affordable end of the scale is no-frills dependable Gaido's Seaside Inn (3700 Seawall Blvd., 409/762-9625, www.gaidosseaside.com, $69 d). Gaido's is perhaps best known for its incredible adjacent seafood restaurant, but the hotel has some tasty amenities, including free continental breakfast, an outdoor pool with a splash shower, and free coffee and juice in the lobby.

Well-regarded is Commodore on the Beach (3618 Seawall Blvd., 409/763-2375, www.commodoreonthebeach.com, $104 d). The Commodore features rooms with balconies facing the beach, a large pool with a welcoming cascading fountain, and several complimentary services, including Wi-Fi access, continental breakfast, coffee, and juice.

Corporate chain hotels are nearly outnumbered by independent establishments on Seawall, but some chains have competitive rates and reliable service, including La Quinta East Beach (1402 Seawall Blvd., 409/763-1224, www.lq.com, $149 d), featuring an outdoor pool, free continental breakfast, and internet access. The accommodations aren't luxurious, but there's something appealing about the comfy beach-town vibe and the ocean view outside your door. Farther down the island is Red Roof Inn Beachfront Palms Hotel (5914 Seawall Blvd., 409/740-1261, www.redroof.com, $177 d), offering a free continental breakfast, free Wi-Fi, and free cappuccino and hot chocolate.

Drop a little more cash at the remarkable ✪ Hotel Galvez (2024 Seawall Blvd., 409/765-7721, www.hotelgalvez.com, $199 d). Known as the "Queen of the Gulf" when it opened in 1911, the Galvez is stunning in its Victorian elegance. Luxurious amenities include a pool with a swim-up bar, a heated saline outdoor pool, courtesy bikes and helmets, marble baths, free Wi-Fi, and an impressive spa and workout facility. Be sure to enjoy an incredible seafood meal at the on-site restaurant and have a cocktail at the classy lobby bar. Head downstairs for a history lesson—the walls are lined with stunning historic

Hotel Galvez

photos and informative exhibits about the Galvez's (and Galveston's) impressive cultural heritage.

Not nearly as historic yet conveniently located adjacent to the fun-filled Moody Gardens is the fancy Moody Gardens Hotel (7 Hope Blvd., 888/388-8484, www.moodygardenshotel.com, $249 d). After a day of exploring cultural attractions in the adjacent pyramids, unwind at the recently upgraded hotel with free Wi-Fi, plush bathrobes, and quality linens. Other amenities include an outdoor heated swimming pool with a jetted tub and a swim-up bar, an indoor lap pool, a full-service spa and salon, a 24-hour fitness center, an outdoor jogging track and sand volleyball courts, and a free weekend shuttle service to the Strand district.

Stylish Hilton Galveston Island Resort (5400 Seawall Blvd., 409/744-5000, www.galvestonhilton.com, $249 d), features large rooms with plush robes, free Wi-Fi, gulf-view rooms with private balconies, a tropically landscaped pool with a swim-up bar, and a fitness center.

STRAND AREA

If you'd rather be within walking distance of shopping than seashells, the exquisite Italianate-style ✪ Tremont House (2300 Ship's Mechanic Row, 409/763-0300, www.wyndham.com, $269 d) is in the heart of the Strand historic district. The Tremont transports guests to Galveston's heyday as the "Wall Street of the South." Notice the lofty 14-foot (4.3-m) ceilings and incredibly tall windows. Wrought-iron beds, marble baths, antique furnishings, and a stylish black-and-white color scheme add to the elegant environment. Modern touches include free Wi-Fi and streaming TV.

Just down the street is the Harbor House (28 Pier 21, 409/763-3321, www.harborhousepier21.com, $269 d), fancy in a different way. It's not historic but offers an amazing vantage point of the busy harbor and bustling marina. One of the better seafood restaurants in town, Willie G's, is across the street, and the hotel provides free passes to a nearby fitness center. Amenities include free Wi-Fi and a free continental breakfast.

BED-AND-BREAKFASTS

With so many impressive historic structures, Galveston is an ideal place to stay in a B&B.

A popular and affordable option is Avenue O Bed and Breakfast (2323 Ave. O, 409/457-4255, www.avenueo.com, from $129), just a few blocks from the beach. This 1923 Mediterranean-style home is on a sizable property surrounded by tropical foliage. Breakfasts are hearty, and snacks are available throughout the day. Avenue O provides bikes for island excursions.

Ranked as Galveston's most popular bed and breakfast is the magnificent ✪ Lasker Inn (1019 16th St., 409/497-4318, www.laskerinn.com, from $239). In one of Galveston's celebrated historic residential districts, the 1870 home originally served as a refuge for homeless children after the 1900 storm. Hospitality endures at the Lasker, where guests enjoy top-notch service and accommodations, including luxury bedding, elegant furnishings, and exquisite breakfasts featuring inventive egg dishes, fresh fruit, and high-quality coffee.

One of the island's newest B&B options is the classy Carr Mansion (1103 33rd St., 409/497-4740, www.carrmansion.com, from $289), a beautifully restored 19th-century

Lasker Inn

Greek Revival home 10 blocks from the Seawall beaches. The property is rich with history, and the mansion hosts a complimentary happy hour every day, including two drinks and an appetizer.

CAMPING

In an RV or tent, Galveston Island State Park (14901 FM 3005, 409/737-1222, www.tpwd.state.tx.us, $7 over age 12, camping $15-25) is on the west end of Galveston Island, 10 miles (16 km) from town, with 140 campsites with electricity and water hookups and 10 screened camping shelters. Park facilities include 4 miles (6.4 km) of hike and bike trails, an interpretive center and nature trail, a concrete boat ramp, a fish-cleaning shelter, restrooms with showers, picnic sites, and Wi-Fi access.

The park is a great place for swimming, hiking, bird-watching, and mountain biking, with 2,000 acres of natural beauty along the Gulf Coast. Educational tours of the coastline's native plants and animals are available by appointment. You'll encounter trout, redfish, croaker, and flounder as well as tropical birds, ducks, marsh rabbits, and armadillos.

Less scenic yet more centrally located is the Bayou Shores RV Resort (6310 Heards Lane, 409/744-2837). Just off the causeway, the RV park offers standard hookups as well as a fishing pier and exercise facility.

INFORMATION AND SERVICES

The Galveston Island Convention and Visitors Bureau (2328 Broadway Ave., 409/797-5144, daily 9am-5pm, www.galveston.com) is a tremendous resource offering brochures and maps with friendly and remarkably helpful staff to answer questions. The website is information-packed and user-friendly. Contact the Galveston Historical Foundation (2228 Broadway, 409/765-7834, www.galvestonhistory.org) for information about the island's impressive historic attractions.

The only way to get to Galveston is via I-45. From Houston it takes about an hour, depending on the traffic. Once you reach the island, the only option is to turn onto Highway 87, which becomes Broadway Avenue.

Brazosport Area

Brazosport isn't a town name but a collection of eight Brazoria County communities southwest of Galveston, an unassuming mix of lightly developed beachfront and petrochemical plants. It's not as bad as it sounds—the beaches are pleasantly uncrowded most days, and the factories are beyond view from the shore. For the record, the Brazosport communities are Clute, Freeport, Jones Creek, Lake Jackson, Oyster Creek, Quintana Beach, Richwood, and Surfside Beach.

The state's earliest European explorers landed on nearby beaches 500 years ago, and Stephen F. Austin's first colony settled along the rich bottomlands of the Brazos, Colorado, and San Bernard Rivers in the early 19th century. The venerable Texas term "Old Three Hundred" refers to the 300 settlers who received land grants for Austin's first colony, where each family received up to 4,000 acres of fertile farm and ranch property in the area.

The massive Gulf Intracoastal Waterway carves a path along the coastal lowlands. This commercial boating canal, constructed in the 1940s, is the most valuable waterway in the country, transporting as much tonnage annually as the Panama Canal. The protected waterway stretches 1,000 miles (1,600 km) from Brownsville to Florida.

Visitors to the Brazosport region enjoy the small-town specialty and antiques shops, beach home rentals, and casual ocean-based recreation. Drive, walk, or swim along the 21-mile (34-km) stretch of beach or watch the seagulls and ocean barges lazily glide by. Other popular recreational activities include fresh- and saltwater fishing, boating, crabbing, and surfing.

SIGHTS

For a destination comprising several communities, the Brazosport Area offers an intriguing mix of cultural attractions. Fortunately, the communities are within a 20-minute drive of each other, so getting from one place to another takes the same amount of time as it does in a big city, just without the traffic or stoplights.

LAKE JACKSON
AREA MUSEUMS

A must-see attraction in the Brazosport Area is the spectacular Sea Center Texas (300 Medical Dr., Lake Jackson, 979/292-0100, www.tpwd.state.tx.us, Tues.-Sat. 9am-4pm, Sun. 1pm-4pm, free), combining several aquariums, an education center, and a fish hatchery along with an outdoor wetland exhibit and a kids fishing pond. The education center's main exhibit is a 50,000-gallon aquarium containing Gulf of Mexico marine animals such as nurse sharks, Atlantic spadefish, red drum, gray snapper, and an enormous moray eel. Other large aquariums house tropical species found in area salt marshes, coastal bays, jetties, and artificial and coral reefs. Kids will love the "touch pool," where they can handle several varieties of crabs, snails, and anemones.

Outside, the wetland exhibit is accessible by a long boardwalk over marsh areas. Families can bring a nature checklist and activity book to identify species, including green tree frogs, turtles, and a variety of birds. The adjacent hatchery has the capacity to produce 20 million spotted sea trout and red drum fingerlings each year for release into Texas coastal waters. Tours are available by advance reservation only.

Culture converges at The Center for the Arts & Sciences (400 College Blvd., Clute, 979/265-7661, www.bcfas. org, Tues.-Sat. 10am-4pm, Sun. 2pm-5pm, free), an all-inclusive facility home to the Brazosport Art League, the Brazosport Museum of Natural Science, the Center Stages Theater, and the Brazosport Planetarium. With so many cultural activities sharing space under one roof, you'll find an array of attractions, including a colossal collection of seashells, an art gallery and studio, and a theater staging regional productions. Most impressive is the natural science museum, containing wildlife, fossils, and an aquarium. Check out the exhibit featuring the lightning whelk (Texas's state shell) and the planetarium, which offers public viewings and previously served as a training facility for astronauts from NASA's nearby Johnson Space Center.

VARNER-HOGG PLANTATION

Strolling beneath outstretched oaks provides a sense of the bygone world of Southern heritage at Varner-Hogg

Varner-Hogg Plantation

Plantation (1702 N. 13th St., West Columbia, 979/345-4656, www.visitvarnerhoggplantation.com, Tues.-Sun. 9am-5pm, $7 adults, $6 students). There's an undeniable charm to the lush grounds and distinguished historic buildings, occupied for most of the 1900s by the larger-than-life Hogg family, including the unfortunately named Miss Ima Hogg.

Owned by the Texas Historical Commission, the site showcases the Hogg family's remarkable 19th-century furnishings acquired from profits associated with the tremendous oil reserves discovered in the 1920s, which at one point brought in nearly $40,000 daily. Recent efforts have turned toward the era of Columbus Patton, the plantation's second owner after namesake Martin Varner. During insightful tours of the historic plantation home, knowledgeable guides educate visitors about the legacies of the three families connected to the property: Varner, Patton, and Hogg.

BRAZORIA NATIONAL WILDLIFE REFUGE

The protected habitats of the sizable Brazoria National Wildlife Refuge (24907 FM 2004, Angleton, 979/964-4011, www.fws.gov, Mon.-Fri. 9am-5pm) host 200 species of birds, one of the highest counts in the nation. In winter more than 100,000 snow geese, Canadian geese, teal, ducks, and sandhill cranes fill the numerous ponds and sloughs. In summer you'll find herons, egrets, white ibis, spoonbills, seaside sparrows, and scissor-tailed flycatchers. Alligators occupy the refuge year-round on Big Slough and in ponds. Look for their trails through the mud and "gator holes" in drier months.

SAN BERNARD NATIONAL WILDLIFE REFUGE

The other major refuge in the Brazosport Area is San Bernard National Wildlife Refuge (6801 County Rd. 306, Brazoria, 979/849-6062, www.fws.gov, Mon.-Fri. 9am-5pm), a 24,000-acre protected area for snow geese, warblers, herons, egrets, ibis, gulls, and terns. Most of the refuge is closed to the public, but the accessible 3-mile (4.8-km) car tour and several miles of hiking trails offer access to high-quality wildlife viewing.

BEACHES

The words "Brazosport Area beaches" don't always prompt excitement or envy. These low-profile beaches can get crowded on summer weekends, but they're not major destinations. At Surfside and Bryan, the beachcombers' bodies aren't designed for a *Sports Illustrated* cover, and the vibe is easy and breezy.

SURFSIDE BEACH

If you don't mind a petrochemical plant just 1 mile (1.6 km) away (fortunately not dominating the view), Surfside Beach (979/233-1531, www.surfsidetx.org) is a delightful getaway for low-key recreation. Most people here are Houston residents looking for a respite from the Galveston crowds. Popular activities include fishing, swimming, sailing, camping, and shell collecting. For information about the village of Surfside Beach, including restaurants, shops, and lodgings, call or visit the website.

BRYAN BEACH

Near the community of Freeport is Bryan Beach, another casual and scenic stretch of sand. Grab a bucket for sand dollar collecting, a pole for shallow surf fishing, or a towel and sunscreen for sunbathing. Primitive campsites are available nearby. To reach the beach from Freeport, travel 2 miles (3.2 km) southwest of town on FM 1495, then 3 miles (4.8 km) south on Gulf Beach Road.

RECREATION

Popular activities in the Brazosport Area are swimming and birding. Fishing is one of the top draws, and kayaking and canoeing are emerging as viable options.

FISHING

Brazosport offers a multitude of facilities for fishing inshore or at sea. There are plenty of jetties, piers, and beaches where you can cast a line for speckled trout, flounder, redfish, sheepshead, and gafftopsail. Nearby marinas and beachside shacks sell tackle and bait. For deep-sea fishing, hire a charter boats to take you out farther for big-time catches, including snapper, marlin, king mackerel, and sailfish. A reputable outfit is Johnston's Sportfishing (979/233-8513).

A popular place for fishing, camping, and lounging is Quintana Beach County Park (979/233-1461, www. brazoriacountytx.gov), on a picturesque barrier island near Freeport. The park's multilevel fishing pier is a favorite among anglers, and the day-use facilities include shaded pavilions, restrooms, showers, and the historic Coveney House, containing a museum and natural history display. Camping sites ($15-27) include full hookups, showers, and laundry facilities. From Freeport, take FM 1495 south 2 miles (3.2 km) to County Road 723, then east 3 miles (4.8 km) to the park entrance.

PADDLING

For low-impact coastal kayaking or canoeing, the Christmas Bay Paddling Trail (515 Amigo Lane, Freeport, 979/233-5159, www.tpwd.state.tx.us) is 19 miles (31 km) long, with a 4-mile (6.4-km) option. Known for fishing and birding opportunities, the trail also has extensive oyster reefs and a salt marsh.

Explore the Brazos River Trail Gulf Prairie Run via kayak. Part of a 125-mile (200-km) system stretching upriver to Houston, the water trail winds through the dense bottomlands, towering trees, and palmetto thickets. Paddlers can experience a wide variety of wildlife species and migrating birds. Launch points in the Brazosport Area are Brazos River County Park in Angleton and Wilderness Park in Lake Jackson.

FOOD

Surfside Beach has several good vacation-style eateries, and the best is Red Snapper Inn (402 Bluewater Hwy., 979/239-3226, www. redsnapperinn.com, Mon.-Fri. 11am-2pm and 5pm-9pm, Sat.-Sun. 11am-9pm, $10-28), a quality surf-and-turf restaurant best known for grilled boneless flounder stuffed with crabmeat dressing, the fried soft-shell crabs with rémoulade sauce, bacon-wrapped oysters, and sautéed garlic shrimp. Turf-wise, most diners opt for the spaghetti and charbroiled Greek-style meatballs or the classic chicken-fried steak.

For a good meal with a great view, head to Seahorse Bar & Grill (310 Ocean Ave., 979/239-2233, daily 8am-9pm, $7-15). The Seahorse has the best deck on the beach, featuring dozens of tables overlooking the surf and sand.

Enjoy a cold beer and hearty burger on the porch.

Just around the corner, you can't miss Kitty's Purple Cow (323 Ocean Ave., 979/233-9161, Mon.-Fri. 10am-8:30pm, Sat.-Sun. 7:30am-8:30pm, $6-12). The food isn't quite as attention-grabbing as the restaurant's facade, a distractingly purple building just a block off the beach. Kitty's specializes in tasty meaty burgers and boiled shrimp on the "app-moo-tizers" menu. Breakfast options include hearty portions of biscuits and gravy and standard egg dishes.

Any beach town worth its weight in sand dollars has a place where locals loiter. Here it's the low-key Jetty Shack (412 Parkview St., 979/233-5300, daily 11am-11:30pm, $7-16), a beachside dive offering a tasty Angus burger, plenty of fried food, grilled cheese, and cold beer.

ACCOMMODATIONS

The Brazosport Area is overrun with local lodging options, with just a few chain hotel signs in sight. Independently owned hotels are the norm, and many travelers rent a beach house or cabin for the weekend.

HOTELS

Clean, comfy, and within walking distance of the beach is the Ocean Village Hotel (310 Ocean Village Dr., Surfside Beach, 979/239-1213, www.oceanvillagehotel.com, from $119). This nice newish spot offers several amenities not found at other accommodations in the area: direct beach access and an attached restaurant and bar, the Sea Horse Grill. The hotel offers ocean-view rooms with large private decks, free Wi-Fi, pet-friendly rooms, and extended-stay suites with kitchens.

More casual and representative of the many sun-bleached and slightly shabby beach hotels is Surfside Motel (330 Coral Court, Surfside Beach, 979/233-4948, www.surfsidemotel.biz, $69-129). The motel offers kitchenette units with two queen beds, one twin, and a full kitchen, or two-room suites with one queen, a pullout bed, a small fridge, and a microwave. Check with the front desk if you need beach towels, board games, or horseshoes.

If slightly shabby isn't your thing, you'll have to venture 4 miles (6.4 km) off the coast to Clute for the chain hotels. One of the better options is La Quinta (1126 Hwy. 332 W., Clute, 979/265-7461, www.lq.com, $59 d), featuring free Wi-Fi, free continental breakfast, and an outdoor pool. A nicer choice is Holiday Inn Express (1117 Hwy. 332 W., Clute, 979/266-8746, www.hiexpress.com, $129 d), offering free Wi-Fi, a workout facility, and free continental breakfast.

BEACH HOME RENTALS

Hundreds of rooms are available in cabins and beach homes along the gulf in the Brazosport Area. The best way to find a place that fits your specific needs regarding pets, kids, and beach access is to contact a rental locating service. Two of the more commendable outlets are Beach Resort Services (800/382-9283, www.beachresortservices.com) and Brannan Resort Rentals, Inc. (979/233-1812, www.brri.com). For a comprehensive list of companies, visit www.visitbrazosport.com and www.surfsidetx.org.

CAMPING

Families and RVers return to Quintana Beach County Park (979/233-1461, www.brazoriacountytx.gov, $15-27), featuring 56 paved and level camping sites, full hookups, primitive tent sites, and a bathhouse with restrooms, showers, and laundry facilities. Cabins ($135-160, depending on the season), complete with TVs, microwaves, kitchenettes, and charming wooden detailing, are also for rent.

A popular option for anglers is Surfside Beach RV Park (102 Fort Velesco Dr., 979/233-6919, www. surfsidebeachrv.com, $25-30), offering full-hookup RV sites, free parking for fishing boats, on-site laundry, and free Wi-Fi access.

INFORMATION AND SERVICES

The Brazosport Convention and Visitors Council (main office 300 Abner Jackson Pkwy., Lake Jackson, 979/285-2501 or 888/477-2505, www. brazosport.org, Mon.-Fri. 9am-5pm) provides details on area attractions, accommodations, and restaurants as well as brochures and maps.

GETTING THERE

From Houston, take Highway 288 south for about 45 minutes to Lake Jackson. From there, take Highway 332 east for 15 minutes to reach the beach.

Corpus Christi

Corpus Christi (population 326,554) is the largest city on Texas's Gulf Coast and one of the most popular destinations in the state for seaside fishing, sailing, swimming, and windsurfing.

The city's precipitous history saw drought and various wars preventing settlement from taking hold until the mid-1800s, when a trading post was established and a small village developed that eventually became known as Corpus Christi, "the Body of Christ." Just when the town started growing, a yellow fever epidemic decimated the population, and for decades it lacked a deepwater port.

In 1916 and 1919, torrential storms destroyed portions of the city, erasing grand hotels and palatial homes. As a result, the "Sparkling City by the Bay" can appear historically lackluster, with few significant structures reflecting its heritage. Historic homes and churches that escaped the hurricanes and wrecking ball exist in downtown

neighborhoods. By the middle of the 20th century, Corpus, as it's known, became a petroleum shipping center. Also contributing to the economy were military bases and six petroleum refineries making use of the 1,500 oil wells in the area.

Despite its population, Corpus retains the feel of a small city, albeit with remarkable museums and top-notch seafood restaurants. Mild year-round temperatures and the inviting tropical climate draw visitors from across the country.

SIGHTS

✪ TEXAS STATE AQUARIUM

The magnificent Texas State Aquarium (2710 N. Shoreline Blvd., 361/881-1200, www.texas stateaquarium.org, Mon.-Sat. 9am-5pm, Sun. 10am-5pm, $37 adults, $35 seniors, $27 ages 3-12) offers a quick break from the beach with the region's fascinating natural resources.

Corpus Christi

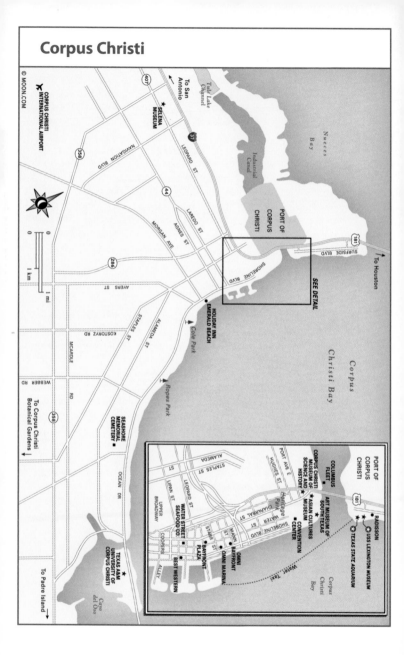

© MOON.COM

CORPUS CHRISTI INTERNATIONAL AIRPORT

SELENA MUSEUM

To San Antonio

Tule Lake Channel

Nueces Bay

PORT OF CORPUS CHRISTI

Industrial Canal

NAVIGATION BLVD

LEONARD ST

LAREDO ST

AGNES ST

MORGAN AVE

AYERS ST

STAPLES ST

ALAMEDA ST

KOSTORYZ RD

SHORELINE BLVD

SURFSIDE BLVD

To Houston

HOLIDAY INN
● EMERALD BEACH

Cole Park

Ropes Park

Corpus Christi Bay

McARDLE RD

WEBBER RD

OCEAN DR

To Corpus Christi Botanical Gardens

SEASHORE MEMORIAL CEMETERY ■

To Padre Island

Corpus del Oso

TEXAS A&M UNIVERSITY OF CORPUS CHRISTI

SEE DETAIL

PORT OF CORPUS CHRISTI

ALAMEDA ST

STAPLES ST

LEONARD ST

UPPER BROADWAY

LIPAN ST

STARR ST

COOPERS ALLEY

PORT AVE E

HUGHES ST

CHAPARRAL ST

MANN ST

WATER ST

SHORELINE BLVD

Heritage Park

COLUMBUS FLEET

CORPUS CHRISTI MUSEUM OF SCIENCE AND HISTORY ★

ASIAN CULTURES MUSEUM ★

CONVENTION CENTER

WATER STREET SEAFOOD CO. ●

BAYFRONT PLAZA ★

OMNI BAYFRONT
OMNI MARINA

BEST WESTERN

RADISSON ●
★ USS LEXINGTON MUSEUM

ART MUSEUM OF SOUTH TEXAS ★

★ TEXAS STATE AQUARIUM

Water Taxi

Corpus Christi Bay

Texas State Aquarium

The layout is clever, leading visitors into Texas's marine world at sea level with exhibits containing birds, alligators, and stingrays, and proceeding to explore the Gulf of Mexico at sequentially deeper levels.

Primary exhibits showcase menacing sharks, a 350-pound grouper, and hundreds of other species that slither and glide around the barnacle-crusted poles of a replicated offshore oil rig. The 350,000-gallon Dolphin Bay habitat uses seawater from Corpus Christi Bay for the Atlantic bottlenose dolphins. A shaded seating area provides respite from the sun for daily interpretive programs, and a lengthy viewing window allows visitors to get nose to nose with the dolphins. Other popular exhibits include Otter Creek, featuring the frisky creatures cavorting on slides and in pools, and Living Shores, allowing kids to handle non-threatening sea creatures. The aquarium also includes terrestrial critters in the Amazon rainforest exhibit, with boa constrictors and poison dart frogs, and in the bird theater, featuring "flight performances" by hawks, falcons, and parrots.

TOP EXPERIENCE

✪ USS *LEXINGTON* MUSEUM

You can't miss the massive USS *Lexington* Museum (2914 N. Shoreline Blvd., 361/888-4873, www.usslexington.com, Labor Day-Memorial Day daily 9am-5pm, Memorial Day-Labor Day daily 9am-6pm, $17 adults, $15 seniors and military, $12 ages 4-12). Looming large in Corpus Christi Bay, the USS *Lexington* was the nation's longest-serving aircraft carrier. This decommissioned World War II vessel is now a 33,000-ton floating museum, transporting visitors back in time with tours of the ship's decks and quarters, educational exhibits, restored aircraft, a high-tech flight simulator, and a collection of historical memorabilia.

The ship served until 1991, when it found a permanent home in Corpus Christi Bay. Its relatively recent use gives visitors an authentic feel for life

French explorer René-Robert Cavelier, Sieur de La Salle, left an enormous legacy in Texas. Well known for his exploration of the Great Lakes region, La Salle's ambition and hubris ultimately led to his demise after a doomed colonization effort on the Texas Gulf Coast. Many artifacts remain from his 17th-century visit, on display in the La Salle Odyssey collection at the **Corpus Christi Museum of Science and History** (1900 N. Chaparral St., 361/826-4667, www.ccmuseum.com, Tues.-Sat. 10am-5pm, Sun. noon-5pm, $12 adults, $9 seniors, $9 ages 3-12).

In 1684, La Salle embarked on a mission to build forts along the mouth of the Mississippi River to attack and occupy Spanish territory in Mexico. His expedition was a series of failures, beginning when pirates in the West Indies captured one of his ships and continuing with sickness, misdirection, and shipwrecks. Searching for the mouth of the Mississippi, La Salle missed his target by 500 miles (800 km) and landed at present-day Matagorda Bay on the central Gulf Coast of Texas. One of his ships was lost offshore, and another, *La Belle,* became stranded on a sandbar during a storm.

La Salle made several more ultimately unsuccessful attempts to find the Mississippi. He eventually established Fort St. Louis near the coast, and his attempt to lead a party in search of reinforcements proved to be his last adventure—he was killed by his own men near present-day Navasota, Texas.

La Salle's legacy would be rekindled 300 years later when the wreck of the *La Belle* was discovered by marine archaeologists with the Texas Historical Commission. The excavation produced an amazing array of finds, including the hull of the ship, three bronze cannons, thousands of glass beads, and even a crew member's skeleton. The artifacts have been carefully cleaned and preserved and are currently displayed at numerous Gulf Coast museums.

aboard the ship through details such as computer monitors, barbershop chairs, and the chow line. The best way to experience the *Lexington* is on one of the self-guided tours, covering 100,000 square feet on 11 decks. The highlight is the flight deck, where you can take your time strolling across the massive former runway while viewing impressive vintage and modern warbirds with a scenic backdrop of the bay and the city skyline.

CORPUS CHRISTI MUSEUM OF SCIENCE AND HISTORY

To get a better sense of the area's colorful past, drop by the **Corpus Christi Museum of Science and History** (1900 N. Chaparral St., 361/826-4667, www.ccmuseum.com, Tues.-Sat. 10am-5pm, Sun. noon-5pm, $12 adults, $9 seniors, $9 ages 3-12), with myriad educational exhibits emphasizing the Gulf Coast's nature and culture. Noteworthy exhibits are maritime-related, including an interactive shipwreck display containing artifacts from three Spanish treasure ships that ran aground on Padre Island in 1554, an exhibit featuring artifacts related to French explorer René-Robert Cavelier, Sieur de La Salle's ill-fated *La Belle* shipwreck, and the Children's Wharf, a bustling learning area for youngsters. The remainder of the museum is a collection of 28,000 shells, Native American crafts, and bird and reptile eggs representing the history and culture of South Texas.

HERITAGE PARK

Just down the street from the science museum is the city's **Heritage Park** (1581 N. Chaparral St., 361/826-3414, www.cctexas.com). These 12 restored Victorian-era historic homes were moved to the city's cultural area to protect them from demolition and to showcase the city's past. The centerpiece is the Cultural Center's Galván House, open for free tours by

USS *Lexington*

appointment. Otherwise, visitors can stroll among the homes to admire the different eras of coastal architecture.

ASIAN CULTURES MUSEUM

Also in the city's cultural district is the Texas State Museum of Asian Cultures (1809 N. Chaparral St., 361/882-2641, www.texasasianculturesmuseum.org, Tues.-Sat. noon-5pm, $6 adults, $5 students, $3 under age 13), offering an interesting array of objects and artwork from across the Pacific. What started as a local resident's personal collection of cultural objects has evolved into a full museum containing thousands of items representing a dozen Asian countries. Billie Trimble Chandler spent decades as a teacher and art collector in Asia, and she brought items back to share with Corpus residents and to educate them about faraway lands. Since then, the museum has grown to include clothing, furniture, paintings, dolls, statues, and other art objects from Japan, Korea, China, the Philippines, and Taiwan. The museum features international traveling exhibits and offers educational classes.

SELENA MUSEUM

Latin-music fans often make a pilgrimage to the Selena Museum (5410 Leopard St., 361/289-9013, Mon.-Fri. 10am-4pm, $4). It's not easy to find—the museum is downtown off I-37 in a warehouse-type building with no sign (look for the painted mural of Selena on the outside). It was created by Corpus resident Abraham Quintanilla to honor the memory of his daughter, the famous Tejana singer who was killed by the president of her fan club in 1995. The museum showcases many of Selena's personal memorabilia, including the outfits and dresses she designed and wore at concerts, her red Porsche, pencil sketches, her prized egg collection, and letters of sympathy from fans across the world.

ART MUSEUM OF SOUTH TEXAS

Culture converges at the Art Museum of South Texas (1902 N. Shoreline Blvd., 361/825-3500, www.stia.org, Tues.-Sat. 10am-5pm, Sun. 1pm-5pm, $8 adults, $6 seniors and military, $4 over age 11). The three-story building is unmistakable, with bright white concrete walls and 13 rooftop pyramids overlooking the bay. Inside are galleries showcasing the museum's 1,300 artworks, primarily paintings and sculpture representing the Americas with a focus on Texas, Mexico, and the Southwest. The museum also contains an interactive kids playroom, classrooms, studios, a gift shop, and an auditorium.

CORPUS CHRISTI BOTANICAL GARDENS AND NATURE CENTER

To appreciate the area's natural beauty beyond the beach, the Corpus Christi Botanical Gardens and Nature Center (8545 S. Staples St., 361/852-2100, www.stxbot.org, daily 9am-6pm, $9 adults, $7 seniors and military, $4 ages 5-12) has exotic gardens and perfectly landscaped lawns, taking full advantage of the tropical climate to produce vibrant colors and lush landscapes. One of the center's showpieces is the Rose Garden, featuring 300 roses, a large pavilion, and a beautiful fountain. Other noteworthy areas are the hummingbird garden, the orchid garden with 2,500 flowering plants, and the hibiscus garden.

BEACHES
CITY BEACHES ON THE BAY

If you're staying downtown and need a quick beach fix, go to Corpus Christi Beach (just north of the USS *Lexington,* 361/880-3480). It's not quite picturesque, and the sand is coarse, but it's great for a leisurely stroll or swim with a pleasant view of Corpus Christi Bay. Local families are playing in the sand and flying kites, and there are several spots offering rinse-off showers, restrooms, and small cabana huts with picnic tables. Much smaller in size yet within walking distance of downtown hotels is Magee Beach (Shoreline Blvd. at Park St., 361/880-3461). This 250-yard (230-m) stretch of sand on the bay isn't designed for shell collecting, but it's a good place to get your feet wet without worrying about the undertow found on larger ocean beaches. Showers and restrooms are on the north end of the beach.

RECREATION
PADDLING

Kayakers are increasingly flocking to Corpus Christi for saltwater kayaking and bay paddling. Both offer beginners and experienced paddlers a fun way to spend a few hours on the water. Saltwater kayaking, a.k.a. sea kayaking, is typically more difficult, since it can involve choppy and unpredictable conditions. It's often more fun, and the waves don't tend to reach intimidating heights. Sea routes can also be longer and less restricted.

Bay paddling is ideal for beginning kayakers, offering calmer conditions and shorter trail options. A good starting point is the Mustang Island State Park Paddling Trail (www.tpwd.state.tx.us), with several routes, including the 5-mile (8-km) Shamrock

Loop to the 8.5-mile (13.7-km) North Trail, that meander through coves and marshes. The park's 7-mile (11.3-km) Ashum Trail traces the Corpus Christi Bay shoreline, offering quality birding and fishing.

Rental and tour options are available at **Coastal Bend Kayak** (1125 S. Commercial St., Aransas Pass, 361/557-7003, www.coastal bendkayaking.com).

FISHING

Corpus is a major destination for anglers, and there are plenty of locations and services to accommodate them. You'll see poles anchored in the sand at city beaches, including Corpus Christi Beach, where fishers gather at the **Nueces Bay Pier** at the end of Hull Street. Lines are also cast from the massive concrete downtown piers (known locally as T-heads), several spots along the seawall, and at lighted breakwater jetties. Another popular spot is **Bob Hall Pier** (15820 Park Rd. 22, 361/949-0499) at Padre Balli Park on North Padre Island. Its prime location and abundance of species (tarpon, mackerel, redfish, and even shark) have drawn anglers to this venerable productive spot since the 1950s.

To get out on the sea for big-game fishing, a charter or rental company can set you up with all the gear, guides, and advice. Deep-sea boats are available to troll for Gulf species such as marlin, sailfish, tuna, and kingfish. Reputable companies include **C&T Bay Charters** (1031 Whispering Sands, Port Aransas, 888/227-9172, www. ctbaycharters.com) and **Deep Sea Headquarters** (416 W. Cotter Ave., Port Aransas, 361/749-5597, www. deepseaheadquarters.com), providing private excursions to anglers of all ages and skill levels.

Corpus Christi, a popular destination for windsurfers

WINDSURFING

Thanks to its constant easy breeze, averaging 15-20 mph (24-32 km/h), Corpus is a mecca for windsurfers. Some try their sails on the bay at city locales like Cole Park (near the 2000 block of Ocean Dr., restrooms available), but most windsurfers head to North Padre Island, particularly Bird Island Basin at the Padre Island National Seashore. This half-mile stretch of beach is internationally recognized as one of the top windsurfing sites on the U.S. mainland. If you've never grabbed hold of a sail, this is the best place to learn, since there's always a breeze. To set yourself up with all the gear, contact Worldwinds Windsurfing (11493 S. Padre Island Dr., 361/949-7472, www.worldwinds. net) or Wind & Wave Water Sports (10721 S. Padre Island Dr., 361/937-9283, www.windandwave.net).

HIKING AND BIKING

Recreational opportunities in Corpus are almost exclusively water-based. With so many options available in the bay and the gulf, the development of organized land-based trails for hiking and biking has not been a priority for governments or private organizations.

The primary hiking and biking option is the Bay Trail (www. ccparkandrec.com), an 8-mile (12.9-km) route hugging the bay. It's extremely scenic, offering views of downtown buildings and bird habitats. Another option is the hike and bike trail on the campus of Texas A&M Corpus Christi (www.tamucc.edu). Although students and faculty are the primary users of the 3-mile (4.8-km) route, it's open to the public and offers a well-lit paved path for safety.

HORSEBACK RIDING

Have you ever wanted to ride a horse on the beach, with the waves crashing at your steed's feet as the ocean breeze whips through your hair? Horses on the Beach (16562 S. Padre Island Dr., 361/949-4944, several rides daily, reservations required), just north of Padre Island National Seashore, has horses for first-timers, children, and experienced riders, and the stable owners also handle lessons. You're welcome to walk, trot, or ride your horse into the surf.

ENTERTAINMENT AND EVENTS

BARS AND CLUBS

Many visitors choose to sip their cocktails on the beach or in the hotel bar, but other options exist for live music and to mingle with the locals. The best place to soak up the scene without feeling like an outsider is the downtown Executive Surf Club (309 N. Water St., 361/884-7873, www. executivesurfclub.com). Adjacent to the Water Street Seafood Co., the Surf Club's decor reflects its name, with vintage surfboards on the walls and refurbished as tables. The scene is lively yet casual, with live music most nights (mainly Texas rock and blues acts, often with a cover charge), more than 30 beers on tap, and a kitchen serving up tasty grub.

Another friendly spot is the more upscale Republic of Texas Bar & Grill (900 N. Shoreline Blvd., 361/886-3515, www.omnihotels.com). On the 20th floor of the Omni Bayfront hotel, the Republic of Texas is dimly lit and heavily wooded in a welcoming way. The views of the bay and city are outstanding, the drinks are expertly made, and the pianist provides a perfect soundtrack. Grab a scotch,

Padre Island National Seashore is undertaking extensive efforts to protect an endearing creature that nests along its shoreline and glides in the gentle waves. The Kemp's ridley is the most endangered species of sea turtle, and it was nearly lost forever in the 1960s due to massive exploitation of its eggs and meat at its primary nesting beach in Mexico. The 16-mile (26-km) stretch of sand at nearby Playa de Rancho Nuevo in Tamaulipas, Mexico, was home to 40,000 Kemp's ridleys in 1947. Fewer than 5,000 currently nest each year.

Park officials incubate turtle eggs and release the little guys into the gulf each summer. The public is invited to view this fascinating natural event—for release dates and directions to the site, call the **Hatchling Hotline** (361/949-7163).

Named for Richard M. Kemp, an angler who submitted the first documented specimen in 1906, the Kemp's ridley has been making a slow resurgence thanks to the devoted scientists of the National Park Service, which operates the Padre Island National Seashore between Corpus Christi and South Padre.

KEEPING KEMP'S

To help save the turtle, the U.S. and Mexican governments have been working together to reestablish a nesting beach at Padre Island National Seashore, utilizing the theory that turtles will return to the beach where they were born to lay their own eggs. In 1978-1988 scientists collected more than 22,000 eggs at Rancho Nuevo and transported them in Padre Island sand to a lab at the national seashore for incubation. The hatchlings were released on the beach, where they then crawled to the surf with the hope they'd be naturally imprinted with the location in their memories for future reference.

Biologists have attempted to gauge the turtles' successful rate of return by marking their shells and fins with identification tags and even GPS devices. Their efforts appear to be productive, since each year more turtles revisit their birthplace. In fact, nearly 60 percent of the species' eggs are now found on Padre Island, making it the most important Kemp's ridley nesting beach in the United States.

Visitors who see a live or dead turtle on the beach should immediately contact a park ranger or the seashore's turtle biologist (361/949-8173). Messing with these endangered turtles in any way is a felony, with fines up to $20,000. Many Kemp's ridleys have been identified and protected as a result of visitors' efforts, so perhaps your next stroll on the beach will yield a finding far more valuable than an intact sand dollar.

---

margarita, or draft beer and soak up the scenery.

With a younger and more boisterous local crowd, **Rockit's Whiskey Bar & Saloon** (709 N. Chaparral St., 361/884-7634, www.rockitscc.com) is on a formerly vibrant stretch of Chaparral Street in the heart of downtown. Rockit's is still thriving, and it's still all about the blues: Live bands from Corpus and across the state play nightly, and the place can get rocking when the bands get rolling. Check the website for a music schedule and cover charges.

PERFORMING ARTS

The grande dame of Corpus Christi's performing arts scene is **Corpus Christi Ballet** (1621 N. Mesquite St., 361/882-4588, www.corpuschristiballet.com), staging several ballets annually, including classics like *The Nutcracker* and children's fare such as *Cinderella*. Corpus Christi Ballet is a first-rate classical company.

One of the most popular classical venues in town is the **Performing Arts Center at Texas A&M Corpus Christi** (6300 Ocean Dr., 361/825-5700, www.pac.tamucc.edu). The $18 million facility is known for its excellent acoustics and amenities. Performers are mainly classical, with featured names from past years including pianist Van Cliburn, mezzo soprano Frederica von Stade, and violinists Itzhak Perlman and Joshua Bell.

Perhaps the most venerable performing arts organization in Corpus Christi is the Harbor Playhouse (1 Bayfront Park, 361/882-5500, www.harborplayhouse.com), a nonprofit community theater that traces its history to 1925. Corpus residents have spent a century enjoying the group's staging of classic musicals and plays such as *Annie, The Sound of Music,* and *A Christmas Carol.*

SHOPPING

Corpus has several standard malls, and vacationers looking for trinkets and T-shirts opt for the souvenir shops in Port Aransas. There are several places that offer quality clothing, jewelry, and beach gear, including Pilar Gallery (3814 S. Alameda St., 361/853-7171), a colorful shop with quality women's clothing, tapestries, rugs, and imported jewelry and folk art from Mexico and around the globe.

Every beach town needs a good surf shop, and Corpus has several rad options. Hodads to heroes will find boards, surf wear, kayaks, skateboards, and surf and skate accessories at Wind & Wave Water Sports (10721 S. Padre Island Dr., 361/937-9283, www.windandwave.net) or Worldwinds Windsurfing (11493 S. Padre Island Dr., 361/949-7472, www.worldwinds.net).

FOOD

Seafood is the favored item for most Corpus Christi diners, and the variety of restaurants in the downtown area offers plenty of options. The city has a large Hispanic population, so

you'll also find high-quality Tex-Mex restaurants.

SEAFOOD

You'll catch the city's best seafood at ✪ Water Street Seafood Co. (309 N. Water St., 361/882-8683, www.waterstmarketcc.com, daily 11am-11pm, $10-26). If you're in Corpus for more than a day, it's practically eat a meal at this legendary downtown locale or at its adjacent sister location, Water Street Oyster Bar. Water Street combines fresh seafood, Mexican influences, Cajun flavors, and Southern cooking. For first-timers, start with fresh catches and daily specials like blackened snapper and broiled flounder. The regular menu features in-demand items such as crab cakes served with spicy rémoulade and mango salsa; seafood jambalaya packed with shrimp, chicken, sausage, and crawfish tails in a creamy tomato sauce; and Southern-fried catfish stuffed with shrimp. For those in search of a simple seafood delight, order a double-size peel-and-eat shrimp plate accompanied by a hoppy pale ale draft.

Slightly more upscale and not quite as family-oriented is the next-door Water Street Oyster Bar (309 N. Water St., 361/881-9448, www.waterstmarketcc.com, Sun.-Thurs. 11am-11pm, Fri.-Sat. 11am-midnight, $13-29), a great spot to have a few cocktails and order some freshly shucked gulf oysters on the half shell. The menu is the same as the Seafood Co.'s, so the aforementioned recommendations apply, and you'll enjoy them in a more refined atmosphere. Two additional recommendations: Order your salad with the walnut-based tangy dressing, and save room for the hot chocolate brownie with ice cream. The freshest addition to Water Street's empire is the Sushi Room, featuring traditional rolls without as strong an emphasis on local sourcing.

One of the fanciest places in town for seafood and ocean views is the Yardarm Restaurant (4310 Ocean Dr., 361/855-8157, www.yardarmrestaurantcorpuschristi.com, Tues.-Sat. 5:30pm-9pm, $13-37). Modestly sized and cozy, it offers tantalizingly fresh seafood, including oysters, shrimp, a snappy snapper papillote, and thick juicy steaks. Due to its limited size and popularity, reservations are recommended.

On the opposite end of the sophistication scale is the consistently tasty yet way casual ✪ Snoopy's Pier (13313 S. Padre Island Dr., 361/949-8815, www.snoopyspier.com, summer daily 11am-

Snoopy's Pier seafood restaurant

10pm, winter daily 11am-9pm, $9-25). If you want to eat like a local and soak up the laid-back beach life, this is the place to be. On the water just below the causeway, Snoopy's is ideal to grab a cold beer and a plate of fried or boiled shrimp. Watch the sun set as you enjoy the flaky goodness of fresh catches such as flounder or drum.

If you're staying on Corpus Christi Beach, you'll find two quality laid-back seafood restaurants within walking distance. Pier 99 (2822 N. Shoreline Blvd., 361/887-0764, www.pier99restaurant.com, Sun.-Thurs. 11am-9pm, Fri.-Sat. 11am-10pm, $10-27) is a Corpus Christi stalwart on the beach across from the massive USS *Lexington.* The portions are nearly as big, particularly the combo plates overflowing with shrimp, crab legs, oysters, crawfish, and catfish. Order a bowl of fresh seafood gumbo. Mellow live music keeps the atmosphere spirited most nights, providing a perfect Margaritaville moment.

Not quite as aesthetically pleasing yet reliable in its good food is the misleadingly named Blackbeard's on the Beach (3117 E. Surfside Blvd., 361/884-1030, www.blackbeards.restaurant.com, Sun.-Thurs. 11am-10pm, Fri.-Sat. 11am-11pm, $9-24), across the street from the Radisson and a couple of blocks from the shore. This is a casual family-friendly place where you'll find a bar full of bric-a-brac and hearty helpings of fresh seafood and Tex-Mex specialties.

AMERICAN

Beach towns are populated with casual eateries, but a special occasion restaurant is Republic of Texas Bar & Grill (900 N. Shoreline Blvd., 361/886-3515, Mon.-Sat. 5:30pm-10:30pm, Sun. 5:30pm-9pm, $14-50). On the 20th floor of the Omni Bayfront, this restaurant serves upscale Texas fare in a refined environment with stunning views. Meat is the main event, in a range of options and methods of preparation. Can't-miss items include château steak with sautéed asparagus and broccoli, pork rib chops in an apple-ginger glaze, Texas crab cake with lobster and cognac sauce, and perfectly prepared venison, buffalo, and redfish.

Katz 21 Steak & Spirits (317 N. Mesquite St., 361/884-1221, www.katz21.com, Mon.-Thurs. 5pm-10pm, Fri.-Sat. 5pm-11pm, $14-44) is a popular traditional steak house specializing in prime grade-A quality cuts of beef as well as fresh seafood, veal, and lamb. Unlike many traditional steak houses, Katz's offers a lighter lunch menu with soups, salads, sandwiches, and pastas. Popular items include the prime rib served au jus with horseradish sauce, bone-in rib-eye, rack of lamb, and veal *piccata*. Reservations are encouraged.

Steak lovers should also consider **Niko's Steakhouse** (5409 Saratoga St., 361/992-2333, www.nikossteakhouse.com, Mon.-Sat. 11am-11:30pm, $19-44). Prime rib is a favorite, but the rib-eye and sirloin steaks are worthy considerations. Sides play second fiddle to the meat, but several notable options include the asparagus and Yukon potatoes.

Slightly more trendy is **Dragonfly** (14701 S. Padre Island Dr., 361/949-2224, www.dragonflycuracaoblues.com, Tues.-Fri. 4pm-9pm, Sat. 5pm-10pm, $10-29), offering a fresh take on seafood and other standard fare, along with an extensive and interesting tapas menu. Dragonfly's salmon features a wonderful curry seasoning and is accompanied by a tasty side of baby bok choy and carrots, while the cheesy lasagna manages to be hearty without being overly filling. Other menu highlights include the slightly spicy shrimp skewer and tasty grilled tuna. Dragonfly doesn't have a kids menu, but they'll whip up a bowl of creamy mac and cheese on request.

Tourist-friendly **Executive Surf Club** (309 N. Water St., 361/884-7873, www.executivesurfclub.com, Mon.-Thurs. 11am-11pm, Fri.-Sat. 11am-midnight, $9-22) specializes in comfort food in a casual atmosphere. Grab a juicy cheeseburger and a Shiner Bock while you contemplate your next beach activity. Standard bar fare is the main draw here, and the Surf Club delivers fish-and-chips, fried shrimp, tortilla wraps, and chicken-fried steak, all served on tables fashioned from old surfboards. Stick around after dinner for some local hot blues and rock bands.

For a hearty breakfast or lunch with colorful local residents, head to **Hester's Café and Coffee Bar** (1714 S. Alameda St., 361/885-0558, www.

Dragonfly restaurant near Corpus Christi

hesterscafe.com, Mon.-Sat. 7am-3pm, $9-24), a reliable spot for semi-fancy comfort food. Hester's offers classics like eggs and hash browns with delectable additions like fresh avocado and thick-cut bacon. Popular lunch options include the stacked Laguna Club sandwich with melted cheese on top, hearty Victoria Pasta, and fresh salads.

ASIAN

Corpus has a long connection with Asia, reaching back a century to the days when shrimpers and rice farmers arrived in the developing coastal town. More recent are Thai, Chinese, and Japanese restaurants, and among the most popular is **Yalee's Asian Bistro**

(5649 Saratoga Blvd., 361/993-9333, Mon.-Fri. 11am-9:30pm, Sat.-Sun. 11am-11pm, $9-22). The counter-service approach may lower expectations, but the food is top-notch, including spicy *ma po* tofu and flavorful standards like *kung pao* shrimp and General Tso chicken.

Sushi fans should head to Aka Sushi (5301 Everhart Rd., 361/851-9191, Mon.-Thurs. 11am-2pm and 5pm-10pm, Fri. 11:30am-2pm and 5pm-10:30pm, Sat. 5pm-10:30pm, $11-27), with classic tuna and shrimp rolls to more elaborate options such as a dragon roll and its off-menu variation known as an ecstasy roll. The seaweed salad is popular, and the sake selection is impressive.

Only a handful of restaurants represent Thai options. Thai Spice (523 N. Water St., 361/883-8884, www.thaispicecc.com, daily 11am-11pm, $10-24) has popular coconut curry options, served in actual coconuts. The flavorful curry is tempered by the sweetness of the coconut and accompanying fresh pineapple. Another notable option is the lemongrass soup, though it can be a bit spicy for some.

Not quite as authentic, a similarly high-quality option is Vietnam Restaurant (701 N. Water St., 361/853-2682, www.vietnam-restaurant.com, Mon.-Thurs. 11am-2pm and 5pm-9pm, Fri. 11am-2pm and 5pm-10pm, Sat. 5pm-10pm, $11-25), the place to go for amazing soups, including *pho* and surprisingly tasty catfish soup. Seafood and veggie dishes are also worth ordering.

TEX-MEX

Unlike its seafood restaurants, most of Corpus Christi's Mexican spots are not on the waterfront. La Playa (5017 Saratoga Blvd.; 7118 S. Padre Island Dr., 361/986-0089, www.laplaya.cc, Sun.-Mon. 11am-9pm, Tues.-Sat. 11am-10pm, $9-24) is the place to go for top-notch traditional Tex-Mex. Feast on chicken enchiladas in a tangy tomatillo sauce or savor the sizzling beef fajitas. You won't regret ordering the stuffed fried avocados. This being a seaside town, you can also order Tex-Mex-style dishes featuring fresh fish and gulf shrimp.

Offering some coastal flair to the Tex-Mex offerings is La Costenita (4217 Leopard St., 361/882-5340, Mon.-Sat. 5:30am-6pm, $9-19), a downtown eatery that's small in size yet huge on taste, particularly the shrimp dishes and traditional enchilada and taco plates. The chips are amazing and the homemade salsa is perfectly spicy. Make sure you arrive before 5:30pm.

Locals flock to Kiko's (5514 Everhart Rd., 361/991-1211, Mon.-Thurs. 6:30am-9pm, Fri.-Sat. 6:30am-9pm, $9-24) for the specialty enchiladas with zesty ranchero sauce. You can't go wrong with most menu items, including the green chili burrito, guacamole salad, and tortilla soup. Sample all the restaurant has to offer with the Kiko's platter, offering a signature cheese enchilada, beef fajita tacos, and a crispy chalupa.

Classic taqueria Solis Mexican Restaurant (3122 Baldwin Blvd.; 5409 Leopard St., 361/882-5557, Mon.-Sat. 6am-9pm, Sun. 7am-3pm, $9-20) draws crowds for its tasty tacos and enchiladas, all prepared with fresh homemade tortillas. Try the stuffed breakfast tacos, served all day, and *licuados* (fruity Mexican drinks).

ACCOMMODATIONS

There's no shortage of lodging in Corpus, and most have decent views, easy access to the bay, and reasonable rates. Budget options are in the airport and greyhound racetrack area, but most leisure travelers stay by the sea. For a nice spot away from the city, consider a condo with nightly rates on alluring Mustang Island or North Padre Island, 10-15 miles (16-24 km) from downtown on the Gulf Coast.

$50-100

Room rates at the beach are more affordable farther down the shore. One of the better deals in town is the barebones Budget Inn & Suites (801 S. Shoreline Blvd., 888/493-2950, www.budgetinnandsuitescc.com, $79 d), within walking distance of Cole Park, a premier windsurfing spot. Amenities include free continental breakfast, free Wi-Fi, and an outdoor pool and sundeck. Closer to the action is Knights Inn (3615 Timon Blvd., 361/883-4411, www.knightsinn.com, $99 d), a couple of blocks off the bay and offering private balconies, several ocean-view rooms, free Wi-Fi, fridges, microwaves, and an outdoor pool.

The best deal in this range is the family-friendly Quality Inn & Suites (3202 Surfside Blvd., 361/883-7456, www.qualityinn.com, $99 d), thanks to its prime location on Corpus Christi Beach in the shadow of the USS *Lexington* and Texas State Aquarium. The hotel features an outdoor beachside pool and hot tub, free continental breakfast, and rooms with microwaves and fridges.

$100-150

Farther up the road in location and price is Days Inn (4302 Surfside Blvd., 361/882-3297, www.daysinn.com, $109 d), a block off Corpus Christi Beach. Amenities include rooms with microwaves, fridges, and free Wi-Fi, along with a complimentary continental breakfast and an outdoor pool. Closer to downtown is the Plaza Inn (2021 N. Padre Island Dr., 361/289-8200, www.plazainnhotels.com, $109 d), offering free hot breakfast in the morning. The Plaza Inn also has an outdoor pool, free Wi-Fi, and is pet-friendly. Just off busy South Padre Island Drive is the Hampton Inn (5209 Blanche Moore Dr., 361/985-8395, www.hamptoninn.com, $109 d), with free internet access, complimentary breakfast, to-go breakfast bags on weekdays, an outdoor pool, and a fitness center.

Another good option in this price range is the Holiday Inn Express (5213 Oakhurst Dr., 361/857-7772, www.hiexpress.com, $139 d), with free Wi-Fi, a complimentary hot breakfast bar, and a fitness center with an indoor pool and whirlpool. A bit farther east is Hilton Garden Inn (6717 S. Padre Island Dr., 361/991-8200, www.hiltongardeninn.hilton.com, $139 d), providing a heated outdoor pool with a whirlpool, complimentary internet, a microwave and mini-fridge in each room, and flat-screen TVs.

Also downtown is the Best Western Corpus Christi (300 N. Shoreline Blvd., 361/883-5111, www.bestwestern.com, $145 d), offering rooms with private balconies and marina views, free Wi-Fi, microwaves, fridges, a free continental breakfast, and an outdoor pool and exercise facility. Farther from the bay is Staybridge Suites (5201 Oakhurst Dr., 361/857-7766, www.staybridgecc.com, $144 d). Features include free hot breakfast, a fitness center, a whirlpool, an outdoor pool, and free Wi-Fi.

The best choice directly on the

beach is the ✪ Radisson (3200 Surfside Blvd., 361/883-9700, www.radisson.com, $149 d). Step out the back doors and onto the sand of Corpus Christi Beach, a pleasant stretch of shoreline on the bay that hosts a large number of frolicking families, flotsam and jetsam, and the USS *Lexington*. The rooms are bright and cheery, with private balconies, microwaves, fridges, and free Wi-Fi. The hotel features a splendid outdoor pool with swim-up bar service, a full-fledged fitness center, and a decent restaurant.

$150-200

Along the bayside is fantastic Emerald Beach Hotel (1102 S. Shoreline Blvd., 800/465-4329, www.hotelemeraldbeach.com, $199 d). This recently renovated hotel offers an independently owned option containing an indoor pool and fitness center along with an indoor recreation area for the kids, with a heated pool, table tennis, billiard tables, and vending machines. Emerald Beach features complimentary Wi-Fi and free meals for children.

Looming large along the Corpus Christi Bay are the Omni Marina and Bayfront (707 and 900 N. Shoreline Blvd., 361/887-1600, www.omnihotels.com, $199 d). Within a block of each other, the towers are connected by a walkway to form a deluxe complex. They're similar in price and amenities, although the Bayfront Tower offers additional upscale room options. Both provide rooms with Wi-Fi access, free meals for kids, an upscale health club, an indoor-outdoor heated swimming pool, an in-house massage therapist, bike rentals, and free covered parking.

CAMPING

For RVers, Puerto Del Sol RV Park (5100 Timon Blvd., 361/882-5373, www.puertodelsolrvpark.com, $29-39) is at the northern edge of Corpus Christi Beach. Amenities include full hookups, a rec room, laundry facilities, restrooms with hot showers, internet access, and a book exchange. Farther out of town at the entrance to Padre Island is Colonia Del Rey (1717 Waldron Rd., 361/937-2435 or 800/580-2435, $29-39), offering a heated pool, a hot tub, a recreation facility, a laundry room, a convenience store, and Wi-Fi. Nearby is the minimal yet affordable Padre Balli Park (15820 Park Rd. 22, 361/949-8121, $15-25), containing 54 paved campsites with water and electric hookups, 12 hardtop campsites for pitching a tent with water and electric hookups, and primitive camping on the beach. A bathhouse and laundry facility are also available.

INFORMATION AND SERVICES

The Corpus Christi Area Convention & Visitors Bureau (101 N. Shoreline Blvd., 361/881-1800 or 800/766-2322, www.visitcorpuschristitx.org, Mon.-Fri. 8:30am-5pm) displays scores of brochures, maps, and helpful information on local attractions and recreation. Similar information is available at the bureau's downtown Corpus Christi Tourist Information Center (1521 N. Chaparral St., 361/561-2000, daily 9am-5pm).

GETTING THERE AND AROUND

For those driving from Central Texas (Austin, San Antonio) to Corpus, take I-35 south, then I-37 south from San Antonio. It takes 3.5 hours from

Austin and 2 hours from San Antonio. Most Houstonians get their beach fix at nearby Galveston, but some travel down the coast via I-69 and U.S. 59 south to Victoria (a 2-hour drive) before heading south on U.S. 77 and U.S. 181 to Corpus (about 1 hour).

Five miles (8 km) west of downtown, the Corpus Christi International Airport (CRP, 1000 International Blvd., 361/289-0171, www.corpuschristiairport.com) offers flights on Southwest, United, and American Eagle, including to Monterrey, Mexico. The city's bus system, Regional Transportation Authority (1806 S. Alameda St., 361/883-2287, www.ccrta.org), provides citywide service. Check the website for fare and route information.

Mustang Island

When people say they're going to Corpus Christi to hit the beach, they're often referring to adjacent Mustang Island. Within 15 minutes, you can move from the city to the sea.

TOP EXPERIENCE

✪ PADRE ISLAND NATIONAL SEASHORE

Just south of Mustang Island is Padre Island National Seashore (3829 Park Rd. 22, 361/949-8068, www.nps.gov/

on the beach at North Padre Island near Corpus Christi

pais, $5 pedestrians and bikers, $10 vehicles), a low-key, nature-oriented, protected shoreline not to be confused with the commercial-minded party atmosphere of South Padre Island, a three-hour drive south. Padre Island National Seashore is the longest remaining undeveloped stretch of barrier island in the world and appeals to naturalists who delight in its primitive shoreline and birding and fishing opportunities. Bird-watchers arrive in droves in the fall and spring migration seasons, when thousands of birds drop by the island, including sandhill cranes, hawks, and songbirds.

The park is also considered the most important nesting beach for the most endangered sea turtle, the Kemp's ridley. Park officials incubate sea turtle eggs found along the coast and release the hatchlings into the gulf during summer. You can watch this fascinating event—for release dates and directions to the site, call the Hatchling Hotline (361/949-7163).

Other popular activities at the park include swimming, fishing, windsurfing, and beachcombing. Visit the website for detailed information about camping locations and fees. To reach the park from Corpus, take South Padre Island Drive (Hwy. 358) to Padre Island, then head south on Park Road 22 for 13 miles (21 km) to the Malaquite Visitor Center.

MUSTANG ISLAND STATE PARK

Don't miss the beautiful shoreline along Mustang Island State Park (17047 State Hwy. 361, 361/749-5246, www.tpwd.state.tx.us, $5 over age 12). Named for the wild horses that escaped from Spanish explorers and roamed free across this 18-mile-long (29-km) island, Mustang Island State Park comprises 5 miles (8 km) of pristine beach for swimming, fishing, sunbathing, hiking, biking, and even low-intensity surfing. Birding is popular on this 4,000-acre island, notable for its distinctive ecosystem of 20-foot-high (6-m) sand dunes that protect the bay and the mainland and can reduce powerful hurricane-driven waves. To get there from Corpus, take South Padre Island Drive (Hwy. 358) to Padre Island, then head north on Highway 361 for 5 miles (8 km) to the park headquarters.

SAN JOSE ISLAND

If you're seriously into beachcombing—we're talking shell collections, mounted driftwood, maybe even a metal detector—San Jose Island is your paradise. This privately owned property across the bay from Port Aransas is almost as untouched as it was when the Karankawa people lived here a thousand years ago. In the 1830s, locals found the remains of a pirate camp on the island, and legend has it that pirate Jean Lafitte's Spanish dagger with a silver spike is still somewhere guarding his booty of silver and gold.

These days, visitors can access "Saint Joe" via a short boat ride to go swimming, fishing, sunbathing, and treasure hunting on this beautiful unspoiled property. To arrange transport, drop by Port A's Fisherman's Wharf (900 N. Tarpon St., 361/749-5448, www.wharfcat.com, call for rates).

PORT ARANSAS

At the northern tip of Mustang Island is Port Aransas, or Port A, as it's known locally, a charming little beach town. Port A took a major hit from Hurricane Harvey in 2017, but it is slowly returning to its status as a laid-back, charming destination.

The origins of Port Aransas (population 4,143) trace to an English farmer who used the area as a sheep and cattle grazing station in the mid-1800s. Decades later, New Jersey entrepreneur Elihu Ropes attempted to organize a massive project to dredge a 30-foot (9-m) shipping channel across Mustang Island to allow access to the deep waters of the gulf. He was ultimately unsuccessful, but his efforts resulted in the town briefly being named Ropesville in his honor.

By the mid-20th century, Port Aransas had become synonymous with recreation, drawing tens of thousands of anglers, swimmers, boaters, and beachcombers to its open sands and seaside village atmosphere. The town's population swelled from 824 residents in 1960 to several thousand by the end of the century. As many as 20,000 vacationers descend on Port Aransas during peak periods, packing the island's motels, beach houses, and restaurants.

To get here from the mainland, travel across the South Padre Island Drive causeway from Corpus on the southern edge of the island, or take the ferry from nearby Aransas Pass (daily 24 hours). Look for dolphins behind the ferry as they tumble over each other in the bay snatching up fish in the boat's wake.

SIGHTS

Port A doesn't have cultural attractions, and the only real destination besides the beach is beach-related. The Marine Science Institute (630 E. Cotter Ave., 361/749-6729, www.utmsi.utexas.edu, Mon.-Fri. 8am-5pm, Sat.-Sun. 11am-3pm, free) is the oldest marine research station on the Texas

Marine Science Institute

Gulf Coast, dedicated to the ecology, biochemistry, and physiology of the plants and animals of the sea. The visitors center offers educational movies (Mon.-Thurs. 3pm) and self-guided tours of marine-related research project exhibits, stunning photographs, entertaining interactive displays for children, and several aquariums containing local sea life, including a funky flounder with two eyes on one side of its body.

RECREATION

When it comes to activities in Port Aransas, the key word is "outside," and there are noteworthy places to explore year-round.

Fishing

Port Aransas is a fishing mecca. Some claim the area is overfished, and it's clear to see why it's popular—easy access to the bay and deep-sea gulf fishing provide fishing year-round. Fish for free from beaches, jetties, or Charlie's Harbor Pier, Ancel Brundrett Pier, and J. P. Luby Pier, all lighted and extending into the Corpus Christi Ship Channel.

It's worth the $2 for the popular well-lit Horace Caldwell Pier (230 North on the Beach, 361/749-5333, www.keepersportaransasfishingpier. com), 1,200 feet (365 m) long and open daily 24 hours, with bait, tackle, rental equipment, and munchies at the concession stand. This is a one-stop-shop for people who don't have much experience fishing. Friendly locals are happy to assist with your bait, offer advice, and, if you're lucky, help remove your catch from your hook.

Many anglers prefer the challenge of the larger deep-sea species, including kingfish, mackerel, flounder, tuna, and shark. Group boats offer

bay and deep-sea fishing, and popular fishing tournaments take place throughout summer. The Deep Sea Roundup, held each July, is the oldest fishing tournament on the Gulf Coast. As a testament to the overwhelming allure of fishing in Port A, the town has several hundred fishing guides. Inquire about group fishing at Fisherman's Wharf (900 N. Tarpon St., 361/749-5448, www.wharfcat. com). To arrange a private rental, contact Woody's Sports Center (136 W. Cotter Ave., 361/749-5252, www. woodys-pa.com).

Swimming

The best swimming is at Mustang Island State Park, but you can access portions of the wide welcoming beach among the condos and private land just off the island's main road (Hwy. 361). Visitors can also swim and camp at the northern tip of the island just outside Port A at 167-acre Magee Beach Park (321 North on the Beach, 361/749-6117, www.nuecesbeachparks. com, $12-20 nightly for camping). Not as breathtaking as other portions of Mustang Island or San Jose Island, it's a good spot to swim. A park office offers limited visitor information, and the beach bathhouse contains publicly accessible showers.

FOOD
Seafood

One of the best seafood restaurants on the Gulf Coast is the unassuming ✪ Shells Pasta & Seafood (522 E. Ave. G, 361/749-7621, www.eatatshells. com, Wed.-Mon. 11:30am-2:30pm and 5pm-9pm, $12-36). Inside a modest building, Shells is a tiny place—nine tables with plastic chairs—with an enormous reputation for quality fresh seafood and pasta. Order from the blackboard or the regular menu, featuring classic seafood such as the signature pan-seared amberjack, grilled shrimp, blue crab cakes, or sumptuous shrimp linguine in a creamy Alfredo sauce. This is elegant food in a casual shorts-wearing environment, and Shells will be a highlight of your trip to Port A.

Locals love Lisabella's (224 E. Cotter Ave., 361/749-4222, Tues.-Sat. 5:30pm-9pm, $10-31) mermaid soup, a tasty concoction of lobster, shrimp, coconut milk, curry, and avocado. The crab cakes and sautéed grouper are similarly enticing.

A casual spot where you can wear T-shirts and flip-flops among old fishing nets, mounted marlin, and a marina is Trout Street Bar & Grill (104 W. Cotter Ave., 361/749-7800, www.tsbag.com, Sun.-Thurs. 11am-8pm, Fri.-Sat. 11am-9pm, $11-30). Sit outside on the covered veranda to watch the ship channel activity while feasting on peel-and-eat shrimp, fish tacos, drum po'boys, grilled amberjack, snapper, tuna, or steak. Complement the fantastic flavors with a local *hefeweizen*. A bonus: Trout Street will cook your fresh-caught fish as long as it's cleaned and ready for the kitchen.

Another venerable seafood spot is Fins (420 W. Cotter Ave., 361/749-8646, www.finsgrillandicehouse.com, Mon.-Fri. 11am-9pm, Sat.-Sun. 11am-10pm, $9-29). The views and menu are amazing, and shrimp is the specialty. Order the Bayou Combo (sautéed whitefish and gulf shrimp topped with a zesty sauce) and savor the flavor. Fins is family-friendly, so bring the whole crew and order some burgers and chicken nuggets.

A popular new destination in town is Tortuga's Saltwater Grill (429 N. Alister St., 361/749-2739, www.

Trout Street Bar & Grill

tortugassaltwatergrill.com, Mon.-Fri. 11am-9pm, Sat.-Sun. 11am-10pm, $10-20). There's something immensely satisfying about sipping well-crafted specialty beer while waiting for your fresh seafood to arrive. Pair it with the shrimp tacos, fried gulf fish, or islander brick-oven pizza.

Italian

Port A has both beach grub and upscale Italian. For a quick slice of pizza in an ultra-laid-back environment, check out the immensely popular Port A Pizzeria (407 E. Ave. G., 361/749-5226, www.portapizzeria.com, daily 11am-10pm, $9-20). The biggest draw is the buffet, allowing diners to devour hot slices. Some diners choose to wait a few minutes for the tasty calzone. The big crowds ensure a quick turnaround.

The fancy Italian option is the consistently top-notch Venetian Hot Plate (232 Beach Ave., 361/749-7617, www.venetianhotplate.com, Tues.-Sat. 5pm-10pm, $13-35). Named for the sizzling iron plates some of the meals arrive on, this upscale spot specializes in tender succulent filet mignon medallions, veal, and lamb. The wine selection is excellent, and desserts are spectacular. Reservations are recommended.

ACCOMMODATIONS

Inns

A memorable experience in this quaint seaside village is the charming ✪ Tarpon Inn (200 E. Cotter Ave., 361/749-5555, www.thetarponinn. com, $99-199). An "inn" in every sense of the term, this historic establishment offers a slice of life in the late 1800s. You won't find a TV or phone in your room, but Wi-Fi is available. Old-fashioned activities include reading, relaxing in a rocking chair, playing croquet and horseshoes, and talking. Rooms are small, with vintage beds and furniture, but are refreshingly uncluttered. Check out the old tarpon fish scales on the wall in the lobby, including those autographed by famous actors and politicians. The trolley stops out front every day to take guests to the beach or nearby shops.

Not quite as charming but appealing in its localness is Alister Square Inn (122 S. Alister St., 361/749-3003, www.portaransas-texas.com, $99-199). A bit rough around the edges, this welcoming accommodation appeals to families and anglers alike with two-bedroom apartments, kitchenette suites, and standard hotel rooms, each featuring microwaves, fridges, and Wi-Fi access. Alister Square is within walking distance of the beach, shopping, and restaurants.

Hotels

In Port Aransas, familiar chain hotels cost more than local inns. Just a couple of blocks from the beach is the Holiday Inn Express (727 S. 11th St., 361/749-5222, www.ichotelsgroup. com, $159 d), offering a fitness center, a pool and spa area, free continental breakfast, and rooms with microwaves, fridges, and free Wi-Fi. Among the more expensive options is Best Western Ocean Villa (400 E. Ave. G, 361/749-3010, www.bestwestern. com, $219 d), within walking distance of beaches, fishing piers, and local shops. Amenities include rooms with microwaves, fridges, and free internet access, along with free continental breakfast and an outdoor swimming pool.

Condos

Condos proliferate on Mustang Island's shoreline like barnacles on a shrimp boat. Condos make perfect sense in a beach environment—visitors can traipse back and forth to the surf, sand gathers on all surfaces, and beers and pizza fill the fridge. Hurricane Harvey damaged many of the condos, but in 2020 individual units were increasingly available via AirBNB.

Among the most popular still taking building-wide reservations is Beachgate CondoSuites & Motel (2000 On the Beach Dr., 361/749-5900, www.beachgate.com, $225-325). Adjacent to Mustang Island—meaning walking the boardwalks or long trails through the dunes isn't necessary—Beachgate offers everything from efficiency-size motel rooms to full-size three-bedroom condos, accommodating everyone from the solo angler to the sizable family reunion. Larger options contain fully equipped kitchens, and all units have small fridges, microwaves, and coffeemakers. Additional amenities include a fish-cleaning facility, boat parking, washers, and horseshoe sets for fun on the beach.

INFORMATION AND SERVICES

Pick up a handy brochure with island info and a map of the trolley route at the **Port Aransas Chamber of Commerce and Tourist Bureau** (403 W. Cotter St., 361/749-5919, www.portaransas.org). The Flexi-B (361/749-4111, $0.25), a.k.a. "the B" and "the 94 shuttle," will take you anywhere in Port A, including the beach, the wharf, shops, and your hotel. It's particularly handy when you're drinking and dinner is calling.

GETTING THERE

The **Port Aransas Ferry System** (361/749-2850) provides free transportation year-round daily 24 hours. It's a unique and charming way to cross the water—you can even get out of your car during the "ride" and look for the dolphins that swim behind the boat. The 15-minute ride connects Port Aransas with the mainland at Aransas Pass, north of Corpus Christi. Six ferries, each carry up to 20 vehicles. During the busy season, particularly holidays and some summer weekends, you may have to wait up to 45 minutes, but typically the wait is no longer than 5-10 minutes.

Kingsville

About 40 miles (64 km) southwest of Corpus Christi, Kingsville (population 25,487) is the birthplace of the American ranching industry. It's the main commercial center of the legendary King Ranch, which sprawls across 825,000 acres and boasts 60,000 head of cattle.

The community is named for the famous riverboat baron and rancher Richard King, who used his business profits to purchase the vast piece of property that would become the eponymous ranch. Kingsville's roots as a city are traced to the St. Louis, Brownsville and Mexico Railway, which put the town on the map when its tracks were laid in the early 1900s. Most of Kingsville's early business was related to the King family, who started a weekly newspaper and built a hotel, an ice plant, and a cotton gin. Kingsville went on to become a busy trade center for ranching families across South Texas.

Kingsville's population grew significantly when Exxon relocated a district office here in the 1960s. A surge in enrollment at the Texas College of Arts and Industries, now Texas A&M Kingsville, brought even more folks to town, with a population of 30,000 by the late 1970s. Exxon closed its regional office in 1985, and the population has slowly declined since then.

Kingsville remains a draw for birders and naturalists, who delight in the area's million acres of habitat. The historic downtown area has boutiques and antiques stores that reflect the heritage of King Ranch.

SIGHTS

TOP EXPERIENCE

✪ KING RANCH

King Ranch is the embodiment of the Lone Star State's legacy. Longhorn cattle, vast ranchlands, and genuine cowboys evoke a sense of mystique and grandeur. America's ranching legacy was revolutionized by a man who arrived on Texas's Gulf Coast

KING'S PEOPLE

At the heart of the King Ranch are the Kineños (King's people), a group of several hundred ranch employees whose families have operated the property for generations, training horses, clearing fields, and promoting the King Ranch's original cattle breed. The Kineños provide a link with the ranch's past and maintain its legacy. To learn more about this remarkable chapter of Texas history, plan a trip to **King Ranch** (2205 Hwy. 141 W., 361/592-8055, www.king-ranch.com, tours Mon.-Sat. 10am, noon, and 1pm, Sun. 12:30pm and 2pm, $20 adults, $15 seniors, $6 ages 5-12).

If you visit the ranch or take one of the tours, you'll get a chance to visit with one of these Kineños. Several now serve as guides, even though they occasionally take on some of their traditional ranching duties. Many of the Kineños are men in their 80s.

Some Kineños spent their early days breaking thoroughbred horses. In the 1940s-1950s, King Ranch trained racing horses and developed well-known successful thoroughbreds. The Kineños also worked extensively with the ranch's quarter horses, using the handling techniques passed down through generations of vaqueros. Others worked closely with the Santa Gertrudis cattle breed, specifically developed and marketed by the ranch, by attending livestock shows around the world. They even slept in the barns with the animals and woke early to clean, feed, water, and brush the cattle in preparation for the shows. Kineños also administered vaccinations, helped in the pastures, and maintained records.

Some of these stories have been captured in print. Pick up a copy of Alberto "Beto" Maldonado's book *The Master Showmen of King Ranch*.

as a preteen stowaway. Richard King, who left New York City in 1835 aboard a cargo ship, went on to become a steamboat baron along the Rio Grande before overseeing his ranching empire.

The origins of King Ranch, now a National Historic Landmark, date to 1853 when Richard King purchased 68,500 acres of property that had been Spanish and Mexican land

historic barn at King Ranch

grants. Between 1869 and 1884 King sent more than 100,000 head of livestock from his ranch to northern markets on now-legendary routes like the Chisholm Trail. Many were marked with the iconic symbol for the King Ranch, the running-W brand, which first appeared in the 1860s. Though the origins of this distinctive shape aren't known, local legends claim it represents the sweeping horns of a longhorn bull, or a slithering diamondback rattlesnake.

One of King Ranch's claims to fame is the development of the western hemisphere's first strain of beef cattle, Santa Gertrudis. Based on the name from the property's original land grant, the breed was developed in the 1920s to produce cows that could withstand the oppressive South Texas conditions—heat, humidity, and biting insects. To accomplish this, breeding experts, including Richard King's grandson, crossed Indian Brahman cattle with British shorthorns.

King was also one of the first ranchers to move Texas longhorns from Mexico to markets in the Midwest, and the innovations developed at his ranch, from breeding and disease control to improving the bloodlines of the quarter horse to well drilling, earned it the title "birthplace of American ranching."

Today, King Ranch sprawls across 825,000 acres, larger than the state of Rhode Island. The King Ranch Visitor Center (2205 Hwy. 141 W., 361/592-8055, www.king-ranch.com, tours Mon.-Sat. 10am, noon, and 1pm, Sun. 12:30pm and 2pm, $20 adults, $15 seniors, $6 ages 5-12) offers daily guided tours along an old stagecoach road past majestic longhorns with the iconic running-W brand on their hindquarters, and a 100-year-old carriage house with a mission-style roofline and distinctive arches. Other highlights include the Victorian-era cabin homes of King's working families, known as Kineños, and a horse cemetery with graves of famous racing thoroughbreds from the 1950s. It gets hot on the ranch, but you'll be in air-conditioned comfort in a plush utility vehicle with water breaks and a friendly guide to answer questions and point out fascinating information. Special tours devoted to birding, wildlife, and agriculture are available in advance by reservation.

A couple of miles down the road is the King Ranch Museum (405 N. 6th St., Kingsville, 361/595-1881, www.king-ranch.com, Mon.-Sat. 10am-4pm, Sun. 1pm-5pm, $10 adults, $8 seniors and students, $4 ages 5-12). Housed in a historic downtown ice plant, the museum contains stunning 1940s photos of the ranch by award-winning photographer Toni Frissell, fancy saddles and firearms, antique coaches and carriages, and other historic ranch items. One of the most intriguing objects is "El Kineño," a custom-designed 1949 Buick Eight hunting vehicle—complete with rifle holders and a shiny running-W hood ornament—made by General Motors especially for Congressman R. M. Kleberg Sr.

Another must-see is the restored 1909 Ragland Mercantile Building that now houses the leather-filled King Ranch Saddle Shop (201 E. Kleberg Ave., 877/282-5777, www.krsaddleshop.com, Mon.-Sat. 10am-6pm). Originally used to supply gear exclusively to the King Ranch Kineños, the store now offers leather goods and clothing to the world, and its website does brisk business. The charming downtown shop also contains exhibits and photos on ranch history and information about the governors, presidents, and foreign dignitaries it has outfitted.

1904 TRAIN DEPOT AND MUSEUM

A block from the saddle shop is the restored 1904 Train Depot and Museum (102 E. Kleberg Ave., 361/592-8515, www.kingsvilletexas.com, Mon.-Fri. 8am-5pm, free), offering a glimpse into Kingsville's bustling past. Photos and artifacts, including an operational telegraph, highlight the historical significance of this hub of regional activity.

KENEDY RANCH MUSEUM OF SOUTH TEXAS

Richard King isn't the only famous rancher in these parts. His longtime pal Mifflin Kenedy also accumulated great wealth and property in commercial and ranching endeavors. His legacy is on display at the Kenedy Ranch Museum of South Texas (200 E. La Parra Ave., Sarita, 361/294-5751, Tues.-Sat. 10am-4pm, Sun. noon-4pm, $4 adults, $3 seniors and ages 13-18). Located 20 miles (32 km) south of Kingsville in the little town of Sarita, the museum showcases Kenedy's illustrious past through exhibits dedicated to family, particularly his wife, Petra Vela de Vidal, of prominent Mexican heritage. Kenedy accumulated 400,000 acres of Gulf Coast property and was among the first ranchers to hold cattle inside wire fences. Housed in the 1927 Kenedy Ranch headquarters, the museum also details the family's philanthropic programs.

JOHN E. CONNER MUSEUM

Regional history and the natural world are the main areas of interest at the John E. Conner Museum (905 W. Santa Gertrudis Ave., 361/593-2810, www.tamuk.edu, Mon.-Fri. 8am-5pm, Sat. 10am-4pm, free). On the campus of Texas A&M-Kingsville, this modest museum offers exhibits devoted to the groups that have occupied the area, from Native Americans to Spanish, Mexican, and American settlers. Native plant and animal species are also on display, as well as artwork from students and Texas artists.

FOOD

AMERICAN

Kingsville isn't a destination for fine dining, but one of the best places to eat in the region is 20 miles (32 km) south of Kingsville in the tiny town of Riviera. ✪ King's Inn (1116 S. County Rd. 2270, Riviera, 361/297-5265, www. mybighouseonline.com, Tues.-Sat. 11am-10pm, $13-29) doesn't look like much from the outside, and the outdated ambience isn't charming, but that won't matter when the food arrives. Order the lightly breaded fried shrimp, accompanied by the famous spicy tartar sauce (the waiter claimed to be sworn to secrecy, though he eventually let it slip that the tartar sauce contained bread crumbs, "lots of eggs," and serrano peppers). This stunning sauce enhances everything

from the interesting choice of fish (drum) to the homemade bread to the avocado salad with accompanying slices of tomato. It's worth the 20-minute detour to eat like a king.

For lunch, just south of downtown Kingsville is the occasionally rowdy Big House Burgers (2209 S. Brahma Blvd., 361/592-0222, daily 11am-10pm, $8-15). The sports bar atmosphere can be overwhelming on weekends, reminding you there's a college in this town, but the noise and blaring TVs are worth it for the immense and flavorful burgers. Try the quadruple burger if you dare. Split some of the crunchy fries or crispy onion rings with a pal.

TEX-MEX

Grab an authentic Tex-Mex meal at El Tapatio Mexican Restaurant (630 W. Santa Gertrudis St., 361/516-1655, Mon.-Sat. 6am-10pm, Sun. 6am-2pm, $9-18), on the edge of the Kingsville A&M campus. The food is standard Tex-Mex fare, with a few items that set it apart. The *carne guisada* has hearty gravy that brings out the rich flavor of the beef. Like the salsa, it has an extra kick and after-bite that leaves your mouth feeling satisfied.

Lydia's Homestyle Cooking (817 W. King Ave., 361/592-9405, Mon.-Sat. 6am-1:30pm, $9-19) is known for its tremendous breakfast taquitos (try the potato, eggs, and sausage) and the *machacado* plate, featuring shredded dry beef scrambled with eggs and grilled onions, tomato, and serrano peppers. Lydia's lunches are legendary, including the *barbacoa* plate, tamales, and chicken flautas. You can also order gringo burgers and sandwiches.

Reputable El Dorado (704 N. 14th St., 361/516-1459, Mon.-Sat. 6am-10pm, Sun. 6am-2pm, $8-15) has traditional Tex-Mex fare that's consistently decent, including the beef tacos, chicken enchiladas, and burritos.

ACCOMMODATIONS

Only a few lodging options are available in Kingsville. On the affordable side is **Best Western Kingsville Inn** (2402 E. King Ave., 361/595-5656, www.bestwestern.com, $69 d). Amenities include a complimentary hot breakfast, free Wi-Fi, standard rooms with microwaves and fridges, and a "soothing outdoor swimming pool and hot tub."

For a little more money, consider **Holiday Inn Express** (2400 S. Hwy. 77, 361/592-8333, www.hiexpress.com, $109 d), offering a free hot breakfast bar, complimentary Wi-Fi, and a heated outdoor pool.

INFORMATION AND SERVICES

For information about area attractions, accommodations, and restaurants, visit the **Kingsville Convention and Visitors Bureau** (1501 Hwy. 77, 361/592-8516, www.kingsvilletexas.com, Mon.-Fri. 9am-5pm, Sat. 10am-2pm).

GETTING THERE

The main route to Kingsville is U.S. 77. From Corpus, get on Highway 44 west for 15 minutes before linking up with U.S. 77, a drive of about 45 minutes total.

South Padre Island

The massive 130-mile-long (210-km) Padre Island is home to the longest sand beach in the United States. Never more than 3 miles (4.8 km) wide, the island was formed by sea erosion and deposition. The northern portion, adjacent to Corpus Christi, has a modest collection of hotels and residences and is mostly recreation-oriented; the central portion is the protected Padre Island National Seashore; and the southern tip is a major resort area lined with hotels and restaurants.

South Padre Island isn't technically an island, but rather the resort community (population 2,830) at the southern portion of the big island. The town is flanked by the Gulf of Mexico to the east, a narrow ship channel to the north, and Laguna Madre, the narrow bay leading to the Texas mainland.

Spanish explorers visited the area in the 1500s, but the seashore remained barren and pristine until the 1950s, when a causeway connected Port Isabel to South Padre Island. It provided access to the nicest beaches on the Texas coast, and the community remained a low-key resort destination until the late 1970s, when insurance companies were required to provide hurricane coverage and the population increased dramatically from 314 to 1,012 residents thanks to the growing emphasis on tourism. For the past two decades, it has become a major spring break destination for college students, who descend on the small town by the thousands for revelry and recreation each March.

SIGHTS

Island time is good for the soul. Everything slows down, priorities shift to beach activities and seafood options, and even tightly wound drivers lay off their car horns. It may take a day or two to assimilate to South Padre mode, but you won't want to leave.

South Padre's soft smooth sand is more inviting and picturesque than the grainier, darker sand farther north. The resort community offers beachcombing, fishing, windsurfing, dolphin-viewing, biking, snorkeling, and scuba diving. Lodging options range from opulent resort condos to pitching a tent on the beach, and restaurants offer gulf-harvested oysters, shrimp, and fish. Make a point of taking a dolphin tour and visiting the sea turtle research center to get an appreciation of the sealife that doesn't end up on your dinner plate.

In winter you'll be surrounded by Midwestern license plates and polite retirees taking advantage of restaurant early-bird specials. In summer, Texas families flock to the island to play in the gentle waves and devour fried shrimp. The beach is pleasant year-round and the vibe is mellow, except during spring break.

It takes some effort to get to South Padre, but maneuvering around the small town is a breeze. After crossing the Queen Isabella Causeway, take a left onto Padre Boulevard to reach the main drag, with hotels, shops, and restaurants. Take a right off the causeway to reach the public beaches and seaside attractions.

SEA TURTLE, INC.

A heartwarming experience awaits at Sea Turtle, Inc. (6617 Padre Blvd., 956/761-4511, www.seaturtleinc.com, Tues.-Sun. 10am-4pm, donation), an unassuming little spot at the end of South Padre's main strip. Inside, tanks are full of various sea turtles, several

native to the nearby Gulf Coast. Each turtle is identified in a separate tank, often with a tear-jerking tale about the unfortunate experience (boat propeller, fishing line, animal attack) that brought it to the rehab site. Arrive at 10am for the informative presentation that offers context about the friendly and fascinating creatures. Kids can feed the turtles, and everyone has a chance for a photo op. Marvel at these prehistoric animals—some can reach 450 pounds—and toss a few extra dollars in the box for this organization that works tirelessly to protect and promote these endangered creatures.

DOLPHIN RESEARCH AND SEA LIFE NATURE CENTER

Kids aren't the only ones who'll learn something at the nearby Dolphin Research and Sea Life Nature Center (110 N. Garcia St., Port Isabel, 956/299-1957, www.spinaturecenter. com, daily 10am-4pm, $3 donation). This low-key locale, just across the causeway from South Padre, contains 20 aquariums filled with sea creatures from the gulf waters. Shrimp, starfish,

Port Isabel Lighthouse State Historic Site

rays, and eels await, and a children's program (11am and 2pm, call ahead to make sure it's available) allows youngsters to handle and feed some of the nonthreatening species in the touch tanks. Knowledgeable staffers educate visitors about environmentally responsible ways to enjoy their time on the island.

✪ PORT ISABEL LIGHTHOUSE

It's worth the 74-step climb up the tight spiral staircase of the historic Port Isabel Lighthouse State Historic Site (421 E. Queen Isabella Blvd., Port Isabel, 800/527-6102, www.thc.texas.gov, daily 9am-5pm), now owned by the Texas Historical Commission. The view stretches from Laguna Madre to the historic downtown Port Isabel. Constructed in 1852 at the request of sea captains frustrated by visibility along the low-lying Texas coast, the lighthouse was prominent until the early 1900s, when newer and more powerful towers were constructed. Sixteen similar lighthouses once graced the Texas coast, but the Port Isabel Lighthouse is the only one still open to the public.

PAN AMERICAN COASTAL STUDIES LABORATORY

Not as family-oriented as other area attractions, the Pan American Coastal Studies Laboratory (100 Marine Lab Dr., 956/761-2644, www.utrgv.edu/csl, Mon.-Fri. 1:30pm-4:30pm, free) is designed with researchers in mind. You'll learn things about the plant and animal life in the Laguna Madre and Gulf of Mexico through interactive displays (shark jaws, turtle shells) and a few aquariums.

BEACHES

The beach is everywhere at South Padre, so you won't have any trouble finding a place to park and tote your gear to the soft white sand (bring plenty of sunscreen and bottled water). Look for public beach access points every few blocks along Gulf Boulevard.

For more amenities—pavilions, picnic tables, and playgrounds in addition to the restrooms and showers—go to one of the county beach parks on the southern or northern ends of the island. The most popular is the southern option—Isla Blanca Park (33174 State Park Rd. 100, 956/761-5494, www.cameroncountyparks.com, daily 7am-11pm, $12 per vehicle). Referred to as the "crown jewel of the system," it features 1 mile-plus (1.6 km) of pristine white sand and bright blue water for swimming, surfing, and fishing. Parking is easily available, and beachcombers can step from the lot onto the beach, where they'll encounter pickup volleyball games, surfers, Frisbee dogs, and friendly folks strolling the low-key surf. There are also nearly 600 RV slots available.

At the northern end is Andy Bowie Park (7300 Padre Blvd., 956/761-3704, www.cameroncountyparks.com, daily 7am-11pm, $5 per vehicle). More rural in nature, Andy Bowie offers access to a beachfront road that eventually opens up to 20 miles (32 km) of scenic driving that qualifies as off-the-beaten-path. Horseback riding is popular, as is wade fishing and windsurfing on the bay side.

RECREATION

WATER SPORTS

Your one-stop shop for all things recreational in South Padre is South Padre Island Water Sports/Air

This low-key, unassuming beach community turns into a raucous party town for several weeks each March. Nearly 100,000 students from across the country descend on South Padre Island approximately March 10-20, prompting locals to leave their quiet seaside homes.

Rivaling Florida's Daytona Beach as the nation's ultimate spring break destination, South Padre has become party central for college students from Texas and the Midwest. The town doesn't have the infrastructure to handle the hordes—eight-hour waits on the causeway are common on peak arrival days—but it ultimately benefits from the millions spent on lodging, food, and DWI tickets (take the Wave shuttle if you've had a few drinks).

One of South Padre's biggest spring break assets is its beach consumption policy—unlike most U.S. seashores, it's legal to drink on the beach if you're 21 or older. The undercover Texas Alcoholic Beverage Commission agents are out in full force looking for minors in possession (MIPs). Rent a hotel with a kitchenette or a condo for easy access to a fridge, ice, and countertops.

Spring breakers often take advantage of package deals offered by travel agencies. Most involve flights and lodging, but several feature mini excursions around the area for a respite after days of drinking and sunbathing. One of the most popular activities is a professionally operated surfing lesson, complete with a board, a wetsuit, and individual instruction. For a change of scenery while downing drinks, sign up for a party yacht cruise, originating at Coconuts Bar and Grill.

Padre (SPIWS, 5709 Padre Blvd., 956/299-9463, www.spiws.com). The company's credo says it all: "Beautiful South Padre island is best seen from the water." The following are compelling options:

Kayaks ($30-95) provide a steady vantage point of island scenery. SPIWS offers many kayaks for rent, including single, tandem, fishing, surfing, and even glass-bottom varieties.

Kiteboarding is another fun way to get a workout at South Padre, though you may spend more time looking at the sky than the sights. The island's steady winds and shallow water are optimal for this activity. SPIWS suggests scheduling an initial lesson (from $99) before venturing out on their rental equipment.

Windsurfing represents a step down in intensity from kiteboarding, though it's still an active pursuit requiring plenty of stamina. Fortunately, the island's steady 18 mph (29 km/h) winds make it easier to move consistently. Combined with Laguna Madre's calm water and shallow sandy floor, windsurfing offers a fun and easy way to zip around.

Traditional surfing remains an appealing option for many island visitors, and you'll see boards on most stretches of beach. The waves aren't major, but they're ideal for honing skills. One of the best ways to get your feet wet is through a SPIWS group lesson, offered daily. You'll find all the equipment you'll need for rent or purchase, including soft-stop surfboards, traditional longboards, and leashes.

Stand-up paddleboarding is low-key and the easiest water sport to experience South Padre. The wide boards help with stability and balance, and the canoe-style paddles provide plenty of propulsion power. SPIWS offers lessons for newbies and rental equipment.

SNORKELING AND SCUBA DIVING

With clear water and fine sand, South Padre Island is a haven for scuba divers and snorkelers. The fish aren't varied or colorful like in tropical locales, but the marinelife among the reefs and rigs is intriguing.

Snorkeling and shallow shore dives are at the Mansfield Jetties, the beach at Dolphin Cove (look for sand dollars), and the adjacent Barracuda Bay. Scuba divers will enjoy the artificial reef (a wreck dive known as The Tug) 7 miles (11.3 km) southeast of the Brazos Santiago Pass Jetties. Farther out and most compelling for experienced divers are the oil rigs, where fish of all sizes are plentiful.

South Padre has several full-service dive shops offering equipment for rent and sale, organized excursions to prime spots, and instruction. One of the most reputable is Southern Wave (201 W. Pike St., 956/772-7245, www.sailspi.com). Another noteworthy option is American Diving (1 Padre Blvd., 956/761-2030, www.divesouthpadre.com).

FISHING

Fishing is a huge draw in South Padre. Everywhere you look are anglers with fishing poles—on the beach, jetty, pier, and chartered boats. Shoreline fishers tend to snag redfish, speckled trout, and flounder, while deep-sea adventurers seek tarpon, marlin, kingfish, mackerel, flounder, and wahoo.

Many anglers use the services of the venerable Jim's Pier (209 W. Whiting St., 956/761-2865, www.jimspier.com), which bills itself as the original South Padre Island fishing-guide company. Jim's provides boat slips, fueling docks, a launching ramp, and fish-cleaning facilities. The company also offers two bay fishing trips daily on its renowned 40-person party boat. To find out more about fishing locations and services, consult the Port Isabel/South Padre Island Guides Association (www.fishspi.com),

offering a list of endorsed professional fishing guides.

DOLPHIN-VIEWING

Laguna Madre is home to myriad bottlenose dolphins, and there's nothing like the thrill of seeing them up close in their natural environment. The best way to get an intimate experience is through an independent tour company like Fins to Feathers (tours from Port Isabel's Sea Life Center, 956/299-0629, www.fin2feather.com, daily 7am-sunset, $25 pp). Enjoy a personalized experience from a small boat, allowing up-close views and interaction with the knowledgeable guide, a colorful character accompanied by a dolphin-finding dog. Anticipate the surge of excitement you'll feel when that first dorsal fin ascends from the water and the sun glistens off the smooth gray surface of these magnificent elegant creatures.

HIKING

South Padre is not a hiking destination, but there's plenty of shoreline to explore by foot. Head to Andy Bowie Park (7300 Padre Blvd., 956/761-3704, www.cameroncountyparks.com, daily 7am-11pm, $5 per vehicle), with access to a beachfront road (watch out for rogue vehicles) that eventually opens up to isolated areas.

BIKING

Cyclists will enjoy the novel challenge of pedaling a Fat Sand Bike on the beach, a surprisingly quick and easy way to navigate the soft sand. Rentals are available at South Padre Island Water Sports/Air Padre (5709 Padre Blvd., 956/299-9463, www.spiws.com), from half days to a week ($40-250).

ENTERTAINMENT AND EVENTS

BARS AND CLUBS

After a day of in the ocean, relax and enjoy cold quality suds at **Padre Island Brewing Company** (3400 Padre Blvd., 956/761-9585, www.pibrewingcompany.com, Sun.-Thurs. 11:30am-10pm, Fri.-Sat. 11:30am-11pm, $9-21). Beer is the main theme, with home-brew supplies such as kettles, burlap sacks, and vintage bottles serving as scenery. It's a refreshing change from the ubiquitous corporate light-beer in most beach establishments. Fortunately, the handcrafted beer is commendable, particularly the Padre Pale Ale and Spotted Trout Stout. Food includes seafood and traditional bar fare like burgers, nachos, ribs, and sandwiches. Look for a seat on the second-floor outdoor deck.

For the ultimate island leisure activity, **Louie's Backyard** (2305 Laguna Dr., 956/761-6406, www.lbyspi.com, daily 11:30am-2am, $10-31) is party central during spring break, with multiple decks of dance floors and swirling light shows. The bartenders work quickly, and the drinks are potent. Before hitting the bar, consider the sumptuous buffet. Choose from boiled shrimp, crab legs, fish, and scallops along with ribs, pasta, and salad. The full menu has better options, including buttery, flaky flounder fillet and crispy fried shrimp. Top off your experience with a stunning view of the sunset over the bay while sipping Louie's signature cocktail, the multi-liquor and aptly named Whammy.

A South Padre favorite bar has returned in a new location. **Parrot Eyes** (5801 Padre Blvd., 956/761-9457, Mon.-Fri. 11am-7pm, Sat.-Sun. 11am-9pm, www.parroteyesspi.com) is Buffett-esque, with a laid-back vibe and beach-loving patrons. Grab a drink and try to snag a spot on the small deck overlooking the bay. If you're feeling adventurous, order the Parrot-Head Paralizer, a crazy concoction of multiple liquors and fruit juices.

For the spring break vibe, head to **Coconut Jack's** (2301 Laguna Dr., 956/761-4218, daily 11am-11pm), with good food but known mainly for water sports rentals and recreation during the day, and in the evening an occasionally raucous bar scene with friendly and generously waitstaff.

EVENTS

The community of South Padre knows a good time, as evidenced by several annual outdoor events. One of the first to draw big crowds each year is early February's **SPI Kitefest** (956/761-1248, www.sopadre.com). Held at the Sand Flats north of the SPI Convention Centre, Kitefest features hundreds of colorful kites punctuating the crisp blue sky. The steady ocean breeze helps keep even beginners' kites aloft, but there are also experts on hand to demonstrate new equipment and kite-flying skills and distribute prizes.

Of course, the community's biggest beach event is **spring break,** when tens of thousands of college students and other partiers descend on South Padre en masse. Revelers arrive throughout March, with the heaviest craziness during Texas Week, the second or third week of March.

Much mellower is the island's annual **Texas State Surfing Championship** (www.surftgsa.org), held in late April-early May, based on surf swell. This invitational competition for all ages is held in Isla Blanca

Park on the southern tip of the island, considered the area's crowning jewel.

FOOD

SEAFOOD

Even before you check in to your hotel room, drop by a low-key local eatery like Palm Street Pier Bar & Grill (204 W. Palm St., 956/772-7256, www.palmstreetpier.com, daily 11am-midnight, $9-20), known for tantalizing seafood and sunsets. Overlooking Laguna Madre, Palm Street Pier specializes in tasty fried and coconut shrimp. Don't miss the cheap margaritas and summertime Friday-night fireworks over the bay. Diners can bring their own fresh catch and have it expertly blackened, grilled, or fried with two side dishes. Palm Street operates on island time, so don't expect your food to arrive quickly.

Venerable and well-regarded Blackbeard's (103 E. Saturn Lane, 956/761-2962, www.blackbeardsspi.com, Sun.-Thurs. 11:30am-9pm, Fri.-Sat. 11:30am-10pm, $9-24) is a swashbuckling-themed spot with surprisingly refined food. Fresh gulf catches are the main draw, including flounder and tilapia, and equally commendable are charbroiled steaks and grilled chicken. The burgers here are some of the best on the island.

A local favorite in a new location is Daddy's Cajun Kitchen & Seafood Market (1801 Padre Blvd., 956/761-1975, http://daddysrestaurant.com, Sun.-Thurs. 11am-9pm, Fri.-Sat. 11am-10pm, $10-25). In a two-story building, Daddy's offers Creole and Cajun specialties such as jambalaya, gumbo, and crawfish étouffée, or one of the in-house lunch specials such as a crispy panko-breaded shrimp or almond-crusted fish fillet topped with crab and cheese sauce.

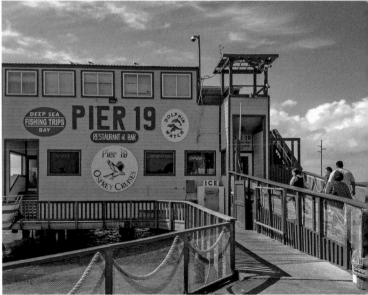

Pier 19 on South Padre Island

South Padre has upscale seafood, but in a casual town like this, you can still wear shorts and sandals. You can't go wrong with anything on the menu at ✪ Sea Ranch Restaurant (1 Padre Blvd., 956/761-1314, www. searanchrestaurant.com, Sun.-Thurs. 4:30pm-9pm, Fri.-Sat. 4:30pm-10pm, $11-46), Options change regularly, focused on wild-caught seafood from the gulf. Signature dishes include grilled flounder, boiled king crab legs, gulf shrimp and bay oysters, and ahi tuna served rare with soy sauce and wasabi. Topping it off is an exceptional view of the sea. Reservations are advised.

Another popular seafood spot is Pier 19 (1 Padre Blvd., 956/761-7437, www.pier19.us, $9-39), at the end of the road past the KOA Kampground. Located on the water, highlights at this restaurant include peel-and-eat, sautéed, and fried shrimp, blackened rockfish, and local flounder, pompano, and amberjack. The Baja tacos (with grilled shrimp) are especially tasty, bursting with the complementary flavors of savory shrimp, spicy jalapeño, and sweet mango. An added bonus: On some weekends, the staff "treats" diners to a pirate-themed show. Also watch for dolphins, known to make occasional appearances in the water below.

BEACH GRUB

If you've exhausted your craving for seafood, your next best bet is beach burgers, pizzas, and fried stuff, and, in South Padre, Tex-Mex. To combine all of these with cold suds is Padre Island Brewing Company (3400 Padre Blvd., 956/761-9585, www.pibrewingcompany.com, daily 11:30am-10pm, $9-21). The handcrafted beer is commendable,

particularly the Padre Island Pale Ale and Spotted Trout Stout, to go with nachos, ribs, and sandwiches. Order a pale ale with a gulf-stuffed flounder, a flavorful fillet packed with crab and topped with creamy shrimp sauce. To enhance the experience, ask for a seat on the second-floor outdoor deck.

For a tasty burger and cold beer, head to Tom & Jerry's Beach Bar & Grill (3212 Padre Blvd., 956/761-8999, daily 11am-10pm, $8-22). The seafood dishes are commendable, but beach grub is the main draw, including burgers, chicken plates, chicken-fried steak, and a club sandwich. After your meal, head to the raised bar, where friendly staffers will pour draft beer or mix frozen concoctions.

ACCOMMODATIONS

HOTELS

Lodging rates are high in the busy season and affordable the rest of the year. The following South Padre accommodations include prices for a weekend stay in midsummer, the busy getaway season in Texas, despite the high heat and humidity.

Among the affordable options is South Beach Inn (120 E. Jupiter Lane, 956/761-2471, www.southbeachtexas. com, $43-129), an independently owned 12-unit establishment among the palms just a block from the beach. One of the oldest hotels on the island, dating to 1961, South Beach offers kitchenettes with full-size stoves, fridges, microwaves, and toasters. Pets are welcome, and Wi-Fi is available.

Close to the Queen Isabella Causeway is the casual and consistent Super 8 (4205 Padre Blvd., 956/761-6300, www.super8padre.com, $129 d), offering a heated outdoor pool, free continental breakfast, free Wi-Fi access, and mini microwaves and fridges. A step up that's closer to the action is the Ramada Limited (4109 Padre Blvd., 956/761-4097, www.ramadasouthpadreisland.com, $159 d), offering a free hot breakfast, an outdoor pool and hot tub, and rooms with microwaves, fridges, and free Wi-Fi. Pets are welcome at the Ramada.

Best Western Beachside Inn (4500 Padre Blvd., 956/761-4919, www.bestwestern.com, $164 d), features clean, simple rooms within walking distance of the beach, an outdoor pool with a hot tub, and kitchenettes with microwaves and fridges. A clean and reliable chain hotel is Holiday Inn Express (6502 Padre Blvd., 956/761-8844, www.hiexpress.com, $179 d). The massive aquarium in the lobby has dozens of colorful fish. Otherwise, the amenities are standard, including an outdoor pool, a fitness center, beach access, free Wi-Fi, and rooms with microwaves and fridges.

RESORTS

A popular and affordable resort option is La Copa Inn Beach Resort (350 Padre Blvd., 956/761-6000, www.lacoparesort.com, $209 d). On the beach, La Copa is a pet-friendly spot with a breakfast buffet that includes a made-to-order omelet station, hot waffles, and free Wi-Fi.

Among the best-known resorts on the island is the Isla Grand (500 Padre Blvd., 800/292-7704, www.islagrand.com, $220 d), with perhaps the best beachfront location in town and excellent services. Rooms include free internet access, microwaves, and fridges. Condo suites have spacious rooms, a living area with a couch and a second TV, a fully equipped kitchen, and separate baths. The hotel's grounds have direct beach access, two outdoor

swimming pools with a cascading waterfall, three whirlpools, four lighted tennis courts, shuffleboard courts, and plenty of lounge chairs.

For a step up, a hotel-to-resort renovation is the Pearl South Padre (310 Padre Blvd., 956/761-6551, www.pearlsouthpadre.com, $289 d). Occupying 15 tropical beachside acres, this former Sheraton is a comfortable fancy spot with ample amenities and several room types: standard guest rooms, kitchenettes, suites, and fully equipped two- and three-bedroom condominiums, all with private balconies. Other amenities include an enormous 6,000-square-foot swimming pool complete with a waterfall and a swim-up bar, a separate oversize whirlpool, volleyball nets, an exercise and weight room, and seasonal parasailing.

Just down the street is the upscale and pricey Peninsula Island Resort & Spa (340 Padre Blvd., 956/761-2514, www.peninsulaislandresort.com, $289 d), featuring one- to three-bedroom units with kitchenettes, a swim-up pool bar, a large pool and hot tub, rooms with fancy Brazilian furniture, a gym, and an on-site convenience store. Seasonal spa services are available.

CAMPING

Beachfront property is too valuable for camping in the commercial part of South Padre. Only a couple of options exist for RV campers.

The South Padre Island KOA (1 Padre Blvd., 800/562-9724, www.southpadrekoa.com, $30-60) is geared to RVs but has a few cabins and lodges available. Site amenities include an outdoor pool, a fitness center, a recreation room, and free Wi-Fi. The adjacent Pier 19 restaurant is one of the best places on the island to enjoy a quality seafood meal.

Another busy option for RVers is Isla Blanca Park (33174 State Park Rd. 100, 956/761-5494, www.cameroncountyparks.com, $25-40), referred to as the "crown jewel of the system," with 600 RV slots. Features include 1 mile (1.6 km) of pristine white sand and bright blue gulf water for swimming, surfing, and fishing.

You can pitch a tent or park an RV on the vast stretch of sand north of the major recreational activity. Officials caution that you should drive on the wet sand to avoid getting stuck in the soft tractionless powder farther from the surf. Bring your garbage back with you, as there are no trash cans in these remote areas, and take the "No trespassing" signs seriously.

INFORMATION AND SERVICES

The incredibly friendly and helpful people at the South Padre Island Convention & Visitors Bureau (600 Padre Blvd., 956/761-6433 or 800/767-2373, www.sopadre.com, Mon.-Fri. 8am-5pm, Sat.-Sun. 9am-5pm) will provide you with brochures, maps, and information about area attractions. Check with them about fishing, boating, and other ocean-based recreation.

GETTING THERE AND AROUND

The Brownsville South Padre Island International Airport (BRO, 700 S. Minnesota Ave., 956/542-4373, www.flybrownsville.com) is 27 miles (43 km) from South Padre and offers several American Eagle and United Airlines flights daily from Houston. Rental cars are available at the airport. The drive to South Padre from Dallas is nine hours, and from Houston or Austin approximately five hours.

Once on the island, you can ditch the car in favor of the city's reliable Island Metro (866/761-1025, www.spadre.com/thewave) transportation system; see the website for stops and schedules. The small buses typically operate 7am-9pm daily among local businesses and services, and late at night during spring break to shuttle impaired revelers. The belligerent scene on the ride back from the bar at 3am is one of the most insane experiences imaginable.

BACKGROUND

The Landscape

As the name implies, the Coastal Plains of Texas include the flatlands that run along the Gulf of Mexico and further inland, part of a larger physical region that starts by the Atlantic Ocean and extends to beyond the Rio Grande. As you drive to the coast from points north and west, the transition is apparent when rolling hills become vast panoramas with little topography.

The official geographic boundary of the Coastal Plains reaches beyond the obvious horizontal stretches near the coast all the way up to San Antonio, Austin, and eastward. A fault line in this area marks the boundary between plains and rocky terrain and is often used to separate Texas into "lowland" and "upland" regions.

In East Texas, the Coastal Plains are largely wooded and once were dense with pine forests before the trees were clear-cut in the early 1900s. Several national forests retain the thick wooded areas representing the western edge of the pine forests that extend across the southern United States.

GEOGRAPHY

The two main geographic areas in this region of the state are the Coastal Plains and Piney Woods. The plains extend westward along the coast from the Louisiana border, reaching inland up to 60 miles. Between the Sabine River (which marks the border between Texas and Louisiana) and Galveston Bay, the demarcation between the Coastal Plains and the Piney Woods is very noticeable, transitioning from towering trees to grassy scrublands.

The Piney Woods area extends about 100 miles into Texas from the east. Geographically, it's rather diverse, with soil ranging from sandy to rocky to mineral rich (iron deposits are mined near Lufkin). Even more significant are the oil fields in the ground beneath several notable sites in East Texas, including the East Texas Oil Field (Smith, Gregg, and Rusk counties) and most famously, Spindletop near Beaumont.

THE GULF COASTAL PLAINS

This area has the lowest elevation in Texas—less than 1,000 feet above sea level—and contains several bands of physical features and soil types formed by the weathering of underlying rock layers. As its name implies, the Gulf Coastal Plains include Texas's entire coastline and the mouths of most of the state's major rivers.

The Pine Belt comprises the eastern portion of this region along the Louisiana border. Pine trees, hay fields, and cattle pastures dominate the area, which is home to several national forests and the state's lumber industry. The region's natural features also include two major oil fields—Spindletop near Beaumont and the East Texas Oil Field.

West of the Pine Belt lie the Post Oak and Blackland Belts. These regions are known for their fertile soil and rolling prairies, and cotton remains the major crop. Settlers coveted the clear streams and quality soil in the Blackland Belt, which stretches east from Del Rio and northward through San Antonio, Austin, Waco, and Dallas. The prime agricultural conditions fueled Texas's growth, and the region retains some of the state's most densely populated areas.

Texas's southern tip is mostly comprised of the Rio Grande Plain, which includes the Lower Rio Grande Valley, known throughout the state simply as "the Valley." The Rio Grande Plain extends southward into Mexico for several hundred miles. Much of the area is covered with cacti, mesquite trees, and wild shrubs. Cattle production is also significant in the southern Rio Grande Plain, including on the famous King Ranch southwest of Corpus Christi. The Valley, meanwhile, thrives agriculturally, thanks to the rich delta soils and absence of freezing weather.

The region's Coastal Prairies stretch across the Gulf of Mexico coastline, reaching as far as 60 miles inland. The eastern portion of this region is thick with vegetation and supports crops ranging from rice to cotton. The southern portion contains grasslands and supports citrus fruits and vegetable farming.

ENVIRONMENTAL ISSUES

Texas probably isn't the first place that comes to mind when talk turns to environmental responsibility, but the state has its fair share of activists and defenders. One of Texas's chief environmental concerns is air pollution, particularly from vehicle emissions.

Since most of Texas's big cities sprawl into outlying wide-open spaces, cars are the preferred method of transportation. The state's steady increase in population has become problematic for environmentalists. Air pollution concerns in Texas's cosmopolitan areas have prompted ozone alerts, and Houston has been jockeying with Los Angeles for the coveted title of "smoggiest city."

Other troublesome issues for Texas environmental activists are water pollution and unsafe waste disposal. The Texas Commission on Environmental Quality, a state agency dedicated to protecting Texas's natural resources, oversees a multitude of monitoring efforts and public awareness campaigns designed to maintain control over potentially dangerous environmental hazards. The agency's air monitoring endeavors, water conservation districts, and efforts to keep tabs on industrial waste are commendable but don't always reach citizens at the local level.

That's where grassroots organizations like the Texas Campaign for the Environment come into play. The group's mission is to inform and mobilize Texans to maintain their quality of life and health. Their primary focus is improving trash and recycling policies to limit air, water, and soil pollution.

The indomitable Texas spirit is also represented in the environmental activism scene. PEER (Public Employees for Environmental Responsibility). The group's informative and entertaining website features information about wetlands, public health, and whistle blowers. The organization's goal is to educate the public about ways environmental hazards impact individual Texas residents.

Plants and Animals

The plant and animal kingdoms in Texas are a source of fascination. Thousands of plant varieties and more than 500 animal species call Texas home, and their compelling assortment is as diverse as the state's landscape. There's the expected (cacti, armadillos, and longhorn cattle) and the unexpected (pine forests, badgers, and cougars).

As is usually the case, the vegetation and wildlife in Houston and the Gulf Coast are tied to the geography and climate. Most of the region's mammals (aside from livestock) live in warmer, forested areas, and many exceptional birds and insects pass through on migratory routes. Hundreds of miles of coastline yields hundreds of varieties of marine animals and associated plants.

TREES AND SHRUBS

Like most vegetation, the abundance and assortment of trees and shrubs in this part of Texas is tied to the quality and quantity of soil and water. Compared to the arid conditions on the opposite side of the state, East Texas seems downright lush. Here, tree species include mesquite, live oak, and pecan, as well as colorfully named shrubs such as blackbrush, whitebrush, and greenbrier. Meanwhile, the forests consist mainly of pine trees, with a healthy mix of oak, elm, and hickory.

GRASSES

The region's grasses, though plentiful, aren't exactly intriguing. Although a fair number of native grasses have been lost to overgrazing, the dozens of remaining varieties in the area endure in spite of Texas's variable weather and topography. Tolerant species such as sideoats grama (the official state grass), Texas grama, buffalo grass, and Indian grass still provide meals for livestock while their hardiness also helps contain soil erosion.

The eastern half of the Coastal Plains are covered with thick grass, but the western half typically has short grass, which appeals to the thousands of grazing cattle in the area, many in the famous King Ranch (southwest of Corpus Christi). The ranch is also home to a good amount of prickly pear cactus, with its spiny paddles and occasional source of nourishment for (somewhat desperate) cattle and goats.

WILDFLOWERS

Wildflowers in the eastern portions of Texas are akin to fall foliage in New England. For most of March and April, nature puts on a brilliant display of iridescent blues, dazzling reds, and blinding yellows across fields and along highways in the region. One of the prime viewing areas is just west of Houston (in the Brenham area), where landscapes are painted with bluebonnets, Indian paintbrush, Mexican poppies, and black-eyed Susan.

These wildflowers have been around for more than 130 million years, and the different species are greatly affected by the differences in the state's soils (for instance, azaleas thrive in acidic East Texas soil but struggle in the chalky earth further west). This biodiversity results in a plethora of springtime wildflowers—nearly 400 varieties in all—and a majority are native species. The scenery is especially prime in East Texas, home to blooming azaleas, yellow jasmine, dogwoods, and wisteria.

MAMMALS

Nearly 150 animal species traverse Texas's terrain, yet only two are emblematic of the Lone Star State. Texas's official small mammal is the armadillo (fun fact: female armadillos always have four pups, and all four are always the same sex), and the state's official large mammal is the Texas longhorn. Mention "mammals" in the Houston and Gulf Coast region, and you may get a few empty stares. But actually quite a few mammals live in this vast expanse of Texas, from the standard variety to the unexpected.

The most interesting mammal by far is the bottlenose dolphin. These curious creatures are common along the Gulf Coast, and many small businesses in the area offer dolphin tours, allowing you to venture out onto the water with an experienced guide who knows where the dolphins tend to spend their time. You can see them for free if you happen to be taking the ferry from Port Aransas to the mainland since the dolphins follow the boat to munch on the fish that are dispersed in its wake.

Slightly less exciting mammals in the region include river otters, which aren't quite as plentiful but can be a source of entertainment if you're canoeing or hiking along one of the rivers outside of Houston. Of the four-legged variety mammals, the occasional coyote may enter the woods outside suburban homes and even a few javelina in the southern sections of the coastline, mostly in search of prickly pear cactus on ranchlands.

BIRDS

Eastern Texas is a destination and crossing point for myriad bird species during migratory seasons. It's also home to hundreds of native varieties. More kinds of birds (approximately 600) are in Texas than any other state— primarily because of its south-central location. Feathered pals from the eastern and western part of the country occupy this region's air space, and international travelers cross the Mexican border, drawing avid birdwatchers to the state from across the United States.

Texas birds can be grouped into five major categories: permanent residents (mockingbirds, roadrunners, screech owls), winter residents (common loons and terns, red-bellied woodpeckers), summer residents (purple martins, yellow-breasted chats, orchard orioles), migrants (snow geese, scarlet tanagers, various sandpipers), and accidentals (greater flamingos, red-footed boobies, yellow-billed loons).

Spring is the prime time for birdwatching. Serious and amateur birders from across the country visit the Gulf Coast and Rio Grande Valley to catch a glimpse of migrating and native bird species. Pelicans, spoonbills, egrets, and herons are fairly easy to spot. Those looking for a unique birding experience can join a boat tour to spy whooping cranes. Boasting a seven-foot wingspan, the massive white birds were nearly extinct before efforts were made to revive the species. Now more than 100 spend their winters in the Aransas National Wildlife Refuge on the Gulf Coast.

MARINE LIFE

An amazing variety of marine animals live in the Gulf of Mexico, home to thousands of fish and shellfish that depend on the coast's diverse habitat for food and shelter. These environs are typically categorized by five distinct water areas—salt marshes, coastal bays, jetties, nearshore waters, and the Gulf of Mexico.

Fish and shrimp enter salt marshes looking for food or for a place to lay their eggs. They're joined by several species of crabs (fiddler, hermit, and stone), snails, mussels, and worms. Coastal bays and beaches are home to two types of jellyfish, the Portuguese man-of-war (stay away from this purplish baggy creature with the poisonous blue tentacles) and the relatively harmless cabbagehead, which looks like its namesake and are occasionally used by dolphins as toy balls.

The beach area also supports oysters, spotted sea trout, and several species of catfish. Jetties, which are used to prevent ship channels from piling up with sand and silt, consist of large stones that provide shelter and food for a wide range of sea life, including sea anemones, urchins, crabs, grouper, and sea trout. Artificial reefs (stone rubble, old ships, oil rigs) make nearshore waters habitable for mussels, shrimp, crabs, and a host of other animals, including the fish that feed on them (tarpon, kingfish, and others).

The Gulf of Mexico is home to some of Texas's heaviest hitters. Great barracuda and hammerhead, lemon, and bull sharks devour smaller varieties like bluefish, striped bass, and tuna. When the currents and temperatures are just right, tropical species such as parrotfish, angelfish, and spiny lobsters also visit the Gulf waters.

REPTILES

Snakes slither across much of Texas's surface, and the state's range of reptiles is rather impressive. Texas is home to 16 varieties of poisonous snakes (including 11 types of rattlesnakes), which can be extremely hazardous to hikers and campers. Other dangerous snakes include cottonmouth, copperheads, and Texas coral snakes.

Snakebites from these varieties require a few basic first-aid techniques if medical care is not immediately available. The American Red Cross suggests washing the bite with soap and water and keeping the bitten area immobilized and lower than the heart. Equally as important is avoiding popular remedy misconceptions: Do not apply hot or cold packs, do not attempt to suck the poison out, and do not drink any alcohol or use any medication.

Texas is also home to hundreds of nonvenomous snake species, some of which mimic their poisonous counterparts. The Texas bull snake realistically imitates a rattlesnake, all the way down to the rattling sound, and the milk snake and coral snake look disturbingly alike, with the same colors but in different orders. A time-honored Texas adage helps differentiate the two: Red and yellow, kill a fellow (the coral snake has red next to yellow stripes); red and black, friend of Jack (the milk snake has red next to black stripes).

Not to be overlooked are Texas's other distinctive reptiles. The official state reptile is the Texas horned lizard (charmingly referred to as the horny toad), which is primarily found in West Texas. The state's other noteworthy reptiles include alligators, sea turtles, geckos, and spinytail iguanas.

INSECTS AND BUTTERFLIES

Nearly 100,000 different kinds of pesky insects buzz around Americans' heads and ankles, and a third of those bugs have been found in Texas. The Lone Star State proudly claims to have more different kinds of insects than any other state.

Texas also has more butterfly species than any other state. Its 400 varieties number more than half the butterfly species in the United States and Canada. The recognizable monarch butterfly makes its annual migratory flight through Texas en route to its wintering grounds in Mexico. The southward flight in late summer and fall can be quite a spectacle, when monarchs fill the air and gather on trees by the thousands.

Texas's insects are just as numerous but not nearly as charming. Most of these winged and antennaed creatures are ecologically beneficial, but the two insects that creep immediately to most Texans' minds are the bothersome mosquito and the squirm-inducing cockroach.

AMPHIBIANS

Like most living things in this region, amphibians are well represented on account of the tremendous diversity in climate and temperature. Frogs, toads, and salamanders are abundant in the relatively wet habitats of the eastern third of the state. Camping near lakes and streams in this area offers visitors an audio sampler of the various croaks and calls of the region's native frog and toad species.

One species worthy of special note (mainly for its subject-appropriate name) is the Gulf Coast Toad. Ranging from two to four inches in size, this local amphibian can be found in open grasslands, wooded areas, residential backyards, and of course, along the shoreline of the Gulf Coast.

Climate

Most of Texas has two main seasons—a hot summer that lasts from approximately May through October and a winter that starts in November and usually lasts until March. Things are slightly different along the Gulf Coast, however, as winter is not really a factor.

Houston can get cold, and it has had a few extremely rare instances of snow. But it mostly gets cloudy during the traditional winter months, and even then, 70-degree days are not uncommon. Further south along the Gulf Coast, the experience of colder weather is even more rare. That's why so many Northerners flock to the region from November through March, comprising a sizable segment of the population known as Winter Texans.

A weather map in winter tells the story of Texas's variable climate in a visually stunning way—the entire spectrum of colors is represented across the state. The rainbow of Texas's diverse climate is a revealing diagram, from the lower Gulf Coast's balmy 90°F reds to icy 20°F blues in the Panhandle.

The average rainfall in the Houston area and East Texas typically exceeds 56 inches annually while parts of West Texas typically receive less than 8 inches each year. One final note of interest: Brownsville, at the southern tip of Texas's Gulf Coast, has no measurable snowfall on record.

CLIMATE REGIONS

Scientists typically divide Texas into three meteorological areas—modified marine (aka subtropics), continental, and mountain. The destinations in this book are mainly located in the subtropics region, which is primarily affected by tropical airflow from the Gulf of Mexico. As a result, Houston and the Gulf Coast are well known for having a humid climate noted for its warm summers.

DANGEROUS WEATHER

Even the weather is extreme in Texas. Menacing hurricanes, treacherous tornadoes, and dangerous floods can strike at any time, and they wreak their havoc swiftly before clear skies and calm conditions return. Fortunately, Texans have learned from previous atrocities, resulting in evacuation plans and safety procedures. Though most of these events are seasonal, there's an unpredictable nature to Texas's nature, so visitors should be prepared for potential flash floods.

Historically, hurricanes have hit Texas's Gulf Coast about once every decade, usually in September or October. Most Gulf Coast communities have evacuation plans in place, along with reinforced buildings and homes to brace against the torrential winds. Many seaside structures are also raised on piers to prevent damage from the crashing waves during a tropical storm.

In the past decade, however, the hurricane activity in the gulf has been more frequent and severe. In addition to the devastation brought by Hurricanes Katrina and

Rita, Hurricane Ike slammed into Galveston Island on September 13, 2008, leaving an enormous swath of destruction in its wake. Ike completely leveled several nearby communities, and its 110 mph winds ripped apart hotels, office buildings, and countless homes in Galveston, Houston, and the surrounding area. Of the nearly 7,000 documented historic buildings in Galveston, upward of 1,500 were seriously damaged. Devastation struck again in 2017, when Hurricane Harvey walloped the city of Rockport near Corpus Christi with 130mph winds. The associated storms resulted in unprecedented flooding in Houston.

Things were quite different a century ago. Galveston experienced the most destructive storm in U.S. history (before Hurricanes Katrina, Rita, and Ike) in 1900, when a hurricane left at least 6,000 dead and leveled most of the city. A storm of equal intensity hit Galveston in 1915, but the city was prepared with its new seawall. The death toll was a comparatively low 275.

Texas also lies in the path of Tornado Alley, with its central corridor running from the Panhandle north through Kansas. The state's worst tornado on record struck downtown Waco in 1953, killing 114 people, injuring 597, and destroying or damaging more than 1,000 homes and buildings. In 1997, a mile-wide tornado (as in *one mile wide*) wreaked havoc on the Central Texas town of Jarrell, leaving only the concrete slabs of dozens of homes in its wake.

Floods have also taken their toll on Texas. Thunderstorms are a major event—they typically come barreling in from the west, spewing lightning and firing occasional hailstones everywhere in their path. Appearing as massive, intimidating red blobs on the radar screen, they furiously dump heavy sheets of rain on Texas's lands, leaving saturated fields and overflowing rivers and streams in their wake.

One of the most destructive rainstorms in Texas history occurred in 1921, when floods in Central Texas killed 215 people. San Antonio was sitting under nearly nine feet of water, and 36 inches of rain fell north of Austin in just 18 hours (a U.S. record).

History

No place has a sense of place quite like Texas, and that sentiment is indelibly tied to the state's fascinating past. Texans are proud of their history, and for good reason. The state was once its own country, and many modern-day residents would likely welcome a return to the idea of isolationism. Above all, there's something reverential about the pride Texans take in their heritage, from the Native American contribution of the word *tejas* (meaning friends), to the state's nearly 400-year-old Spanish mission buildings, to the aforementioned Republic of Texas, to the role Texas played in the Civil War, to its ranching and oil heritage.

Being proud of what a state represents is somewhat distinctive to Texas. Not to take away anything from other states' history, but a term like "Rhode Island pride" or the concept of a proud Idaho heritage just doesn't resonate the way Texas Pride does. It's a badge of honor, and the state's rough-and-tumble past makes it a deserved title.

Everyone knows about the Alamo, but those who set out to discover Texas's dynamic heritage will encounter fascinating stories, like the 4,000-year-old Native American pictographs in a rock shelter along the Rio Grande, the discovery of the 1686 Gulf Coast shipwreck of French explorer La Salle, the influence of Mexican *vaqueros* on Texas's cowboys, and life in an oil boomtown in the 1930s. And that's just scraping the surface.

PREHISTORIC ERA

Depending on the source, Texas's prehistoric past can be traced as far back as 13,000 years. That's 11,000 BC. Most archaeologists and historians divide the state's prehistoric era into three periods: Paleo-Indian, Archaic, and Late Prehistoric.

The Paleo-Indian period is significant for containing references to the earliest known inhabitants of the state (circa 9200 BC). Archaeologists have discovered numerous distinctive Clovis fluted points (a type of arrowhead) from this era, which were sometimes used for hunting mammoth.

The longest span of Texas's prehistory falls under the Archaic period (circa 6000 BC-AD 700). It's noted for the changes in projectile points and tools, and the introduction of grinding implements for food preparation. A significant weapon used during the Archaic period was a spear-throwing device known as an atlatl.

The bow and arrow were introduced during Texas's Late Prehistoric period (AD 700 to historic times). Pottery is present during this period among the hunters and gatherers in Central, South, and coastal Texas.

Bison hunting was also very important to people living in most regions of the state's present-day boundaries.

NATIVE AMERICANS

Historians have identified hundreds of Native American groups in Texas. The validity of their naming is problematic, however, because explorers used different languages (mainly Spanish, French, and English) to record what they heard of the newly "discovered" tribes they encountered.

Regardless, most historians agree that European diseases decimated Texas's native people. Anthropologist John C. Ewers identified at least 30 major epidemics (mostly smallpox and cholera) that wiped out as much as 95 percent of the state's Native Americans between 1528 and 1890. Until then, the four major tribes playing roles in Texas history were the Apache, Caddo, Comanche, and Kiowa.

The Apaches arrived in the area that would become Texas circa AD 1200. They were a nomadic tribe subsisting almost completely on buffalo, dressing in buffalo skins and living in tents made of tanned and greased hides. The Apaches were a powerful tribe that raided most groups they encountered. Eventually, their aggressive behavior turned their neighbors into enemies, and the Apaches had fled before the Comanches entered the region.

The Caddo were a collection of about 30 distinct groups, including the Tejas Indians, from whom Texas got its name, who had a similar language, political structure, and religious beliefs. Based in the current-day East Texas Piney Woods, the Caddo were mainly agricultural, living in permanent villages (as opposed to being nomadic). They weren't especially warlike, except for minor territorial conflicts they had with smaller nearby tribes over hunting grounds.

The Comanches were known as exceptional equestrians who played a prominent role in Texas frontier history in the 1700s and 1800s. They occupied much of what is now North, Central, and West Texas. Because of their trading skills, the Comanches controlled much of the region's commerce by bartering horses, buffalo products, and even captives for weapons and food. They lived in portable tepees constructed of tanned buffalo hide stretched over as many as 18 large poles.

The Kiowas acquired horses, slaves, and guns from the Spanish and eventually evolved a nomadic, warring lifestyle until they became one of the most feared tribes in the region that became Texas. By the late 1700s, the Kiowas had made a lasting peace with the Comanches and continued to live in the area until peacefully joining the Comanches with the Southern Cheyennes and Arapahos.

Before Texas became a state in 1845, most of the Native American groups were either eradicated by European settlers or moved to reservations in present-day Oklahoma. As a result, only three reservations currently exist in Texas today. They are the Alabama-Coushatta near Houston, the Tigua east of El Paso, and the Kickapoo along the Rio Grande between Del Rio and Laredo.

EUROPEAN EXPLORATION AND SETTLEMENT

The arrival (via shipwreck) of Spanish explorer Alvar Nunez Cabeza de Vaca in 1528 was one of Texas's first contacts with the Old World. His subsequent trek across the land that would become the Lone Star State offered Europeans some of the first clues about this newfound foreign region.

By 1685, the French were in on the action, dispatching explorer Robert Cavelier, Sieur de La Salle to find the mouth of the Mississippi River. He missed it by a long shot, ultimately wrecking his ship *La Belle* in a bay between present-day Houston and Corpus Christi. More than 200 years later, the Texas Historical Commission discovered the contents and remains of *La Belle,* which offered a rare glimpse at the material culture of a 17th-century New World colony in the form of glass trade beads, dinnerware, gunflints, and even a human skeleton.

By the early 1700s, the Spanish had solidified their presence in the region with several new mission buildings (the Alamo being one of them) used primarily to "civilize" the area's Native American tribes by converting them to Christianity. It didn't work as well as they'd hoped. By the early 19th century, European diseases had decimated most of the state's Native Americans, and many tribes had mixed in with other cultural groups, rendering the missions' objective obsolete.

Around this same time, the first wave of Germans arrived in Texas. Word spread quickly about Texas's bountiful land and ideal climate (perhaps they visited in springtime), prompting thousands of Germans to take root along rivers and streams in the state's fertile prairies and scenic hills.

THE REPUBLIC OF TEXAS AND STATEHOOD

An 1835 skirmish between colonists and Mexicans over ownership of a cannon is generally considered the opening battle of the Texas Revolution; subsequently, a provisional government was established in 1836 when delegates adopted the Texas Declaration of Independence on March 2 (which remains a state holiday). Texas's most famous battle occurred a week later with the 13-day siege of the Alamo. Mexican troops led by Gen. Antonio Lopez de Santa Anna eventually killed the remaining Texas defenders.

Later that month, about 350 Texan prisoners were executed by order of Santa Anna at Goliad. With these setbacks in mind, the Texans, led by Sam Houston, defeated Santa Anna's Mexican army on April 21 with rallying cries of "Remember the Alamo!" and "Remember Goliad!" Houston reported 630 Mexican troops killed, with only nine Texan lives lost. The revolution's end became official in May 1836 when both sides signed the Treaties of Velasco.

A year later, the United States, France, and England officially recognized the new Republic of Texas, and plots of land were soon sold in the republic's new capital, named for Stephen F. Austin, the state's preeminent colonist. In 1845, Texas became a U.S. state after Congress passed an annexing resolution, which was accepted by the republic's Texas Constitutional Convention and overwhelmingly supported by Texas voters.

From 1846 to 1848, Texas and Mexico engaged in a boundary battle known as the U.S.-Mexican War, which ultimately established the current international boundary. A decade later, the federal government moved Native American tribes in West and Central Texas to Indian Territory (now Oklahoma).

THE CIVIL WAR AND RECONSTRUCTION

Texas struggled with complexities during the Civil War. Some people supported the Union, including Governor Sam Houston, who refused to take an oath of allegiance to the Confederacy. It cost him his office. For the most part, however, Texans identified with the rest of the southern United States, and in early 1861 that support became official when Texas seceded from the Union and became the seventh state accepted by the provisional Confederate States of America government.

After four years of border skirmishes, Gulf Coast naval battles, and prisoner of war camps, Texas troops marked the true end of the Civil War with a battle near Brownsville, more than a month after the war officially ended (due to the time involved for the news to reach Texas). In June, it was announced that slavery had been abolished, an event still commemorated today during Juneteenth festivals in African American communities statewide.

Much of Texas's history during the late 1800s centers around the arrival of the railroads, which put towns on and off the map depending on their routes. Cattle rustling was an important part of Texas's commerce and identity before railroads took over the responsibility of moving cattle northward. Texas's development was made possible by the railroads, and they continued to sustain the local economy for decades since so many areas of the state still needed railroad service, including the lower Rio Grande Valley, the South Plains, the Panhandle, and West Texas.

THE 20TH CENTURY AND BEYOND

The 20th century kicked off with a boom—a 100-foot oil gusher blew in at Spindletop near Beaumont in 1901, boosting Texas into the petroleum age. Oil wells would be discovered for several decades, turning small communities into boomtowns with tens of thousands of wildcatters and roughnecks arriving overnight to work on the rigs.

The Wild West arrived in West Texas when the Mexican civil war (1911-1920) spilled across the border; as a result, supply raids and refugee harboring became common occurrences. The notorious Mexican general Pancho Villa was involved with some of these skirmishes.

By the 1950s and 1960s, Texas was gaining a reputation for its intellectual resources, resulting in the Dallas-based development of the integrated circuit (used in semiconductors and electronics) and the opening of the National Aeronautics and Space Administration's Manned Spacecraft Center in Houston.

In one of the darker moments of Texas and U.S. history, President John F. Kennedy was assassinated in Dallas. It marked the end of the optimism of the nation under the Kennedy administration and ushered in a new president—Texan Lyndon B. Johnson. Johnson would go on to play a major role in advancing the country's civil rights movement. The final two decades of the 20th century were notable for two additional Texans being elected to the U.S. presidency: George H. W. Bush and his son George W. Bush.

Government and Economy

GOVERNMENT

Texas was annexed to the United States as the 28th state on December 29, 1845. From Reconstruction (the late 1800s) through the early 1960s, the Democratic Party dominated Texas politics. Keep in mind, the Democrats of those days differed considerably from the current political party. For almost a century, Texas Democrats consisted mainly of white conservatives, who prevailed in almost all statewide elections.

A Texas-worthy phrase was used during this era to describe the especially dedicated party members: "Yellow Dog Democrats" were the state's die-hard partisan loyalists who would vote for a yellow dog if it ran on the Democratic ticket. The phrase is now used to describe any Democratic loyalist, although the recent dominance of Republicans in Texas is rendering the term nearly obsolete.

Texas's bicameral legislature is comprised of 31 Senate members who serve for four years, and the House of Representatives, with 150 members elected for two-year terms. The legislature meets for its regular session in the spring of odd-numbered years, but the governor may convene a special session for the legislators to address particular issues. The governor of Texas is elected to a four-year term in November of even-numbered, non-presidential election years.

Texas is divided into a whopping 254 counties that average nearly 1,000 square miles in size. West Texas's Brewster County is especially enormous—at 6,169 square miles, it's roughly the size of Delaware and Rhode Island combined.

ECONOMY

Cotton, cattle, and crude (oil)—Texas's venerable "Three Cs" dominated the state's agricultural and economic development until the mid-20th century, and these land-based resources continue to support much of the state's wealth. Other factors contributing to Texas's economy are various industries not exclusive to the Lone Star State, such as retailing, wholesaling, banking, insurance, and construction.

Many national corporate headquarters have relocated to Texas (especially to the midcontinental location of Dallas), and petroleum companies continue to search for new sources of energy to provide fuel. In addition, Houston is home to many federal air installations and the NASA Space Center, while Austin is home to Dell Computers and other esteemed high-tech companies. Tourism has also become a major business, particularly in San Antonio, and Texas has become a leader in the areas of medicine and surgery.

AGRICULTURE

Cattle and cotton remain staples of Texas's agricultural economy. The state's wide-open spaces allowed both commodities to spread freely when settlers arrived in the mid-1800s, and Texas's remaining abundance of available land continues to make it the most important cattle-raising state in the country.

Nearly all of the state's 254 counties derive more revenue from cattle than any other agricultural commodity; those that don't almost always rank cattle second in importance. Cattle dominates Texas's livestock production, contributing approximately 70 percent of the state's livestock and products sales. And if those aren't enough agricultural accolades, consider this: Texas ranks first nationally in production of cattle, beef cattle, sheep, lamb, wool, goats, and mohair.

Cotton, meanwhile, became a prominent crop due to the immigration of settlers from the Deep South, who continued their plantation system of agriculture when they arrived in Texas. Cotton production grew steadily after 1900, and the crop became a major economic factor when suitable varieties were developed for the West Texas climate. Since that time, Texas has led all states in cotton production virtually every year, and it provides approximately one-quarter of the country's cotton supply.

In total value of farm crops, Texas has consistently ranked in the top five among the states since the mid-20th century and has been a leading producer of grain sorghums, peanuts (groundnuts), and rice. Incidentally, nearly all of the mohair produced in the United States comes from Texas's Angora goats.

MANUFACTURING AND INDUSTRY

Texas's manufacturing roots lie with its agricultural processing—cotton gins, cottonseed mills, meatpacking plants, flour mills, oil field equipment, and canning plants. These days, the state's largest employment sector is categorized as the "trade, transportation, and utilities industry," which includes jobs in retail, wholesale, and finance.

Jobs in the petroleum, construction, and service industries are also typically steady across the state. Texas's top exported products are chemicals, petrochemicals, and transportation equipment. The state's remarkable number of exports is attributed to its proximity to Mexico, which receives nearly half of Texas's products. Texas is also responsible for a large number of U.S. exports to Mexico (approximately 50 percent).

PETROLEUM

Oil changed everything for Texas. It transformed the state from a backwoods frontier to an industrial giant. In January 1901, a gusher blew in at Spindletop near Beaumont, and the Texas oil boom erupted into the nation's consciousness. Thirty years later, an even more significant event occurred—the discovery of the enormous East Texas Oil Field. Within two years, 5,600 wells had been drilled near the cities of Kilgore and Longview, and 25,000 wells were in place by 1938.

Oil became the basis for Texas's mammoth petrochemical industry and provided the funding to develop the state's educational and highway systems. On the flip side, a massive drop in oil prices in the early 1980s resulted in a decline in Texas's economy.

Regardless, oil and natural gas remain the state's most valuable minerals, contributing nearly 20 percent of the country's oil production and 30 percent of its gas production in recent years. Texas leads all other states in oil and natural gas production. It also ranks first in oil-refining capacity. In 2017, Texas accounted for 37 percent of the country's crude oil production and 24 percent of the nation's marketed natural gas production.

TRAVEL

The state's official travel slogan aptly captures its allure: "Texas, It's Like a Whole Other Country." More than 72 million people from out of state visit Texas annually. International travelers account for approximately 10 percent of Texas's total visitor spending.

The five countries with the highest visitation numbers are Mexico, Canada, the United Kingdom, Germany, and France. The top five destination cities for out-of-state visitors are Dallas-Fort Worth, Houston, various "rural Texas destinations," San Antonio, and Austin. Among the top tourist sites include the Alamo, the San Antonio River Walk, the Magnolia properties in Waco, The Texas State Capitol in Austin, and the Six Flags Over Texas amusement park near Dallas.

People and Culture

PEOPLE

The people of Texas equally reflect and defy all stereotypes associated with their dynamic nature. For every good ol' boy set in his ways, there's a progressive genius building her web-based empire. For every brash oilman making millions, there's a humble educator affecting lives. Intense football coaches coexist peacefully with environmental activists.

Like anywhere else, people in Texas have their differences, but there's one thing that transcends obstacles and is unique to this state—the common bond of being Texan. Not that it solves all problems, but most Texans look kindly upon their fellow citizens and genuinely display the spirit of Southern hospitality. It's infectious—"Y'all come back" becomes a true expression of kindness rather than a silly stereotype.

Transplants from the northern and eastern United States may initially be taken aback by random strangers in the grocery store commenting on their purchases, but they'll later find themselves doing the same thing. Offers of assistance are genuine rather than obligatory, and people make direct eye contact when they mutter a polite "Howdy."

There are many ways to categorize Texans—by age, ethnicity, religion, income level, etc.—but labels don't capture the soul of the state's residents, who aptly represent the character of the word *friend* in the origins of the word *Texas*.

POPULATION

Texas's rate of population growth has exceeded the nation's in every decade since Texas became a state (1845), and recent population increases have been substantial. Population has more than doubled in the past 25 years, from roughly 11.2 million to nearly 29 million. Estimates based on recent growth rates suggest the state is surging by nearly 500,000 people annually.

Texas is the second most populous state in the U.S. and it's getting bigger, leading the nation in population growth. According to the most recent estimates by the U.S. Census Bureau, the population of Texas increased by nearly 2 million or 7.2 percent over roughly the past decade.

Texas boasts several accents within its borders, from the slowly stretched-out East Texas drawl, to border-hopping Spanglish known as Tex-Mex, to the tight twang of the Panhandle and West Texas.

Even though Texans like to brag about their accomplishments, they can't take credit for the Southern accent that prevails below the Mason-Dixon Line. However, residents of Houston and the Gulf Coast region can claim some of the spice that makes the Southern dialect unique. For the most part, the following examples are found in rural areas of the state, though you'll occasionally hear a "yessir" or "fixin' to" in a downtown urban environment.

Let's start with the obvious: "Howdy, y'all." It's the quintessential Texas/Southern phrase, usually invoked by Northerners with a mocking twang. The truth is, Texans actually say these words often, but usually not together. "Howdy" is typically muttered as a polite greeting as opposed to a loud welcome, and its use as a friendly salutation is one of many cultural traditions taught at Texas A&M University. As for "y'all," it just makes sense—why refer to a group of people (women and children, in particular) as "you guys"? The common Texas phrase "all y'all" takes things to whole new level.

Rural Texans also use "sir" and "ma'am" regularly, just not in a formal or subservient way. It's common to hear men respond to each other with a simple "yessir" or "nosir," and it's just plain polite to express appreciation to someone—a police officer, fellow pedestrian, or store clerk—with a simple "thank you, ma'am." Up North, these terms take on military or old maid connotations, but in Texas it's just being cordial.

Like other Southerners, Texans of all ages refer to their parents as "mother" and "daddy." It's somewhat strange to hear a grown man talk about his "daddy's" influence, but it's charming, nevertheless.

Another Texas phrase that gets the Yankees giggling is "fixin' to." It's a handy term that's quintessentially Southern, indicating someone is getting ready to do something without fully committing to carrying out the task ("I'm fixin' to pay those bills soon"). Incidentally, the "fixin" also refers to food in Texas, garnishes in particular. If you order a burger or barbecue plate with all the fixins, you'll get onions, pickles, peppers, and any number of sides or sauces piled on the plate.

Speaking of food, occasional confusion arises when Texans refer to "dinner" and "supper." These are interchangeable in other parts of the country, but around here, "dinner" can mean lunch, while "supper" almost always refers to the evening meal.

Other examples of Lone Star speak are evident in the pronunciation of words. You can tell a Texan by the way they emphasize the first syllable in words like **umbrella** (UM-brella), **insurance** (IN-surance), and **display** (DIS-play). Others are subtler, like the tendency to flatten out the vowel sounds in words like **mail** (mell), **wheel** (well). Sometimes, entire letters disappear, like the L in "help" ("can I hep ya?").

Finally, you'll occasionally hear Texans using traditional rural sayings like "over yonder" (over there), "pitch a hissy fit" (a dramatic reaction), and even "gaddum" and its derivative "dadgum." Fortunately, Texans are such a friendly bunch, they won't pitch a hissy fit if you sound like a dadgum Yankee.

Interestingly enough, this growth has been anything but uniform, with some counties in West Texas losing population and others around Dallas and Austin growing by more than 60 percent. In fact, recent demographic reports associated reveal that nearly 85 percent of the state's population lives east of the I-35 corridor, which stretches north-south from Dallas to Laredo.

ETHNICITY

Since the mid-1800s, most Texas residents have been of European descent, but for the first time in state history, their numbers are no longer the majority. Currently, about 41 percent of the population is of northern European ancestry; roughly 38 percent are Hispanic, and approximately 12 percent are African American.

The healthy pace of Texas's increased population is largely due to international immigration, which represented more than half of the state's population growth in recent years. Of note is the rapid growth of foreign-born residents in Texas's major metro areas compared to border metro cities.

According to recent reports, Hispanics accounted for two-thirds of Texas's growth over the past decade and now represent about 38 percent of the state's total population. Also of interest is the considerably younger age of the state's Hispanic population (approximately 25 years for the median age versus 38 for Anglos). The effect on Texas's population is a statewide median age of 34.

RELIGION

For the most part, Texas is a devoutly religious state, with Christianity dominating the spiritual scene. Although it mirrors national trends showing slightly declining congregation numbers, residents in the rural areas of the state remain committed churchgoers. In fact, a 15-county area in Texas's southeastern Panhandle is designated as a candidate for the "buckle of the Bible Belt," a wide band of the entire U.S. South where a majority of people identify themselves as Baptists.

The two primary religious groups in Texas are Baptist (approximately 22 percent) and Catholic (roughly 21 percent). The percentages are far lower for other religions—Muslim, Hindu, Buddhist, Jewish, and other faiths—which are mostly located in the state's urban areas. Texas's big cities also had the largest number of people claiming not to be affiliated with a religious group.

LANGUAGE

English speakers in Texas account for 65 percent of the population, with Spanish running a distant, yet still notable second (29 percent). People speak Vietnamese and German in a few small pockets of the state, but for the most part, it's Spanish and English (and a few interesting varieties of the two).

A fair number of Hispanics in South Texas speak an unofficial language known as Tex-Mex, which combines Spanish and English words without any rigid guidelines determining when to use each. It's a distinctive regional practice, resulting from an impulsive tendency to toss in an English or Spanish word when the translation isn't immediately on the tip of the tongue, and it's most evident on Tejano radio stations in Corpus Christi and the Lower Rio Grande Valley, where rapid-fire DJs pepper their announcements in Spanish with random yet instantly recognizable English words.

Learning to speak Texan is an entirely different endeavor. Though the dialect sounds Southern on the surface, there are distinct variations in different parts of the state. In East Texas, vowels are more drawn out, and the slower cadence includes inflections of the Deep South. People in West Texas, meanwhile, speak with more of a tight twang. Pronunciation of the word *Texas* is an example—in East Texas, it can sound like "Tay-ux-us," and in West Texas it's often pronounced "Tix-is."

Just to make things interesting, young adults in the state's metropolitan areas tend to combine elements of their own Texas dialect with California's. Dallas-born actor Owen

Wilson's accent is the quintessential example of this style of speech.

ARTS AND CULTURE

One of the specialty license plates available to Texans features a bold image of the state flag with the phrase "State of the Arts" at the bottom. This motto might not be the first attribute people associate with Texas (California and New York immediately jump to mind), but it's absolutely befitting of the Lone Star State.

Hundreds of world-renowned writers, artists, musicians, and actors call Texas home, and their influences and styles are as far-reaching as the stars in the West Texas sky. Having 4 of the country's 10 largest cities also helps maximize exposure for artists and art aficionados. Premier exhibits and tours always include Texas on their schedule, and the dynamic magnetism of the state itself serves as an inspiration for a diverse mixture of creative endeavors. Anywhere that can claim Pulitzer Prize-winning (and Oscar-winning) writer Larry McMurtry and alternative rockers the Butthole Surfers is bound to be brimming with eclectic culture.

LITERATURE

Larry McMurtry, famed author of the cattle-drive epic *Lonesome Dove* and drama *Terms of Endearment,* as well as screenplay writer for *The Last Picture Show* and *Brokeback Mountain,* is emblematic of the literary state of Texas. He approaches his craft with the sweeping majesty of one of his favorite subjects—the mythic Old West, with Texas as a focal point.

Another celebrated literary genre in Texas is folklore, and J. Frank Dobie (1888-1964) was and still is considered the foremost figure in the field.

Dobie painted fascinating portraits of cowboys, cattlemen, hunters, and countless other Texas characters and critters. From an intellectual perspective, many Texans cite Pulitzer Prize-winning journalist, essayist, short story writer, and novelist Katherine Anne Porter (1890-1980) as the state's most accomplished writer. She is perhaps best known for her acute insight about complex subjects in her works *Pale Horse, Pale Rider* (1939) and *Ship of Fools* (1961).

An essential book about Texas by a non-Texan is H. G. Bissinger's *Friday Night Lights: A Town, A Team, A Dream* (1990), which accurately and compellingly chronicles the positive and negative aspects of Texas's passion for high school football. Texas journalist Molly Ivins (1944-2007) gained national fame as a sharp and scathing critic of the country's right-wing political movement in the early part of the 21st century. President George W. Bush was a frequent Ivins target, and her book *Bushwhacked: Life in George W. Bush's America,* was a success in liberal enclaves of the United States and especially her hometown of Austin. The latest legendary tome is 2013's The Son by Philipp Meyer. This incredible story, a finalist for the Pulitzer Prize in 2014, chronicles 200 years of Texas history through the fictional account of a powerful Texas family. Texas can even make a (partial) claim to acclaimed writer George Saunders, an Amarillo native, whose 2017 novel Lincoln in the Bardo is considered by many a modern-day classic.

MUSIC

Texas has perhaps the most compelling music legacy in the country, and many of the state's artists have become influential figures in popular

Texas is immortalized in song perhaps more than any other state. Several sources list nearly 100 tunes with **Texas** (or **Lone Star** or Texas cities) in the title.

With all the options to choose from, it's unfortunate the official state song, "Texas, Our Texas," is unrecognizable by most people, including some Texans. Adopted by the legislature after being selected in a statewide competition, the song features inspirational (and poorly written) lyrics with simple rhymes like "all hail the mighty state" paired with "so wonderful, so great."

Our country's national anthem is rather difficult to sing due to its extremely wide tonal range and occasionally confusing lyrics, so Texas's official state song should be something recognizable and easy on the vocal chords. Some Texans have even proposed adopting an updated official tune to rouse the troops at athletic competitions and school or government events.

There are plenty to choose from, including iconic classics such as "Deep in the Heart of Texas," made famous by Gene Autry (and Pee Wee Herman); "The Yellow Rose of Texas," as performed by Bob Wills; Ernest Tubb's version of "Waltz Across Texas"; or even the fiddle-filled old-school dance craze "Cotton Eyed Joe." Collegiately patriotic Texans will insist their school fight songs are the most iconic Texas tunes, particularly "The Eyes of Texas" (University of Texas) and the "Aggie War Hymn" (Texas A&M University).

The 1970s were a golden time for Texas-themed songs, particularly in the country music scene. Though the following options haven't attained "official song" consideration status, they're known well enough in pop culture as ambassadors of Texas mystique. Highlights include Willie Nelson's adaptation of "San Antonio Rose," Marty Robbins's "(Out in the West Texas town of) El Paso," "Streets of Laredo" by Buck Owens, "Luckenbach, Texas (Back to The Basics of Love)" by Waylon Jennings, Glen Campbell's "Galveston," ZZ Top's "La Grange," and a couple of George Strait classics, "Amarillo by Morning" and "All My Exes Live in Texas." Unfortunately, there's also Alabama's hit, "If You're Gonna Play in Texas (You Gotta Have a Fiddle in the Band)."

The Texas-themed songs haven't been quite as prolific lately, but the state's music scene remains vital. Perhaps in the near future we'll see a remixed version of a Texas classic or a new Lone Star legend penned by one of Austin's indie rock sensations. Stay tuned.

music history. Texans have contributed essential volumes to the world's music catalog by introducing and refining styles such as rhythm and blues, Western swing, Tejano, country, and rock. The state's musical giants are recognizable by a single name—Buddy, Janis, Willie, Selena, and Beyonce—and each have influenced generations of future musicians while getting plenty of boots scootin' and toes tappin' in the process.

Texas's documented musical history began with its initial wave of settlers in the late 1800s. A fascinating mix of cultures, including German, African American, Czechoslovakian, Mexican, and Anglo, resulted in an equally intriguing blend of musical styles. The best-known types of music in the U.S. South—blues and country—evolved into new and intriguing genres when accompanied by a Texas twist. Appalachian "fiddle music" migrated westward with pioneers and merged with distinctly Texan influences such as yodeling, accordions, and 12-string guitar, resulting in unique styles such as Western swing, conjunto, and rockabilly.

One of Texas's most influential musicians was Blind Lemon Jefferson, who introduced his signature country blues in the 1920s with his raw, potent track "Black Snake Moan." Borrowing the flamenco-influenced guitar work he heard from Mexican migrant workers, Jefferson's fast fingers and ear for melody inspired fellow Texas blues legends Huddy "Leadbelly" Ledbetter and Lightnin' Hopkins. Their work paved the way for generations of Texas blues heroes, including Albert Collins, Freddy King, Clarence "Gatemouth" Brown, and Buddy Guy. Legendary Austinite Stevie Ray Vaughan led a blues revival in the 1980s with his soulful guitar wizardry, scoring national hits with albums *Couldn't Stand the Weather* and *In Step* before he was tragically killed in a 1990 helicopter crash at the age of 35.

A wholly distinct sound from Texas is conjunto music (aka Tejano, Tex-Mex, norteno), which combines accordion and 12-string guitar to produce lively dance melodies with South Texas soul. The style originated with Texas and Mexican working-class musicians who adopted the accordion and the polka from 19th-century German settlers. Conjunto music was popular along the Rio Grande and throughout Latin America for decades before artists began reaching larger audiences in the late 1960s. The genre's best-known artist is Leonardo "Flaco" Jiménez, who has performed with renowned acts such as the Rolling Stones, Bob Dylan, Willie Nelson, Buck Owens, and Carlos Santana. An underappreciated Mexican-influenced style, dubbed "Chicano soul" or the "San Antonio West Side sound," emerged from the late-1950s influences of rhythm and blues and doo-wop. The instantly catchy sound represented an innovative blend of soulful Motown-style harmonies and melodies with Mexican-influenced accents from brass and reed instruments.

Although country music has its true origins in Anglo-based folk balladry, Texans took the style and made it their own. Several of country music's offshoots are Texas products, including Western swing, honky-tonk, and outlaw country. Bob Wills pioneered the jazz-based Western swing style of music in the 1920s, and Ernest Tubb's walking bass lines were a crucial component of 1940s honky-tonk country. In the late 1960s, Austin became the laid-back capital of outlaw country in response to the slick, produced material coming out of Nashville. A raw and loose version of country music emanated from the city's storied Armadillo World Headquarters, which regularly featured legendary outlaws like Willie Nelson, Waylon Jennings, and Jerry Jeff Walker. Overall, Texas's contributors to country music reads like a track listing from the style's greatest hits: Gene Autry, Buck Owens, George Jones, Kenny Rogers, Larry Gatlin, Barbara Mandrell, Townes Van Zandt, Kris Kristofferson, George Strait, Mark Chestnutt, Lyle Lovett, and Pat Green (and that's just volume one).

Rock 'n' roll also received a big ol' Texas brand on it during its formative years. Lubbock's Buddy Holly and the Crickets refined the country-blues style into a distinct rockabilly sound, which influenced the Beatles in ways far beyond their insect-inspired name. Another West Texan, Roy Orbison, made an impact in Memphis with a smoother approach to rockabilly. Port Arthur's Janis Joplin wowed Austin with her bluesy swagger in the late 1960s before moving to San Francisco, where she played a major role in solidifying the city's psychedelic sound. In the 1970s, Texas contributed to the future classic rock scene with artists such as the Steve Miller Band, ZZ Top, and Don Henley (of The Eagles).

During the past 20 years, Texans have continued to make their marks on myriad musical styles. Selena Quintanilla-Perez (1971-1995), known simply as Selena, led a surge in the Latino music scene's popularity in the early 1990s with her dancy pop tunes that drew thousands of converts to her spirited shows. The Dixie Chicks rose from relative obscurity to become one of the world's most popular country music acts with a sound inspired by traditional country, folk, and bluegrass. Their album *Wide Open Spaces* sold 12 million copies, becoming the best-selling album in country music history from a duo or group. Other significant Texas contributions to contemporary music in the early 21st century were Houston acts like Destiny's Child, Dallas songstress Kelly Clarkson, Fort Worth soulster Leon Bridges, northeast Texas native Kacey Musgraves, and artists from Austin such as Spoon, Explosions in the Sky, and Gary Clark Jr.

FILM

More than 1,300 film projects have been made in Texas since 1910, including *Wings,* the first film to win an Academy Award for Best Picture (made in San Antonio in 1927). Film production in Texas has been a vital part of the state's economy for decades, bringing thousands of jobs and hundreds of millions of dollars to the state each year.

With mild winters and more than 267,000 square miles of diverse landscape to work with, Texas is an extremely versatile place to shoot movies, TV shows, music videos, commercials, and other independent film projects. Texas locations have doubled for the American Midwest; Mexico; Washington, D.C.; Vietnam; Afghanistan; Bolivia; Africa; Florida;

and a host of other places throughout the world.

The Texas Film Commission, a division of the governor's office, lends filmmakers a hand by providing free information on locations, crews, talent, state and local contacts, weather, laws, sales tax exemptions, housing, and other film-related issues. The assistance certainly pays off, with the state receiving more than $2 billion in film-related expenditures during the past decade.

Filmmakers look kindly upon Texas because the state has experienced crew members, equipment vendors, and support services. On most features shot in Texas, 75 percent of the crew is hired locally, and the production company is exempt from state and local sales taxes on most of the services and items they rent or purchase. In addition, Texas has several regional film offices that court the major studios and provide production assistance.

Dozens of acclaimed and influential films have been shot on location in Texas (of the hundreds of projects completed), and several have become celluloid classics. Most notable are the 1956 movie *Giant,* starring Elizabeth Taylor, Rock Hudson, and James Dean, and John Wayne's 1960 film *The Alamo. Giant* was filmed in West Texas, and its legacy is still celebrated in Marfa, where the stately 1930 Hotel Paisano served as home base for the cast and crew. A glass case in the lobby displays movie-related magazine clippings and photos, and guests clamor to stay in James Dean's hotel room.

Other significant film projects shot in Texas include *The Last Picture Show* (1971, screenplay by Texan Larry McMurtry), *The Texas Chainsaw Massacre* (1973), *Urban*

Cowboy (1979), *Terms of Endearment* (1983, based on McMurtry's novel), David Byrne's brilliant *True Stories* (1986), McMurtry's *Lonesome Dove* (1990), Austinite Richard Linklater's generation-defining *Slacker* (1990), David Lynch's *Wild at Heart* (1990), Austinite Robert Rodriguez's groundbreaking *El Mariachi* (1992), Linklater's classic *Dazed and Confused* (1992), Christopher Guest's hilarious *Waiting for Guffman* (1995), Dallas native Wes Anderson's masterpiece *Rushmore* (1997), Steven Soderbergh's *Traffic* (2000), Rodriguez's *Predators* (2010), Terence Malick's *The Tree of Life* (2011), *Texas Chainsaw 3D* (2012), *Transformers 4* (2013), and *Boyhood* (2014).

In addition to its mighty movie credits, Texas has hosted noteworthy television shows. Perhaps most significant of them all is *Dallas* (1978-1990, and again in 2013), which entranced audiences around the globe with its Texas-worthy dramatic storylines centered around oil magnate J. R. Ewing and his family. Equally as remarkable yet more artistically viable is PBS's venerable *Austin City Limits* (1975-present), showcasing top-notch country, roots, and alternative music across the United States and spawning its thriving annual music festival. In 2011, the program made a dramatic venue change, from the University of Texas's communications building to a swanky new theater on the ground floor of the upscale W hotel. Other notable Texas TV shows include Office Space (1999), NBC's critically acclaimed *Friday Night Lights* (2006-2011), HBO's *The Leftovers* (2014-2017), Netflix's documentary Cheer (2019), and finally, in the bizarro category, *Barney and Friends,* filmed in Dallas (1992-2010).

VISUAL ARTS

The visual arts scene in Texas is particularly captivating, due in large part to available funding from the state's land and oil barons. World-class artwork is regularly exhibited throughout Texas in big cities and small towns, where philanthropists give generously to construct ornate museums and draw exceptional exhibits.

In addition, the Texas Commission on the Arts state agency funds education and cultural programs. Its grants help fund projects to educate Texas citizens about the importance of art, and the agency has been lauded for its work with at-risk youth and children with disabilities.

For the most part, Texas's fine arts opportunities are located in its metropolitan areas. Some of the country's best art museums are in Houston and Dallas-Fort Worth. Of particular note is Fort Worth's Kimbell Museum, where the facility housing the artwork is as impressive as the work it holds. Designed by architect Louis I. Kahn, its softly arching ceilings provide the perfect amount of natural light to complement the interior artwork by masters such as Picasso, Monet, Rembrandt, El Greco, Cézanne, and others in addition to its impressive collections of Asian and African art.

Other must-see art museums in Fort Worth are the Amon Carter Museum, showcasing high-quality Western art (Georgia O'Keeffe, Ansel Adams, Winslow Homer), and The Modern Art Museum of Fort Worth, a glass structure designed by famed Japanese architect Tadao Ando that seems to float in a surrounding shimmering pool. Inside are more than 26,000 works by renowned artists such as Picasso, Andy Warhol, and Jackson Pollock.

Dallas's premier art attraction, the Dallas Museum of Art, features an impressive $32 million two-acre sculpture garden showcasing the work of Miró, Rodin, Moore, de Kooning, and many others. The facility is also known for its Museum of the Americas, which showcases an impressive collection of historic art from North, Central, and South America.

Houston is the other main hub for Texas's fine arts, with nearly 20 major museums and galleries. The city's Museum of Fine Arts houses approximately 31,000 works of American, European, Latin American, Native American, and Asian art spanning 4,000 years. Its concentration is on the Renaissance and impressionism, but there are treasures hiding around every corner, especially the primitive Native American pieces.

Other worthy Houston museums are the Contemporary Arts Museum, which rotates exhibits every six weeks, offering visitors a fresh experience year-round, and the Menil Collection, which features rotating displays along with its permanent 10,000-piece collection including a stunning mix of styles, from African and Byzantine to surrealist and contemporary.

ESSENTIALS

Transportation

GETTING THERE

Texas is far removed from the transportation hubs on the East and West Coasts, but it's easily accessible by plane and relatively so by car.

AIR

Houston is so big, it has two airports. The rest of the cities along the Gulf Coast aren't that big, but

several have small regional airports to save travelers the long drives across the seemingly endless coastal plains.

The major air hub in the region is George Bush Intercontinental Airport (2800 N. Terminal Rd., 281/230-3100, www.fly2houston. com), located just north of Houston. This is one of United Airlines' major hubs, and since it offers nonstop service to and from more than 170 cities around the world, it's typically hustling and bustling at all hours of the day and night. The city's old airfield, William P. Hobby Airport (7800 Airport Blvd., 713/640-3000, www. fly2houston.com) is now the center of activity for Southwest Airlines and hosts flights from several other major carriers. Located 10 miles southeast of downtown, Hobby is more accessible than Bush, but it's showing its age. That's often forgiven by travelers who prefer the facilitated accessibility and cheaper cab fares (nearly $20 less than the trek from Bush to downtown Houston).

To reach the mid-Gulf Coast area, book a flight to Corpus Christi International Airport (1000 International Blvd., 361/289-0171, www. cctexas.com/airport). The Brownsville South Padre Island International Airport (700 S. Minnesota Ave., 956/542-4373, www. flybrownsville.com) is the closest airport to South Padre. At 27 miles away, it's not too far, especially if you need to get to the beach in a hurry and don't feel like making the five-hour trek from Houston. T

CAR

The interstate highway system in Texas is pretty impressive for a state this huge. You can get from most major cities to the others (excluding El Paso) by noon. Two major U.S. interstates, I-10 and I-45, lead to Houston, making it easily accessible from the north, west, and east. The roads tend to be in good shape since they don't often experience icy conditions, but as in most states, construction is a perpetual issue in Texas's metro areas. Increased truck traffic from Mexico has taken its toll on some of the freeways, and rural roads between smaller cities can get a bit rough, but that doesn't deter Texans from going 90 mph. The Texas Department of Transportation (www. txdot.gov) oversees all aspects of vehicular travel.

Since the majority of the coastline is underdeveloped, no major freeways link major cities south of Houston. State Highway 35 is the closest option, stretching between Houston and Corpus Christi and passing through dozens of small towns along the way. The lengthy Padre Island National Seashore is only accessible by a park road near Corpus Christi; otherwise, the trek to South Padre beaches is more than 20 miles inland via U.S. Highway 77 through Kingsville, Harlingen, and Brownsville.

BUS AND TRAIN

Houston is large enough to make accessibility by bus and train a viable option (thanks to the frequency in arrivals and departures). Those interested in traveling by bus can contact Houston Greyhound (2121 Main St., 800/231-2222, www.greyhound.com). The venerable Dallas-based bus line has an easily navigable online reservation system (not always the case with bus companies) and hosts bus stops in cities across the country. Fares tend to run about half the price of a plane ticket, often a welcome option for travelers on a tight budget (and willing to make the trip in more time with less glamour). Greyhound can assist travelers with fares and schedules via email (ifsr@greyhound.com) and can serve Spanish-speaking travelers via phone (800/531-5332).

Passenger trains arrive in town via Amtrak's Sunset Limited line, which runs cross-country between Orlando and Los Angeles. Look for arrivals and departures at the Houston Amtrak station (902 Washington Ave., 800/872-7245, www.amtrak.com). Be forewarned: Traveling by train in Texas is not nearly as charming as it sounds. Trains stop frequently between destinations and for long periods of time.

BOAT

Texas's Gulf Coast has several major shipping ports, including Houston, Galveston, Corpus Christi, Beaumont, and Brownsville. Virtually all the activity is industrial, but cruise ships occasionally dock in Houston and Galveston. Contact the cruise lines (Carnival, Royal Caribbean, etc.) to see if they plan voyages to the Lone Star State.

GETTING AROUND

Texans love their cars—and trucks. In a state this big, a vehicle is virtually a necessity, despite some advances in metropolitan public transportation systems. To get anywhere in Texas's sprawling cities and widespread landscape, a vehicle is the most practical approach. In fact, the state is so spread out, travelers occasionally hop on planes to get from place to place. The drive from Lubbock to Corpus Christi would take about 13 hours by car but only 2 hours via plane. Other small cities with airports include Tyler,

Waco, San Angelo, Amarillo, and Brownsville.

CAR

Texas's major interstates are well maintained, and drivers are largely courteous, if a bit lead footed. At time, I-10 east and west of Houston can resemble a racetrack, with cars and semi trucks regularly buzzing along at a 90 mph clip. That being said, some Texas drivers are notorious for hanging in the passing lane at 55 mph, forcing cars to line up behind them and pass on the right when there's a break in the "fast" lane. Incidentally, freeway ramps are unpredictable in Texas—some are only a few hundred yards short, while others seem to stretch for miles. Once you're off the interstate, be sure to keep an eye out for police, since some small Texas towns rely on speeding ticket fines to help fund their municipal budgets.

Toll Roads

Unlike other states with well-established turnpike and tollway systems, much of Texas is relatively new to the fees-for-freeways concept. Small stretches of highways in Dallas and Houston have charged tolls for decades, but only recently have other cities jumped on board. Houston's main toll road is a lengthy 70-mile outer loop known as the Sam Houston Tollway. Like most tollways, it offers a convenient option if you're in a hurry or you don't mind the pay-to-play approach.

For the most part, the tollways are welcome (unless they're placed or proposed on a previously public road) because they ease congestion on busy nearby interstates. Still, they rub some Texans the wrong way and can be underused due to perceived expense. The Texas Department of Transportation's system is surprisingly convenient and innovative (yet occasionally confusing), with electronic gates allowing drivers to cruise through the tolls and receive a bill in the mail several weeks later. Fees are reasonable: from 75 cents to several dollars, depending on the length of the toll road.

If you're renting a vehicle, be sure to ask the rental company if they have a toll tag or if you can purchase a prepaid tag. Otherwise, you may be unpleasantly surprised to later find you've been charged a $50 "convenience" fee for the company to handle the arrangements. If you don't have a tag, be sure to look for the highway signs letting you know if there's an option for paying an actual person at a toll gate; otherwise, you may want to take a more convenient route on a true freeway.

For more information about Houston's toll roads, contact the Harris County Tollroad Authority (HCTA, 713/587-7800, www.hctra. org) for toll road maps and information about the organization.

BIKE

Texas has a considerable number of bicyclists, but its roadways aren't considered very bike-friendly. The best spots for riding are municipal and state parks, which contain well-designed and scenic hike and bike trails. The state's tremendous geographical diversity allows for a good variety of terrain. Before planning to spend most of your time attempting to navigate Houston on two wheels, it's advisable to contact a local cycling advocacy organization to inquire about accessibility and issues in the areas you'll be visiting. One of the most reputable groups is Bike Houston (713/364-6074, www.bike-houston.org).

BUS

For those interested in traversing Texas by bus, it's worth contacting Trailways (319/753-2864, www. trailways.com). The company operates eight regional routes in Texas, offering passengers the option of making personalized trips using independently operated bus companies. This is an ideal option for travelers interested in exploring cities or smaller towns at their own pace without having to rely on a major bus tour operation with existing (and less-than-adventurous) itineraries. In addition, Greyhound (www.greyhound.com, 800/231-2222) has over 150 bus stations and stops throughout Texas.

Corpus Christi's metropolitan bus system, Regional Transportation Authority (1806 S. Alameda St., 361/883-2287, www.ccrta.org), provides citywide service. Check the website for updated fare and route information.

PUBLIC TRANSPORTATION

Houston has a decent public transportation system, but it can be confusing for out-of-towners who haven't yet developed a strong sense of direction. Regardless, a little homework can be helpful in strategizing plans via the Metro, aka the Metropolitan Transit Authority of Harris County (713/635-4000, www.ridemetro.org), which offers local and commuter bus service. Tickets are available in vending machines located at each station. Metro's red line services 16 stations near downtown's busiest commercial and recreational sites.

In Galveston, a unique public transportation service, the Galveston

Island Trolley (www.galvestontrolley.com) offers transportation from the Seawall to The Strand district and Pier 21. The cars are charming replicas of those used in Galveston from the late 1800s to the 1930s.

In South Padre, you can ditch the car in favor of the city's reliable Island Metro (866/761-1025, www.spadre.com/thewave) transportation system; see the website for stops and schedules. The small buses typically operate 7am-9pm daily among local businesses and services, and late at night during spring break to shuttle impaired revelers. The belligerent scene on the ride back from the bar at 3am is one of the most insane experiences imaginable.

Recreation

Texans spend a lot of time enjoying outdoor activities, despite the intolerably hot summers. For sports, football is the undisputed king, but baseball, basketball, and golf are also popular since they can be played year-round. The state's mild climate also allows nonprofessional (recreational) sporting activities to continue throughout the year. Campers, hikers, and mountain bikers flock to state and local parks year-round—especially in winter for the warm tropical climate of the Gulf Coast and Rio Grande Valley. The *Recreation* and *Camping* sections for specific cities in this guide provide detailed information about available resources.

PROFESSIONAL SPORTS

Professional sports are a major attraction in Texas (the *Recreation* sections in the metropolitan areas contain detailed information). Once home to the storied Houston Oilers football franchise (before they bolted for Tennessee and became the Titans), the city has been home to the NFL's Houston Texans since 2002. The Texans have become a formidable franchise that continues to draw substantial crowds to NRG Stadium (1 NRG Pkwy.).

Sports fans are also drawn to the venerable Houston Astros. In 1965, the Astros became the primary occupants of the then-futuristic Astrodome, billed as the "Eighth Wonder of the World." Their current home in downtown's Minute Maid Park (501 Crawford St.), a classic urban ball field with a modern retractable roof.

Basketball isn't as big a draw in Texas as football, but the Houston Rockets have always had a considerable following. The Rockets hold court at the downtown Toyota Center (1510 Polk St.).

ECOTOURISM

One of the most popular ecotourism destinations in the country is emerging in South Texas, particularly the Lower Rio Grande Valley. The Valley's immense biodiversity and ecological complexity make it a natural crossing point for migratory birds, which traverse the region each fall and spring en route to and from their winter homes in the tropics.

Much like the birds that arrive in the Valley from the East Coast and Midwest, the birders who track and document their feathered friends flock from across the country in search of their favorite and rare species. The McAllen area is home to several acclaimed birding sites catering to the thousands of ecotourists who arrive annually, including the World Birding Center's Quinta Mazatlan, the highly regarded Santa Ana National Wildlife Refuge, and the Bentsen-Rio Grande Valley State Park. These parks retain the region's natural state by maintaining the distinctive woodlands, which draw species popular with the birding crowd, such as chacalacas, green jays, and broad-winged hawks.

PARKS

Most big cities have a showcase central park offering an inviting natural oasis among the harsh urban environs. Houston's version is Hermann Park. Located in the heart of the Museum District just southwest of downtown, Hermann Park is a 400-acre magnet for joggers, dog walkers, bikers, and families in search of some rare green space in a city known for its rampant development. Trails and trees are abundant here, as are the amenities and services, including a theater, golf course, and garden center. The park is filled with statues, too; look for monuments to Sam Houston, Mahatma

Farther outside of town but worth the 30-minute drive is Armand Bayou Nature Center. Located near NASA on the west side of Galveston Bay, the nature center offers residents and visitors a chance to learn about native plant and animal species, hike on the discovery trails, or see the live animal displays featuring the likes of bison, hawks, and spiders. The main area of the park contains a boardwalk traversing the marshes and forests

and providing a glimpse of the beautiful bayou region of East Texas. The best way to experience this natural wonder is by boat—consider taking a tour on the Bayou Ranger pontoon boat or signing up for a guided canoe tour.

CAMPING

As in many other states, funding for parks is scarce in Texas, but the Parks and Wildlife Department manages to run a decent operation with limited resources. For years, Texans complained mightily about the hassles of making campground reservations via antiquated systems such as phones. TPWD's online reservation system (http://texas.reserveworld.com), has provided added convenience.

Houston's best camping is about 30 miles (48 km) southwest of the city at Brazos Bend State Park (21901 FM 762, 979/553-5102, www.tpwd. state.tx.us, $7 over age 12). Covering 5,000 acres, this popular park offers hiking, biking, equestrian trails, and fishing on six easily accessible lakes. Visitors are cautioned about alligators, which are numerous in some areas of the park. Facilities include restrooms with showers, campsites with water and electricity, screened shelters, primitive equestrian campsites, and a dining hall.

FISHING

Like other outdoor activities in Houston and the Gulf Coast region, fishing is a popular recreational endeavor due to the mild year-round temperatures. The area of East Texas just north of Houston (especially near the four national forests) are well known in angler circles for its freshwater reservoirs and streams packed with largemouth bass, smallmouth bass, crappie, and panfish (bluegill, sunfish). The Gulf Coast, meanwhile, is an angler's paradise for tarpon, amberjack, red drum, and spotted sea trout.

For detailed information about fishing reports, tides, and advisories, visit the Texas Park and Wildlife Department's comprehensive website (www.tpwd.texas.gov).

There are many locations to obtain a fishing license (a requirement). Anglers can purchase a license at most bait and tackle shops, as well as local sporting goods stores, grocery stores, and even some department stores. Recreational licenses are available on a daily basis (fees vary by location, but usually cost around $7) or with an annual permit ($30 for freshwater, $35 saltwater, $40 "all-water"). These licenses can also be purchased in advance by phone (800/895-4248 Mon.-Fri. 8am-5pm) or via TPWD's website. In addition, the site offers a handy service that identifies the nearest local license vendor based on the city.

HUNTING

Hunting is huge in Texas, and the state's sheer size provides countless opportunities to grab a gun and wait patiently for your critter of choice. Deer hunting is one of the biggest draws, and deer season has a major cultural and economic impact on much of the state. Pick up a community newspaper during the winter, and you'll find plenty of photos of hunters, ranging in age from 8 to 88, in the back of their pickups proudly displaying the rack of the buck they just killed.

There's something for every kind of hunter, from waterfowl along the Gulf Coast to quail and pheasant in South Texas to feral hogs in East Texas. The best place to find all the information you'll ever need about hunting in Texas—seasons, permits, regulations, restrictions, hunting lodges, and hunting leases—is the Texas Parks and Wildlife Department's website (www.tpwd.state.tx.us).

Like fishing licenses, Texas's hunting licenses are required and can be obtained across the state. Hunters can purchase a license at a local gun shop, sporting goods store, grocery store, or department store. Resident licenses are available for $25 (fees for out-of-staters are slightly higher) and allow hunting of "any legal bird or animal (terrestrial vertebrates)." The licenses can also be purchased in advance by phone (800/895-4248 Mon.-Fri. 8am-5pm) or via TPWD's website. As with the fishing licenses, the website offers a service that identifies local vendors based on the closest city.

Though most locals are well versed in the procedures associated with field dressing and transporting a deer after it's been killed, visitors may need a crash course on the state's requirements. To find out everything you need to know about appropriate tags, processing (four quarters and two backstraps), and keeping the deer in "edible condition," visit www.tpwd.texas.gov.

Food

Food lovers love Texas. Turn on the Food Network, and you'll probably soon be watching a feature about Texas barbecue, the many varieties of Mexican food in Texas, or recipes for the perfect Lone Star chili. Here's a quick overview of how they came to be culinary icons in Texas.

BARBECUE

The prime representation of Texas cuisine, barbecue is all about the meat—beef (brisket and ribs), pork (sausage, ribs, and chops), and turkey, chicken, mutton, goat, or anything else a Texan can put in a barbecue smoker. The tradition originated in the Caribbean as a method to cook meat over a pit on a framework of sticks known as a *barbacot*, and it eventually made its way across the southern United States, where it picked up various cultural influences on the way. Even in Texas there are several different methods for barbecuing meat, and there's plenty of debate about who does it the right way. Fortunately, everyone wins since all styles of Texas barbecue are exceptionally pleasing to the palate.

In general, the East Texas approach is aligned with delectable African American traditions of the South—the sauce is tomato based and somewhat sweet, and the sides (potato salad and coleslaw, in particular) are mayo based and sweet. Central Texas-style 'cue is considered the ideal representative of the Lone Star State, originating in the German and Czech communities in the Austin area. Based on traditions from European meat markets, the sausage and beef are smoked and served on waxed paper along with side items

inspired by the former grocery store/butcher shops where they originated—bread slices, beans, tomatoes, cheese, and jalapeños. In West Texas, some restaurants and ranches still serve their meat "cowboy style," where an entire slab of beef is cooked over hot coals on open pits and basted with a "mop" of oil and vinegar.

TEX-MEX

For most people, Mexican food means tacos, burritos, and nachos. In Texas, Mexican food can mean a variety of things—cuisine from the interior of Mexico with savory sauces and various meats, Southwestern-style Mexican food with green chiles and blue corn, or border-inspired Tex-Mex with gooey cheese, seasoned beef, and tortillas.

Though interior Mexican food is certainly worth sampling if you can find an authentic restaurant, it's Tex-Mex that prevails in Texas, and it's not hard to find a good representation of this regional comfort food in most cities across the state. In fact, mom-and-pop Tex-Mex restaurants are much like Italian eateries on the East Coast and in the Midwest—the best food is often in the most unassuming spot, like a strip mall or small house on a side street.

The main ingredients in Tex-Mex are ground beef, chicken, cheese, pinto beans, and tortillas. These items are combined differently for tasty variations, including a crispy or soft beef taco; a beef, cheese, or chicken enchilada; a bean chalupa; cheese quesadilla; or beef and chicken fajitas. Salsa, guacamole, lettuce, tomato, and sour cream are typically added as flavorful accompaniments.

SOUTHERN

Texas doesn't hold exclusive rights to this category, but Southern food is considered somewhat exotic to more than half the country, and, like just about everything else, Texas puts its own distinct spin on this style of down-home country cuisine.

It's unfair to generalize Southern cooking as being mostly fried, even though a good portion of it is encased in crispy goodness (just not always of the deep-fried variety). One of the best examples of Southern cookin' done right in Texas is chicken-fried steak, a thin cut of cube steak that's tenderized, breaded in egg batter or a seasoned flour mixture, pan fried in lard or vegetable oil, and served smothered in peppered cream gravy. The name likely refers to the similar process used in frying chicken. Other fried favorites include pork chops, catfish, okra, and chicken.

Another Southern cooking tendency is to include meat in veggie dishes (vegetarians should consider themselves warned). Beans, greens, and black-eyed peas are often spruced up with ham hock or bacon, and lard or bacon grease can add an extra dimension of flavor to just about any vegetable or bread recipe. Incidentally, if you order tea in a Texas restaurant, you'll get iced tea (occasionally sweetened), and you should never skip an opportunity to order a fruit cobbler or pecan pie for dessert.

CHILI

Texans take their chili seriously—maybe too seriously. But since Texans claim bragging rights to many things, it should be no surprise they profess to have the best chili, too. The main point of pride with the Texas variety is the absence of beans. It's meat and spices only. Beans are for wimps and Yankees.

There's no denying the results, however. A meat-based chili puts the emphasis where it belongs, on tender beef (occasionally venison) enhanced by a blend of fiery peppers and flavorful seasonings like garlic, onions, and oregano. Chili cook-offs are traditionally cultural celebrations in Texas towns, and winners become local celebrities.

Not surprisingly, Texans claim to have the original chili recipe, though food historians trace the dish to Incan, Aztec, and Mayan cultures. The Texas connection is tied to Canary Islanders, who arrived in San Antonio in the early 1700s with traditional meals of meat blended with herbs, garlic, wild onions, and other veggies, including pungent local peppers. These days, Texans typically opt to prepare their chili at home, since restaurants could never duplicate the perfect combination of ingredients passed down through the generations in family recipes.

SEAFOOD

Although the holy trinity of Texas food—barbecue, Tex-Mex, and Southern—is available in all areas of the state, Houston and the Gulf Coast region are the only places where seafood is a viable fresh option. In fact, for many travelers, a visit to the Gulf Coast is incomplete without including shrimp in every meal. One of the best ways to kick off a visit to the coast is by going directly to a seaside restaurant and ordering a plate of peel-and-eat shrimp accompanied by a hoppy local brew. To continue your mealtime quest, consider ordering shrimp in breakfast tacos, in a lunchtime enchilada dish, and in the traditional fried form for dinner.

It's possible that you'll be seeking other varieties of fresh-caught seafood while visiting the area. Feel free to ask a waiter about potential specials that may not be listed on the menu.

In some cases, especially in traditional fishing communities like Port Aransas, the restaurants are happy to cook your own fresh-caught fillet, a handy option if you're staying in a hotel or somewhere without easy access to a cooking source. Call ahead to find out the procedures in place for each location.

Travel Tips

For the most part, traveling in Texas is similar to traveling in the rest of the United States, with the main exception being issues associated with crossing the Mexican border (which is avoided by most people these days). Otherwise, it's smooth sailing across state lines, with visitor information centers located on the Texas side of most major freeways entering the state.

BORDER CROSSING

Years ago, people were able to easily cross the Rio Grande sans passport or auto insurance, free to roam Mexican border towns. These days, people in border communities are wary of the violence across the border associated with warring drug cartels, even though they remain safe on the Texas side.

The violence and unrest in Mexico has been severe enough in recent years to warrant statewide warnings against visits to the neighboring country. Since this affects most tourists, it is advisable for travelers in Texas to remain in the state for safety's sake. Even longtime residents of Texas's border communities are reluctant to cross the border, unless a family or business emergency necessitates it.

If the volatile conditions in Mexico subside (as most border communities hope, since their tourism has historically been tied to border hops), visitors will once again return to Mexico's *restaurantes* and *tourista* areas. Meanwhile, many of these destinations (restaurants, in particular) have addressed the drop in business by opening new locations on the Texas side of the Rio Grande. It may not offer the same international flavor, but it provides visitors with something equally as palatable: safety.

INTERNATIONAL TRAVELERS

Since Texas shares an enormous border with another country, international travel has traditionally been commonplace in the Lone Star State. Not anymore. With the recent rise in violence associated with the warring drug cartels, visitors are advised against traveling to Mexico.

Overseas travel is a different story—recent numbers compiled by state government show Texas ranks seventh as a destination point among mainland U.S. states for overseas travelers, with New York, California, and Florida taking the top spots.

Before international travelers arrive

in Texas, they're encouraged to address several issues that will make their experience more pleasant and convenient. Suggested action items include consulting their insurance companies to ensure their medical policy applies in the United States; making sure they have a signed, up-to-date passport and/or visa; leaving copies of their itinerary and contact info with friends or family for emergencies; and taking precautions to avoid being a target of crime (don't carry excessive amounts of money, don't leave luggage unattended, etc.).

SPECIAL CONSIDERATIONS

TRAVELERS WITH DISABILITIES

Travelers with disabilities shouldn't have much trouble getting around in Texas; in fact, the only places that may not be wheelchair accessible are some outdated hotels and restaurants. Otherwise, parks, museums, and city attractions are compliant with the Americans with Disabilities Act, providing ramps, elevators, and accessible facilities for public-use areas.

Texas law requires cities to appoint one member to a transit board representing the interests of the "transportation disadvantaged," a group that can include people with disabilities. As a result, most cities have addressed accessibility issues in airports and public transportation services. For detailed information, contact the municipal offices in the city you're visiting or the Texas Department of Transportation's Public Transportation Division at 512/416-2810 or www.txdot.gov.

Other handy resources for disabled travelers en route to Texas are the Handicapped Travel Club (www.handicappedtravelclub.com),

providing information about campgrounds with accessibility; and the Society for Accessible Travel and Hospitality (www.sath.org), containing a resources page with handy travel tips for anyone with physical limitations.

SENIOR TRAVELERS

For seniors, it's always a good idea to mention in advance if you're a member of AARP or if you qualify for a senior discount (typically for ages 65 and older, but occasionally available for the 60 and older crowd). Most museums in Texas offer a few dollars off admission fees for seniors, and many public transportation systems also provide discounts.

If you haven't done so already, inquire about travel options through Road Scholar (877/426-8056, www. roadscholar.org), an organization providing several dozen programs in Texas with seniors in mind. Excursions lasting 4-12 days are available, ranging from birding trails to heritage-based tours to art, nature, and fishing trips.

LGBTQ+ TRAVELERS

Texas's rural communities (and even some of its smaller cities) aren't quite as open-minded as its metropolitan areas. Houston, Dallas, and Austin have sizable gay communities, with bars, restaurants, and services catering exclusively to gay clientele.

To learn more about resources related to gay and lesbian travel in Texas, including accommodations, restaurants, and nightclubs, visit the following travel-related websites: www. gaytravel.com and the McKinney, Texas-based www.gayjourney.com. For additional information, contact the International Gay & Lesbian Travel Association (www.iglta.org).

Health and Safety

Texas isn't any more dangerous or any safer than other U.S. states, but there are several environment-related issues (weather, animals) that set it apart. Travelers with medical issues are encouraged to bring extra supplies of medications and copies of prescriptions—local visitors bureaus can recommend the best pharmacy or medical center, if needed.

CRIME

Although it's still often considered a Wild West state, Texas is similar to the rest of the nation regarding crime statistics and trends. According to a recent report by the Texas Department of Public Safety, criminal activity in Texas was separated into the following categories: violent crimes (against people—robberies, assaults, etc.), which represented more than 10 percent of the reported offenses, and property crimes (burglary, car theft), representing the remaining circa 90 percent.

THE ELEMENTS

Eastern and Southern Texas's weather is as volatile as its landscape. Summers regularly reach triple digits, and winters are marked by near freezing temperatures (and the occasional snowfall). The biggest threat to travelers in winter is ice—bridges and overpasses become slick and are usually closed when a rare ice storm barrels through the state. Since Texans in this region are unaccustomed to dealing with such slippery conditions, they often disregard the danger and plow across a patch of ice in their big fancy trucks. The results are predictably disastrous.

Heat is by far the most serious threat to travelers. From the sticky humidity of marshy East Texas to the intense sun further south, the summer months (May-September in Texas) can be brutal. Hikers, bikers, and campers are encouraged to pack and carry plenty of water to remain hydrated.

WILDLIFE, INSECTS, AND PLANTS

Texas has some bizarre fauna and flora, which can occasionally pose a danger to travelers, particularly those who venture to the state's parks and natural areas. Of primary concern are snakes, which nestle among rocks and waterways throughout Texas (though rattlesnakes are largely found only in western portions of the state).

The most dangerous plant in Texas is cactus. There are many varieties in all regions of the state, and even though some appear harmless, they may contain barely visible needles that get embedded in your skin and cause major irritation. With cactus, the best approach is to look but don't touch.

Information and Services

The best way to find out about activities and services in the city you're visiting is through the local convention and visitors bureau, or in smaller communities, the chamber of commerce. Each destination in this guide includes contact information for visitor services, and even the most rural areas have discovered the value of promoting themselves online.

MONEY

It's always a good idea to have cash on hand for tips, valets, and parking lots, but you can get by in most Texas cities with a credit or debit card. Some smaller towns still don't accept them (old-fashioned restaurants in particular), but they're typically modern enough to have ATMs. Also available, yet not quite as accessible, are wire transfers and travelers checks. Call ahead for the bank's hours of operation since some institutions close at odd hours.

MAPS AND TOURIST INFO

Convention and visitors bureaus are the best resource for planning a trip to Texas. Call ahead to have maps and brochures sent before your trip, or check the town's website for walking tours and street maps. It's also a good idea to check these sites or call in advance to find out if the city you're visiting is randomly hosting its annual pecan days or biker festival at the same time. Depending on your outlook, this can enhance or hinder your excursion.

RESOURCES

Suggested Reading

GENERAL INFORMATION

State Travel Guide. Each year, the Texas Department of Transportation publishes this magazine-size guide with maps and comprehensive listings of the significant attractions in virtually every town, including all the local history museums in Texas's tiny communities.

Texas Almanac. Published annually, this handy book includes virtually everything you'd ever need to know about Texas—current and historical information about politics, agriculture, transportation, geography, and culture, along with maps of each county (all 254 of 'em).

Texas Monthly. With a higher-end subscriber base, this monthly magazine features some of the best writers in the state offering insightful commentary and substantive feature articles about the state's politics, culture, history, and Texas-ness. It's available at most bookstores.

LITERATURE, FICTION, HISTORY

Bissinger, H.G. *Friday Night Lights.* Boston: Addison-Wesley, 1990. This book will tell you more about Texas than you could ever experience in a visit to the state. It's not just about football, but the passionate emotions involved with family, religion, and race in Odessa through the eyes of journalist Buzz Bissinger.

Dobie, J. Frank. *Tales of Old-Time Texas.* Austin: University of Texas press, 1955. Known as the Southwest's master storyteller, J. Frank Dobie depicts folk life in Texas unlike any other author, with 28 inspiring stories of characters (Jim Bowie) and culture (the legend of the Texas bluebonnet).

Fehrenbach, T.R. *Lone Star.* Cambridge, MA: Da Capo Press, 2000. Considered the definitive book on Texas history, this enormous book by the highly respected late historian covers Texas's lengthy and colorful heritage in fascinating and accurate detail.

Harrigan, Stephen. *The Gates of the Alamo.* London: Penguin Books, 2001. This is gripping historical fiction, with detailed history about the actual people and events associated with the Battle of the Alamo weaved with a dramatic narrative resulting in a completely compelling read.

Harrigan, Stephen. *Big Wonderful Thing: A History of Texas,* University of Texas Press, 2019. This 944-page book brings Texas' enormous legacy into the 21st century by acknowledging its multi-cultural past with thoughtful analysis and masterful storytelling.

McCarthy, Cormac. *All the Pretty Horses*. New York City: Alfred Knopf, 1992. Tracing a young man's journey to the regions of the unknown (though it technically takes place along the Texas-Mexico border), this novel depicts a classic quest with plenty of good, evil, and Texas mystique.

McMurtry, Larry. *Lonesome Dove*. New York City: Simon & Schuster, 1985. Beautifully written by Pulitzer Prize-winning novelist Larry McMurtry, this period piece (late 1800s) chronicles two ex-Texas Rangers on a cattle drive, leaving readers with a yearning for the compelling characters and the Texas of the past.

Meyer, Philipp. *The Son*. New York City: Harper Collins, 2013. This incredible story, a finalist for the Pulitzer Prize in 2014, chronicles 200 years of Texas history through the fictional account of a powerful Texas family. From tensions with Native Americans to border relations to oil barons, The Son captures Texas' complicated past in a fascinating novel.

MUSIC AND FOOD

Govenar, Alan. *Meeting the Blues: The Rise of the Texas Sound*. London: Penguin Books, 1994. This semi-obscure, thoroughly researched book provides fascinating insight about the development of the Texas blues through historical narrative, interviews, and photos.

Marshall, Wes. *The Wine Roads of Texas: An Essential Guide to Texas Wines and Wineries*. San Antonio: Maverick Books, 2002. Covering more than 400 Texas wines and the top wineries in Texas, this book offers a comprehensive sampling of wines from Big Bend to the bayous.

Porterfield, Bill. *The Greatest Honky Tonks of Texas*. Houston: Taylor Publishing Company, 1983. You'll likely have to do some searching to dig up a copy of this book, but it's worth it for the engaging text about the colorful culture associated with the state's iconic honky-tonks and historic dance halls.

Walsh, Robb. *Legends of Texas Barbecue*. San Francisco: Chronicle Books, 2002. This book is as fun to read as it is to use—learn about the fascinating history of the many different styles of Texas barbecue while trying out some of the state's best recipes and cooking methods.

Walsh, Robb. *The Tex-Mex Cookbook*. Emeryville, CA: Ten Speed Press, 2004. Well researched and comprehensive in approach, this informative book includes cultural information about classic and unknown Tex-Mex dishes and plenty of authentic recipes.

OUTDOORS

Tekiela, Stan. *Birds of Texas Field Guide*, 2004. Designed for amateur birders, this handy guide is color coded (corresponding to the birds' feathers) with helpful photos, maps, and descriptions.

Tennant, Alan. *A Field Guide to Texas Snakes*, 2002. This thorough guidebook provides essential information about understanding and appreciating Texas's venomous and nonvenomous snakes through identification keys and color photos.

Internet Resources

GENERAL TRAVEL INFORMATION

Office of the Governor, Economic Development and Tourism
www.traveltex.com
This indispensable site provides background and contact information for virtually every tourist attraction, major and minor, in the state.

Texas Department of Transportation
www.txdot.gov
Visit this site for information about road conditions and travel resources (maps, travel info center locations, etc.).

Texas Monthly
www.texasmonthly.com
The site of this award-winning magazine offers samples of feature articles and recommendations for quality dining and lodging options throughout the state.

HISTORIC PRESERVATION

Texas Historical Commission
www.thc.texas.gov
The official state agency for historic preservation, the THC provides helpful guidelines about its preservation programs and essential travel information about popular historic properties across the state.

Texas State Historical Association, *The Handbook of Texas* **Online**
www.tshaonline.org/handbook/online
The Handbook of Texas has long been considered the definitive source for accurate information about Texas's historical events, sites, and figures.

OUTDOORS

Texas Parks and Wildlife Department
www.tpwd.texas.gov
You can get lost (in a good way) exploring this site, with its comprehensive listings of state parks and detailed information about outdoors activities.

National Parks in Texas
www.nps.gov
Texas's national parks are astounding, and this site provides enough information to put these intriguing locales on your must-visit list.

Texas Campgrounds
www.texascampgrounds.com
Use this site to help find a commendable RV park or campground anywhere in the state.

Texas Outside
www.texasoutside.com
This site contains helpful info and links to outdoor activities in Texas such as hiking, biking, camping, fishing, hunting, and golfing.

Index

WXYZ

List of Maps

Photo Credits

Craft a personalized journey through the top National Parks in the U.S. and Canada with Moon!

In these books:

Coverage of gateway cities and towns

Suggested itineraries from one day to multiple weeks

Advice on where to stay (or camp) in and around the parks

MOON

GREAT SMOKY MOUNTAINS NATIONAL PARK

HIKING · CAMPING · SCENIC DRIVES

JASON FRYE

MOON

JOSHUA TREE & PALM SPRINGS

JENNA BLOUGH

MOON

YELLOWSTONE & GRAND TETON

HIKE, CAMP, SEE WILDLIFE

BECKY LOMAX

MOON

YOSEMITE SEQUOIA & KINGS CANYON

ANN MARIE BROWN

MOON

ZION & BRYCE

W. C. McRAE, JUDY JEWELL

SHARE YOUR TRAVELS AND TAG US ON SOCIAL MEDIA!

ROAD TRIP GUIDES FROM MOON

Moon Baseball Road Trips
The Complete Guide to All the Ballparks, with Beer, Bites, and Sights Nearby

Sunshine, hot dogs, friends, and the excitement of the game: Baseball is called America's pastime for a reason. Experience the best of the MLB cities and stadiums with strategic advice from road tripper and former baseball writer Timothy Malcolm.

For when your friends want your recommendations.
Keep track of your favorite...

Restaurants and Meals

Neighborhoods and Regions

Cultural Experiences

Walks or Outdoor Activities

Day Trips or Scenic Drives

Photo Ops or Scenic Spots

MAP SYMBOLS

═══	Expressway	▭▭▭	Unpaved Road	┤┤┤	Railroad
═══	Primary Road	-------	Trail	≈≈≈	Pedestrian Walkway
═══	Secondary Road	·········	Ferry	▪▪▪▪	Stairs

○	City/Town	ⓘ	Information Center	▲	Park
◉	State Capital	Ⓟ	Parking Area	↕	Golf Course
⊛	National Capital	⛪	Church	✛	Unique Feature
✪	Highlight	🍇	Winery/Vineyard	⌇	Waterfall
★	Point of Interest	TH	Trailhead	Λ	Camping
•	Accommodation	🚉	Train Station	▲	Mountain
▼	Restaurant/Bar	✈	Airport	🎿	Ski Area
■	Other Location	✗	Airfield	⬭	Glacier

CONVERSION TABLES

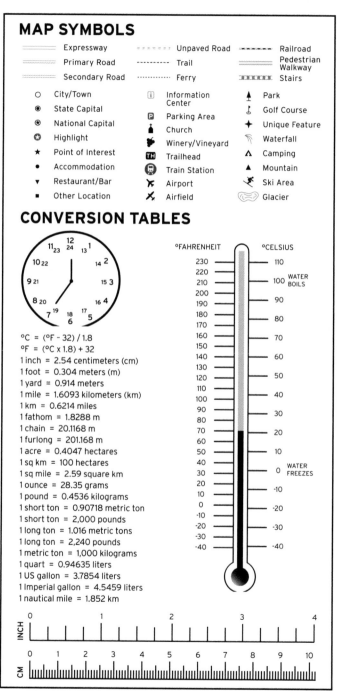

°C = (°F - 32) / 1.8
°F = (°C x 1.8) + 32
1 inch = 2.54 centimeters (cm)
1 foot = 0.304 meters (m)
1 yard = 0.914 meters
1 mile = 1.6093 kilometers (km)
1 km = 0.6214 miles
1 fathom = 1.8288 m
1 chain = 20.1168 m
1 furlong = 201.168 m
1 acre = 0.4047 hectares
1 sq km = 100 hectares
1 sq mile = 2.59 square km
1 ounce = 28.35 grams
1 pound = 0.4536 kilograms
1 short ton = 0.90718 metric ton
1 short ton = 2,000 pounds
1 long ton = 1.016 metric tons
1 long ton = 2,240 pounds
1 metric ton = 1,000 kilograms
1 quart = 0.94635 liters
1 US gallon = 3.7854 liters
1 Imperial gallon = 4.5459 liters
1 nautical mile = 1.852 km

MOON HOUSTON & THE TEXAS GULF COAST
Avalon Travel
Hachette Book Group
1700 Fourth Street
Berkeley, CA 94710, USA
www.moon.com

Editor: Rachael Sablik
Acquiring Editor: Nikki Ioakimedes
Series Manager: Leah Gordon
Copy Editor: Christopher Church
Graphics Coordinators: Suzanne Albertson and Darren Alessi
Production Coordinators: Suzanne Albertson and Darren Alessi
Cover Design: Faceout Studios, Charles Brock
Interior Design: Megan Jones Design
Moon Logo: Tim McGrath
Map Editor: Albert Angulo
Cartographers: Andrew Dolan and John Culp
Indexer: Rachel Kuhn

ISBN-13: 978-1-64049-400-8

Printing History
1st Edition — February 2021
5 4 3 2 1

Front cover photo: downtown Houston at sunset © agefotostock / Alamy Stock Photo
Back cover photo: Houston Zoo exhibit © Mossaab Shuraih | Dreamstime.com

Printed in China by RR Donnelley